CAROL BROWN GOLDBERG

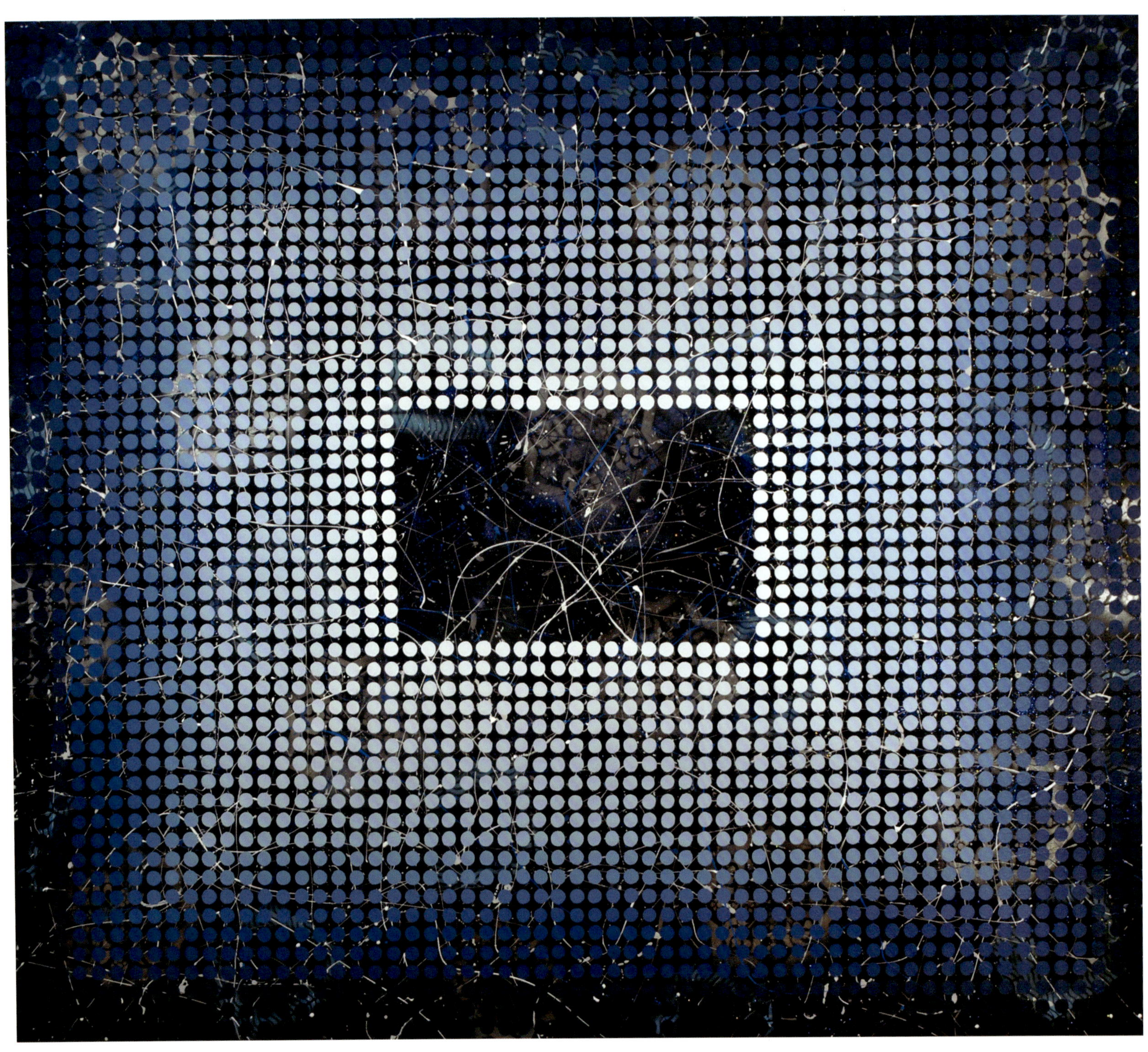

The Aroma of Snow Through a Rusty Screen, 2007
Acrylic on canvas with reflective chips
84" x 96"

CAROL BROWN GOLDBERG

INTERNATIONAL ARTS & ARTISTS
WASHINGTON, DC

This catalogue was published to coincide with an exhibition of the most recent work of Carol Brown Goldberg at American University, September 2007.

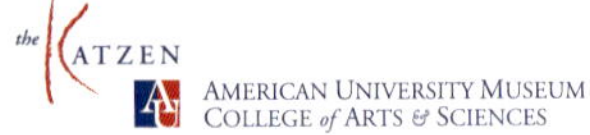

In 2009, The Suzanne H. Arnold Art Gallery at Lebanon Valley College in Annville, PA will host an exhibition of recent paintings by Carol Brown Goldberg. The touring exhibition is organized by the Exhibitions Department of International Arts & Artists, Washington, DC.

Cover: *What's the Fastest Elevator in the World?*, 2006, Acrylic on canvas, 96" x 108"
Photography: Recent work by Greg Staley and Brandon Webster
Early work by Joel Breger and Edward Owen
Editor: Penny Kiser, International Arts & Artists' Design Studio
Designer: Katie Dahl, International Arts & Artists' Design Studio
Text: Franklin Gothic Book/Adobe Jenson Pro
Printer: Badger Press, Fort Atkinson, WI

Library of Congress Cataloging-in-Publication Data

Kuspit, Donald B. (Donald Burton), 1935-
Carol Brown Goldberg / Donald Kuspit, Barbara Rose, Jack Rasmussen.
p. cm.
Includes bibliographical references.
ISBN 0-9767102-5-0
1. Goldberg, Carol Brown--Catalogs. 2. Painting, Abstract--United States--Catalogs. I. Rose, Barbara. II. Rasmussen, Jack, 1949- III. Goldberg, Carol Brown. IV. International Arts & Artists. V. Title.
ND237.G5798A4 2007
759.13--dc22

2007022552

CONTENTS

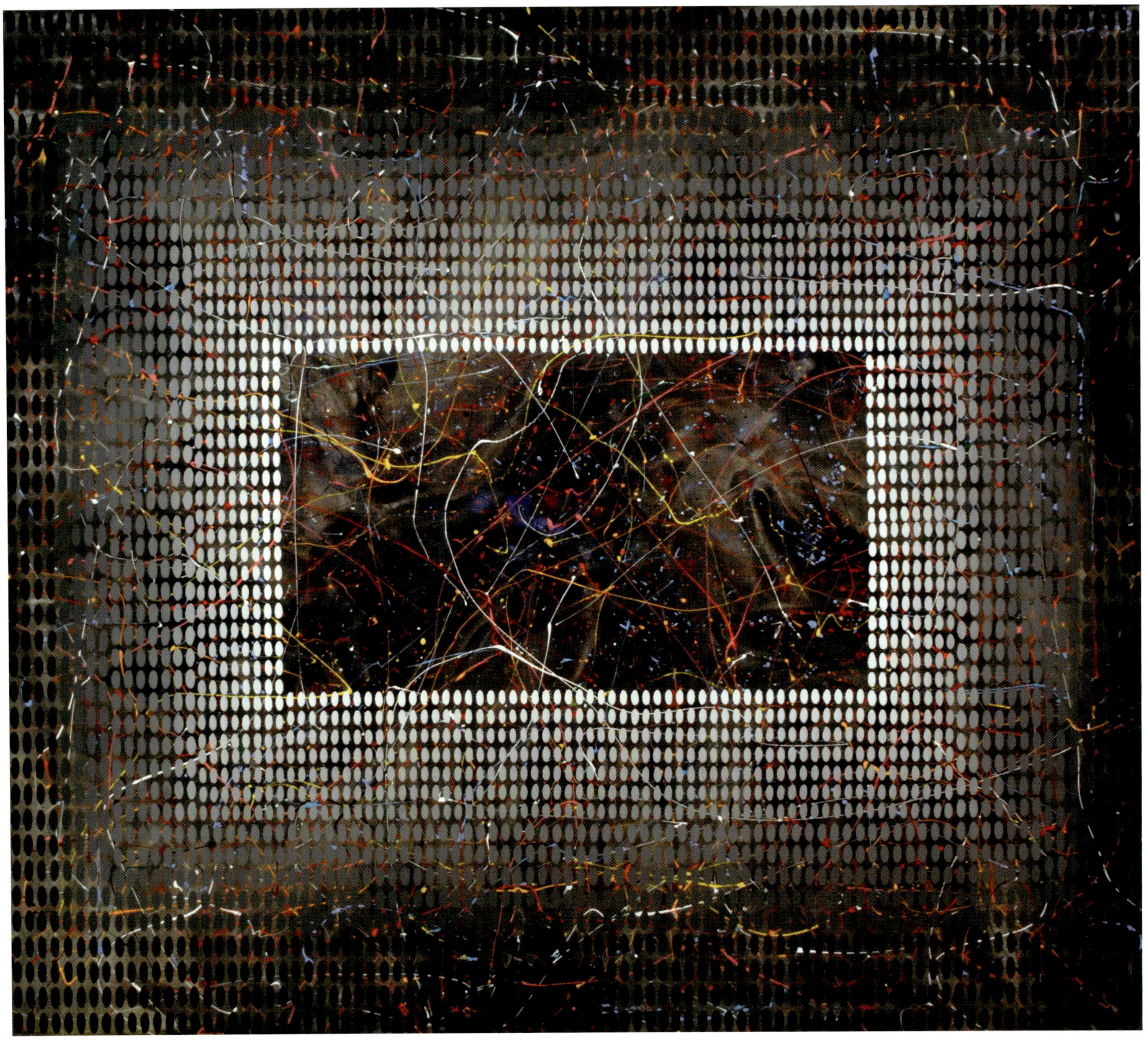

Five O'clock at 4 North Eutaw Street, 2007
Acrylic on canvas with reflective chips
84" x 96"

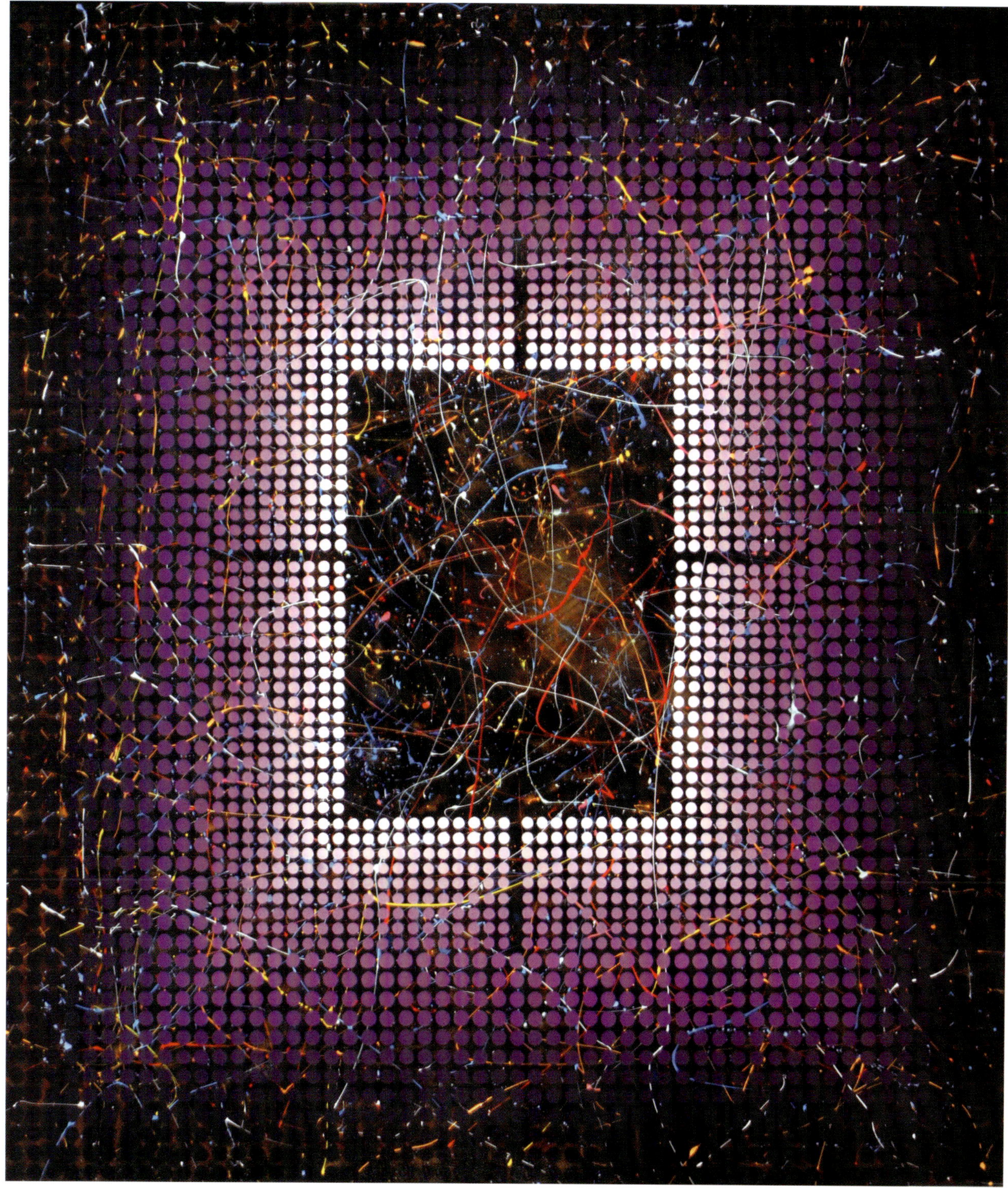

Brother's Portugal, 2007
Acrylic on canvas with reflective chips
84" x 96"

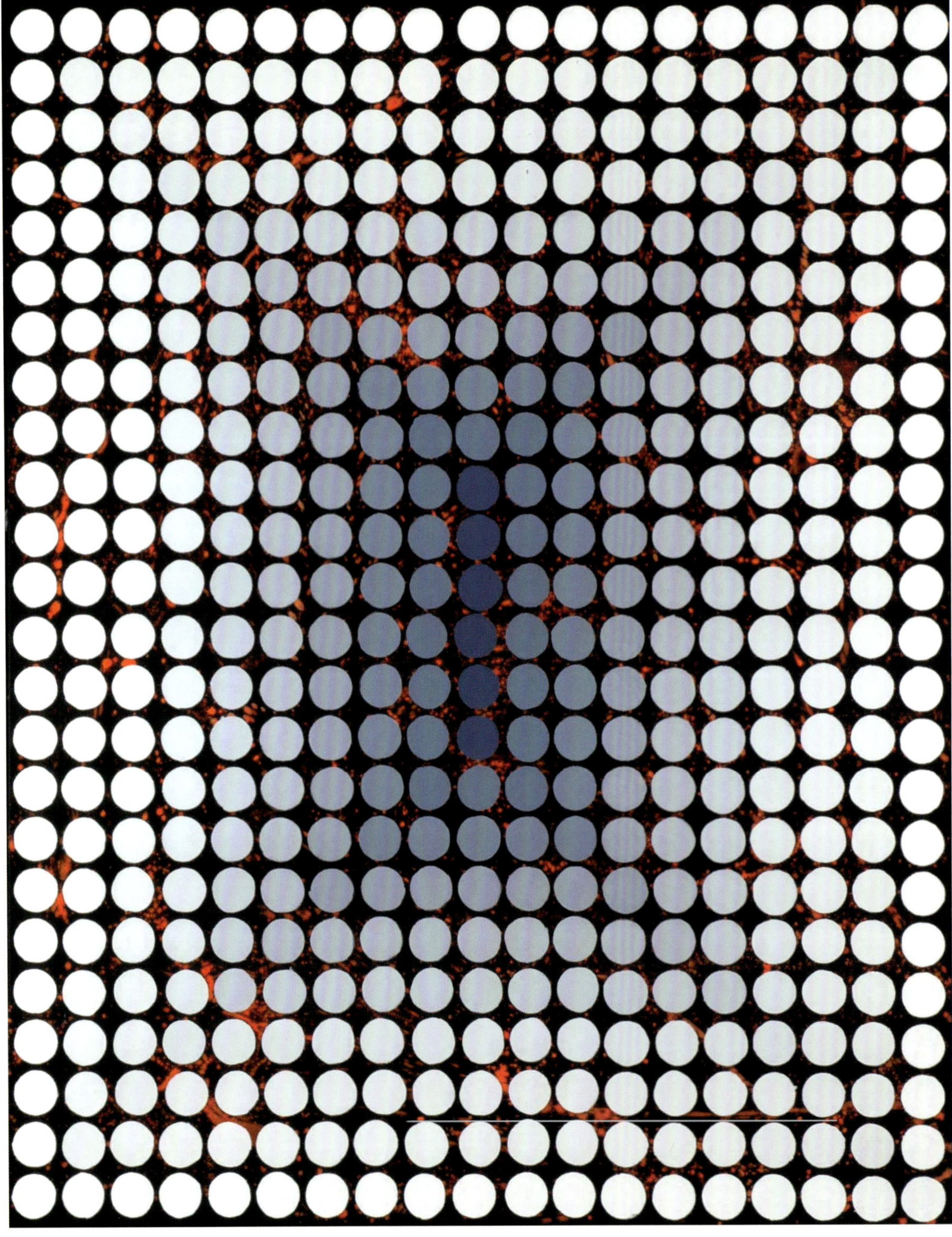

Jackie Takes Me to the Movies, 2005
Acrylic on canvas
60" x 48"
Collection of the DC Commission on the Arts and Humanities

Recent Work continues through the essay to page 34 ►

Painting As Meditation

In her most recent paintings from 2005-2007, Carol Brown Goldberg returns to concerns she first investigated in her earliest abstractions. In those paintings, she investigated the relationship of bright colored, eccentric, volumetric shapes to the space through which they were hurtling with careening speed. Her new paintings, on the other hand, while still radiating life and energy, do so with a subtle rhythmic pulsation of circles that seem to move imperceptibly as we look at them.

Undoubtedly in these new paintings there is a relationship to the retinal stimulation of "op art." However, rather than dazzling the eye with a superficial brilliance derived from the interaction of adjacent colors, these paintings draw us in with their darker mystery. They permit, indeed they require, an extended duration in order to be fully perceived. In this sense, they are more related to Ad Reinhardt's icons for meditation than they are to hard edge geometric painting. There is an evident structure derived from an underlying grid, but it is not mindlessly adhered to. The circles, which seem to shift as we observe them, constitute only one of the complex series of intertwined illusions that the artist, now certain of what she has to say and equipped with the wisdom of experience, is able to realize. The degree of sophistication required to master such a task informs us that it is the result of building on what has gone before, transforming the unguided energy of youth into the discipline of an ordered sense of space and a more conscious awareness of time.

– Barbara Rose

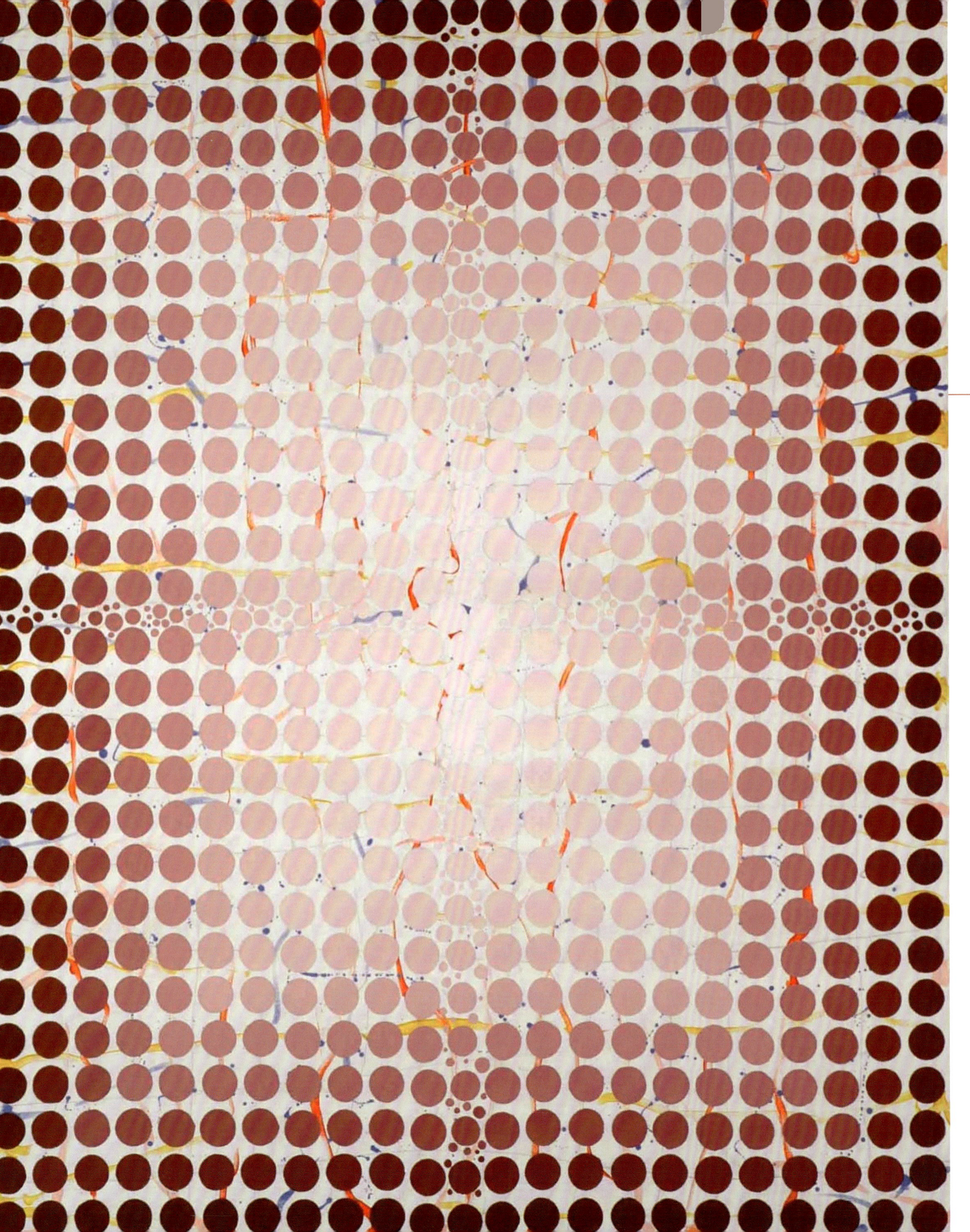

Reinventing Aura: Carol Brown Goldberg's Abstract Paintings

By Donald Kuspit

Non-objective paintings are prophets of spiritual life.

Hilla Rebay, "The Beauty of Non-Objectivity" [1]

This treatment of order in terms of similar differences and different similarities appears to be broad enough not only to cover all the orders found thus far in physics, but it seems to be valid in much broader areas of experience. For example, an order of colours can be expressed as similar differences, as can an order of musical tones.

The musical theme can clearly be seen in terms of similar differences and different similarities in patterns of notes, going all the way up to an order that can be found in highly organized compositions. Similar (but different) orders can also be seen in thoughts, which often develop in terms of patterns of similar differences and different similarities.

David Bohm and Basil Hiley, *The Undivided Universe* [2]

The basic relationship of quantum theory and consciousness is that they have the implicate order in common. The essential features of the implicate order are...that the whole universe is enfolded in everything and that each thing is enfolded in the whole.

However, under typical conditions of ordinary experience, there is a great deal of relative independence of things, so that they may be abstracted as separately existent, outside of each

Listening to Ivy; Remembering Brookville, 2005
Acrylic on canvas
60" x 48"

other, and only externally related. However, more fundamentally, the enfoldment relationship is active and essential to what each thing is, so that it is internally related to the whole and therefore to everything else.

Nonetheless, the explicate order, which dominates ordinary common sense's experience as well as classical physics, appears to stand by itself. But actually this is only an approximation and it cannot be properly understood apart from its ground in the primary reality of the implicate order, i.e. the holomovement. All things found in the explicate order emerge from the holomovement and ultimately fall back into it.

They endure only for some time, and while they last, their existence is sustained in a constant process of unfoldment and re-enfoldment, which gives rise to their relatively stable and independent forms in the explicate order.

David Bohm and Basil Hiley, *The Undivided Universe* [3]

Artistic perception...begins by observing the whole fact in its full individuality, and then by degree articulates the order that is proper to the assimilation of this fact....[It] can become what could perhaps be called the normal way of doing scientific research.

David Bohm, Wholeness and the Implicate Order [4]

1

Are non-objective (abstract) paintings still "prophets of spiritual life," as Hilla Rebay, the founder of the Museum of Non-Objective Art (now the Solomon R. Guggenheim Museum), said? If "spiritual life"—a life informed with spiritual consciousness—means consciousness of the implicate order (a convincing "new model of reality," as the theoretical physicist David Bohm demonstrates), are there convincing signs of spiritual life or spiritual consciousness in contemporary abstract painting, that is, painting by the epigoni of the pioneering abstractionists Kandinsky and Malevich (the innovator of pure gestural abstraction and the innovator of pure geometrical abstraction)? Not many, if any, apart from Goldberg's new abstract paintings.

I will argue that they are an epigenetic leap forward in the development of abstract painting, rescuing it from decadence—supposedly inevitable after becoming mainstream—by breathing new

Three Towers, 2006
Acrylic on canvas with reflective chips
72" x 48"

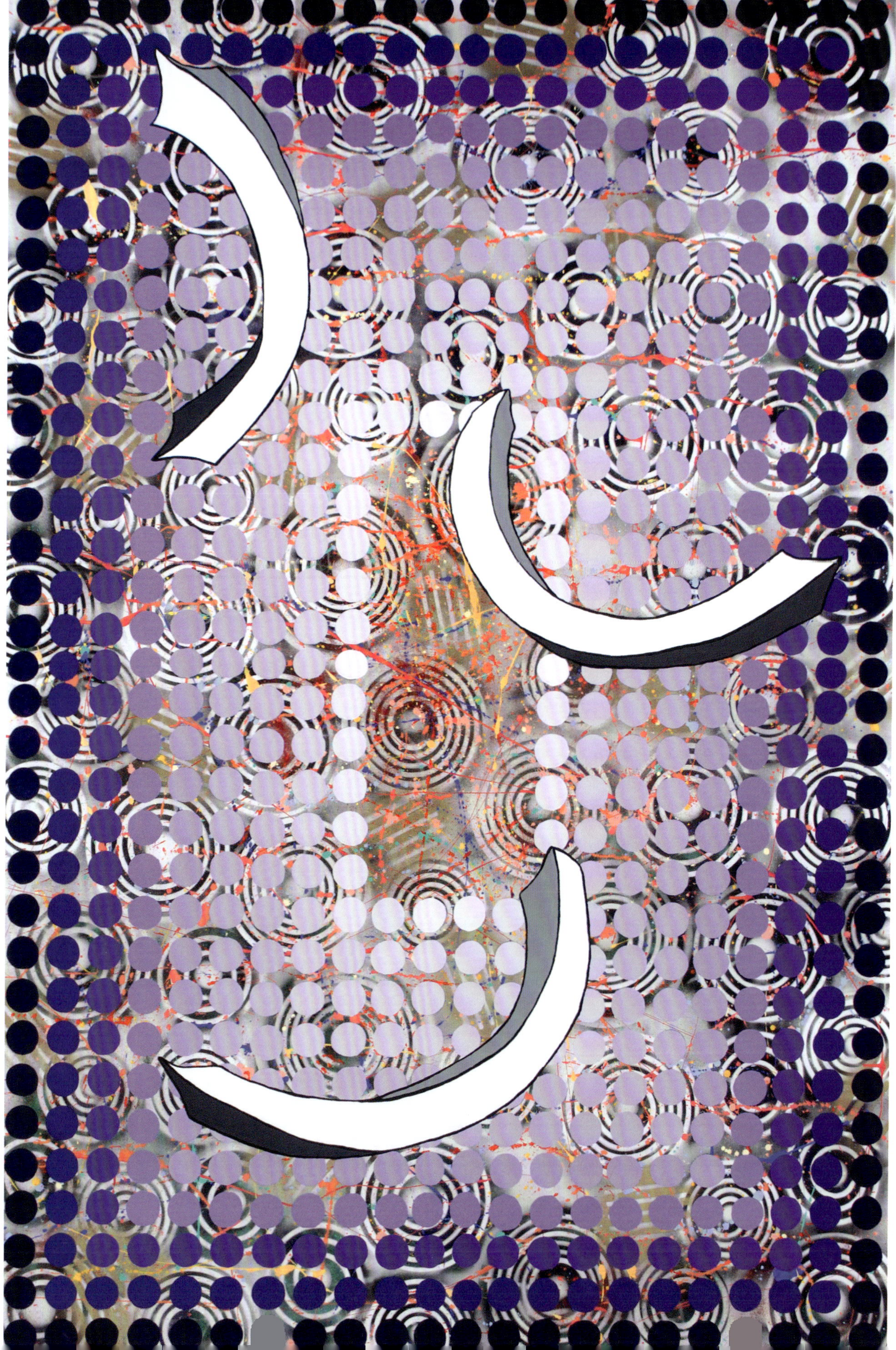

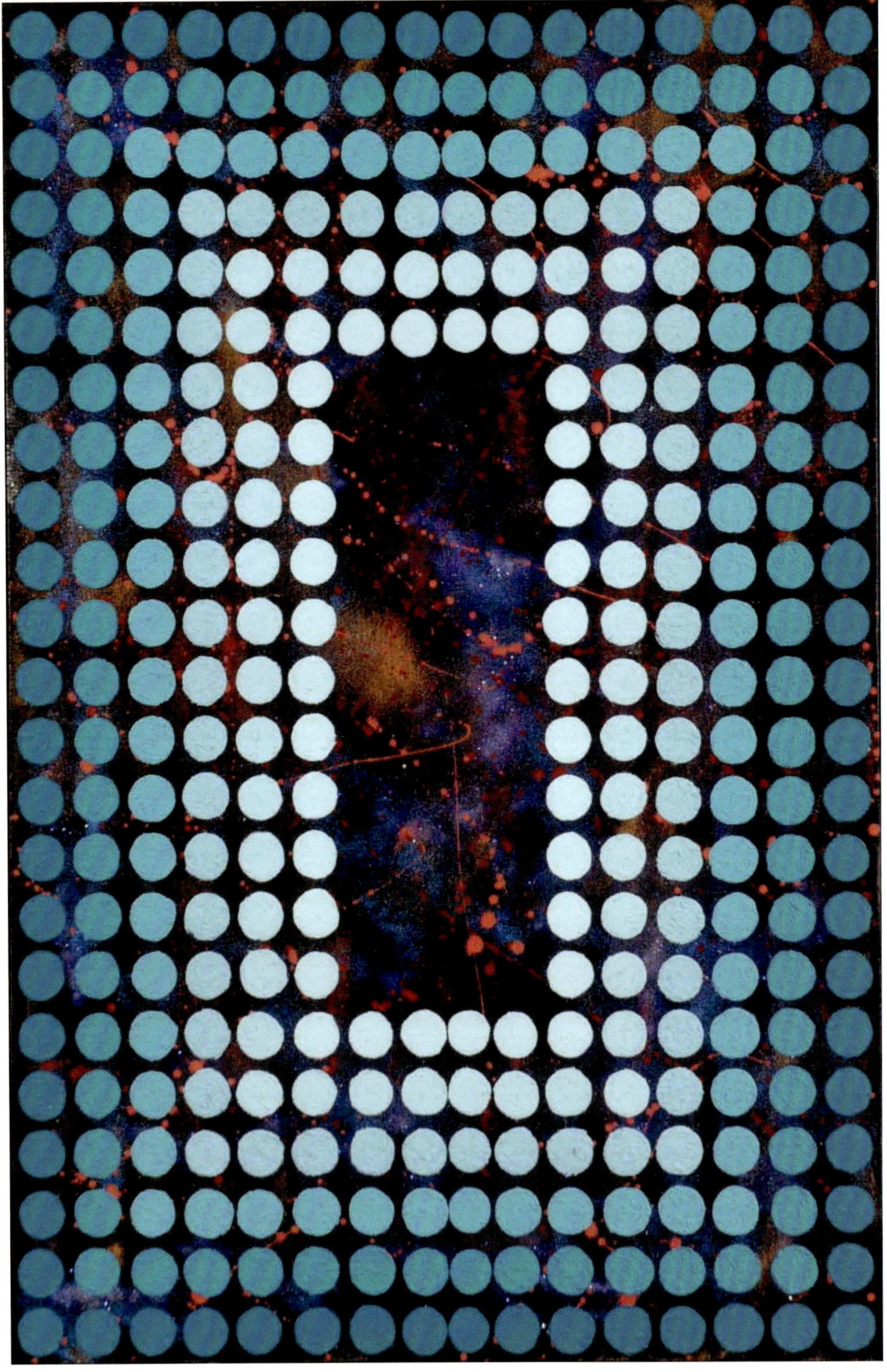

The Carnival at Our Lady of Lourdes, 2006
Acrylic on canvas with reflective chips
36" x 24"

spiritual life and understanding into it. Indeed, I will argue that Goldberg's new abstract paintings are the consummate realization of the spiritual intention that brought abstract art into existence. In fulfilling its mission she clarifies the meaning of spiritual consciousness, which remained an unclear ideal, attached to anachronistic religious beliefs, in the writings of Kandinsky and Malevich. Goldberg's new abstract paintings are scientifically grounded, indicating that spiritual consciousness is not a groping toward the unknown—blindly mystical, as it were—but enlightened cognition of scientifically known reality. What was an old-fashioned religious dream in new formal dress in Kandinsky and Malevich has become modern insight into subtle reality in Goldberg's abstractions. They show the scientific spiritual truth—they are not just sublimated fantasy, as Kandinsky's impulsive and Malevich's utopian abstractions have been called (suggesting that their spirituality has more to do with the unconscious than full consciousness)—and that art can articulate it. It is safe to say that Goldberg's new paintings are scientific research carried out through artistic perception—scientific research as artistic revelation (and vice versa).

Abstract painting has come to an ironical end—become familiar and historical, "simply one element in a purposive [decorative] arrangement," as Max Horkheimer put it[5]—and with that lost the spiritual meaning, however inchoate, it had when it was experimental and unexpected. But now that the end is here or near, it is time to return to its risky, desperate beginning, if it is not to disappear into meaninglessness altogether. It is necessary to renew the originary ambition that inspired its revolutionary break with traditional representation: the urge to distill the spiritual in life and communicate it, in fresh and unique purity, through the esthetics immanent in the paint medium—the "beauty of colors and forms," as Rebay said, unique to its materiality and responsible for its spiritual effect when endowed with ecstatic presence and purity. Only such a renewal of spiritual resonance can de-reify abstract painting, saving it from complacency and conventionality, from the hardening of esthetic arteries that announces obsolescence, from the formulaic objectification of colors and forms, the authoritarian assumption that abstraction is the grand climax of modern art, the conclusive direction in which it was inevitably heading—the view that became a truism in Alfred Barr's famous diagram of the development of modern style.[6]

If abstract painting is once again to make a spiritual difference it must re-acquire the "esthetic shock"[7] it had before it became fashionably familiar. There are few—any—contemporary abstract paintings that have the esthetic shock—the spiritual electricity, as it were, to recall Kandinsky's idea that art must now be based on the modern "theory of moving electricity" rather than the traditional theory that "matter...was the basis of everything"[8] (one of his rationalizations for his gestural dynamics)—that Goldberg's have.

The belief that pure art alone is authentically modern, even the only authentic art—for it alone treats the formal fundamentals of art as ends in themselves (rather than as a means to a representational end)—sidesteps the fact that it was initially regarded as an incomprehensible aberration, suggesting that spiritual purpose was beside the modern point. Pure painting may have been achieved by what the art critic Clement Greenberg called "dialectical conversion"[9]—the unwitting realization of esthetic purity in the course of the effort to represent every perceptual nuance and insistent sensation of external experience—but its declaration of independence from representation seemed to preclude dialectical engagement with it, and with that its human relevance. Abstract painting stood alone and supreme in esthetic autonomy, convinced of its superiority to other art, but its hermetic unworldliness made it obscure and mute—aristocratically inaccessible and ineffable, and with that humanly useless. As the historian Eric Hobsbawm writes, radical purity is "on the way to nowhere. What could painting do once it abandoned the traditional language of representation, or moved sufficiently far from its conventional idiom to make it incomprehensible? What could it communicate?"[10] For Hobsbawm, abstraction is a narcissistic revolt against social reality: it catalyzed the belief "that anything was legitimate as art, so long as the artist claimed it as a personal creation"[11]—a delusion that we now seem stuck with.

But the claim emphasizes the creative as well as the personal, suggesting that both are implicit in any definition of art. The seemingly narcissistic insularity of abstract painting—what has been called its introspective aspect, its turning toward interior reality and away from exterior reality—involves an effort to fathom the creativity innate to the self, indeed, without which it is not true to itself and thus fully alive.[12] The expressive interplay of formal fundamentals that occurs in pure art is a spontaneous communication of primary creativity. The dialectics of pure art and of primary creativity correlate and coordinate. Both reveal the co-implication of individual fact and assimilative order, to refer to the final epigraph by Bohm, a real wholeness that can only be perceived by artistic perception, as he says. Representations demand that art communicate commonsensical facts—its insistence that art must engage the conventionally intelligible explicate order in which everyone socially lives if it is to be humanly meaningful (Hobsbawm's point)—undermines the attempt to engage and communicate the dialectical creativity of true selfhood (and true humanness) that abstraction undertakes. Representation narrows the focus of artistic perception to individual facts, resulting in one-dimensional art, while abstraction uncovers their dialectical integration in the implicate order, and with that their creative place in the whole of being.

2pm at Hanlon Park, 2006
Acrylic on canvas with reflective chips
72" x 60"

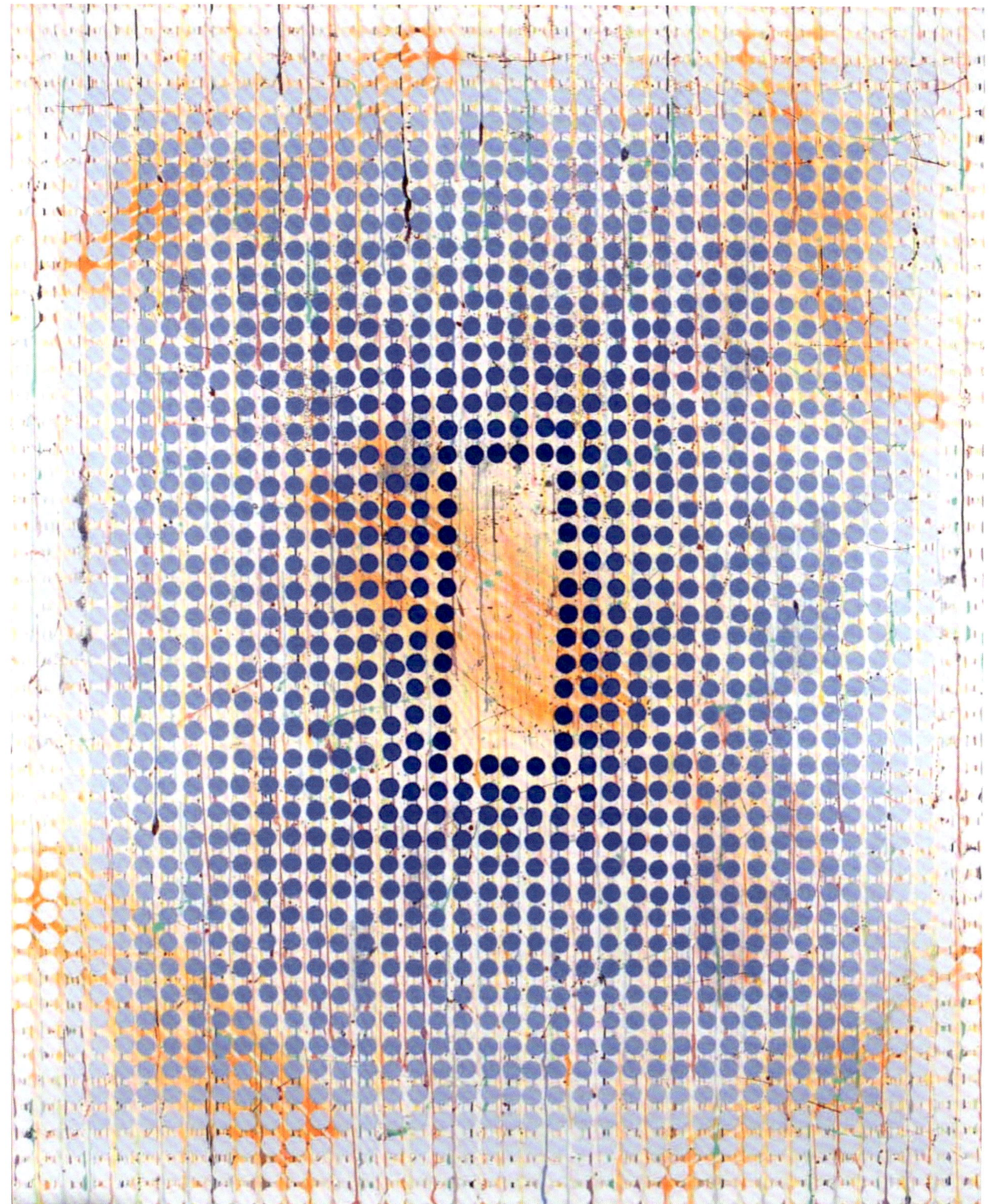

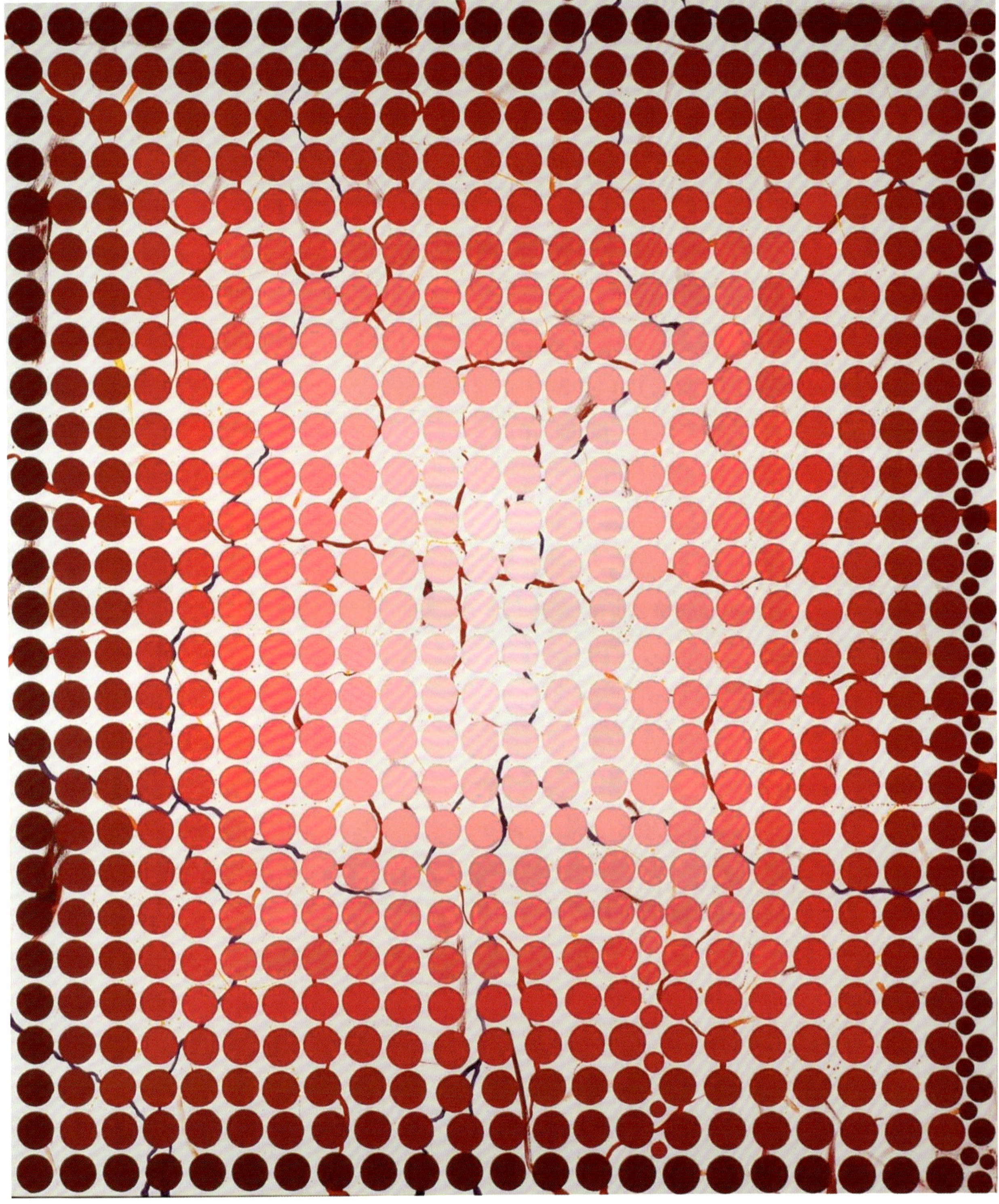

The Summer Parade, 2005
Acrylic on canvas
48" x 60"

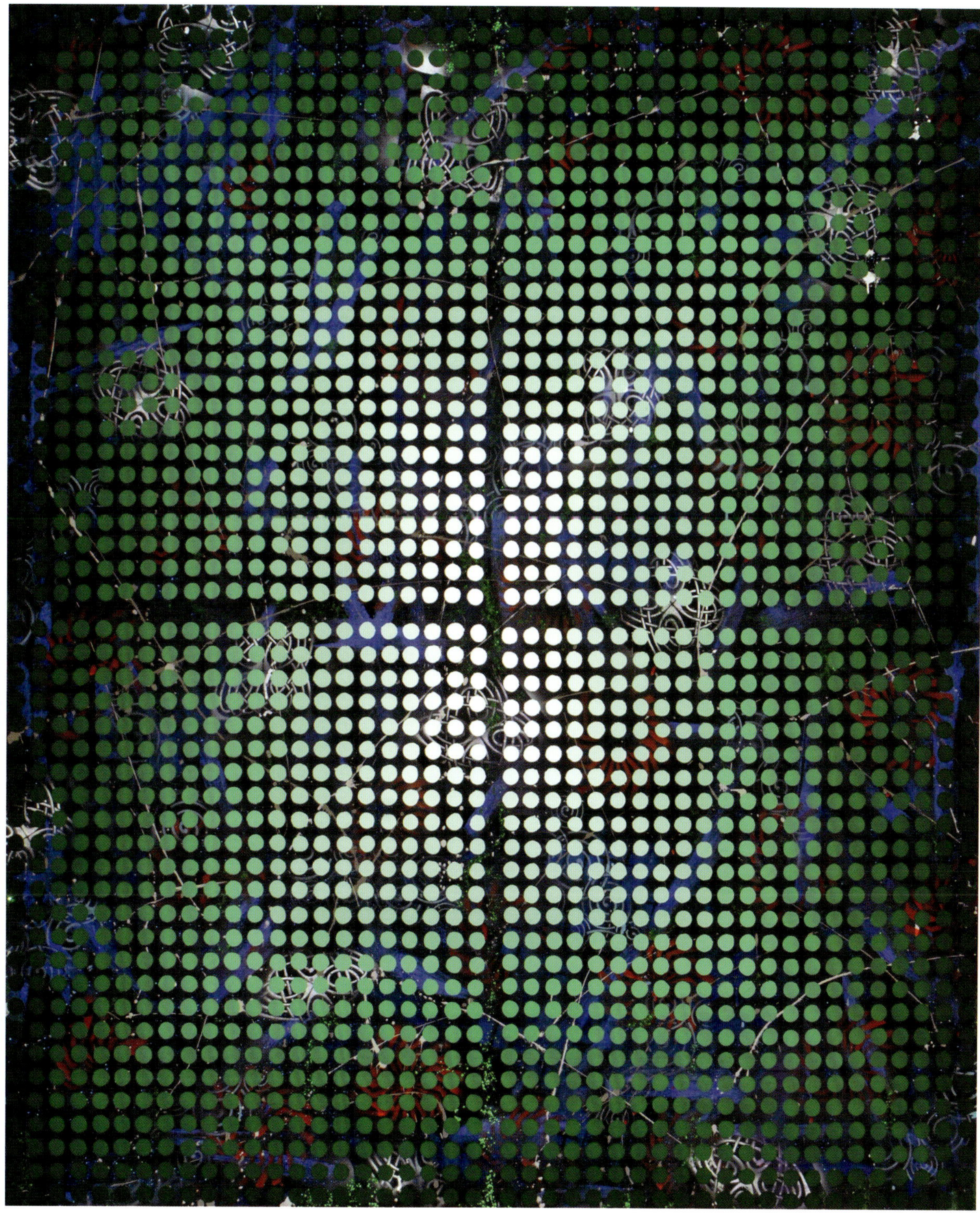

The Night of Mu Sig's June Week, 2007
Acrylic on canvas with reflective chips
72" x 60"

Abstraction starts by attempting to grasp the primary creativity of the self and ends with the consciousness that creativity is inseparable from being. It begins as a narcissistic adventure and ends with spiritual consciousness, which involves recognition of the truth that the self is a minor aspect of being. The self's creativity is a secondary expression of universal primary creativity—of being perpetuating itself by dialectically integrating all beings in the implicate order. The ultimate creative "act" is clearly the creation of the cosmic order of similar differences and different similarities. Goldberg's new abstract paintings are a convincing attempt to represent that cosmic order in its dialectical essentials. Perception of particular facts—the colorful and formal details of sense experience, meticulously articulated—and their assimilative conception in an over-all or all-inclusive (cosmic) order, so that each factual detail seems implicated in and inseparable from every other, become parallel lines of consciousness that converge in the holomovement of Goldberg's paintings.

In a sense, representation turns our attention away from our own core creativity, the source of whatever originality of being we have, toward other beings, who seem socially constructed and thus unoriginal—we tend to narcissistically privilege ourselves by assuming that we alone are true creative selves while others are false compliant selves—suggesting that, however hard representation struggles to convey the spontaneous aliveness that is the sign of their originality and creativity, it never unequivocally succeeds in doing so, in sharp contrast to abstraction, which turns our attention toward our own creativity—a more authentic narcissism, as it were—and with that our innate originality.

Abstract painting is unusual—at least when it is unusual—in that it thematizes and evokes, through the dialectical use of pure form, art's inherent creativity. Its ultimate aim is to create "an abstract picture of the immortal soul," to use Otto Rank's words,[13] that is, of the creative part of the soul—the part that links it with the whole of Creation or reality, and thus its most spiritual part, as Rebay would say. Rank writes: "artistic productivity, not only in the individual, but probably in the whole development of culture, begins with one's own human body and ascends to the creation and artistic formation of a soul-endowed personality."[14] If abstract painting at its best is artistic productivity at its purest, then one can say it transforms material paint into "soulful" presence, that is, endows it with immortality and personality. Through projective identification, Goldberg invests her primary creativity—the core of her soul—in paint, bringing it to uncanny life. Given the aura of life, paint is unconsciously experienced as organic body rather than inorganic matter, the vital embodiment of true selfhood rather than a medium whose properties cannot bear witness to

Saturday Morning at the Hippodrome
Acrylic on canvas
48" x 48"

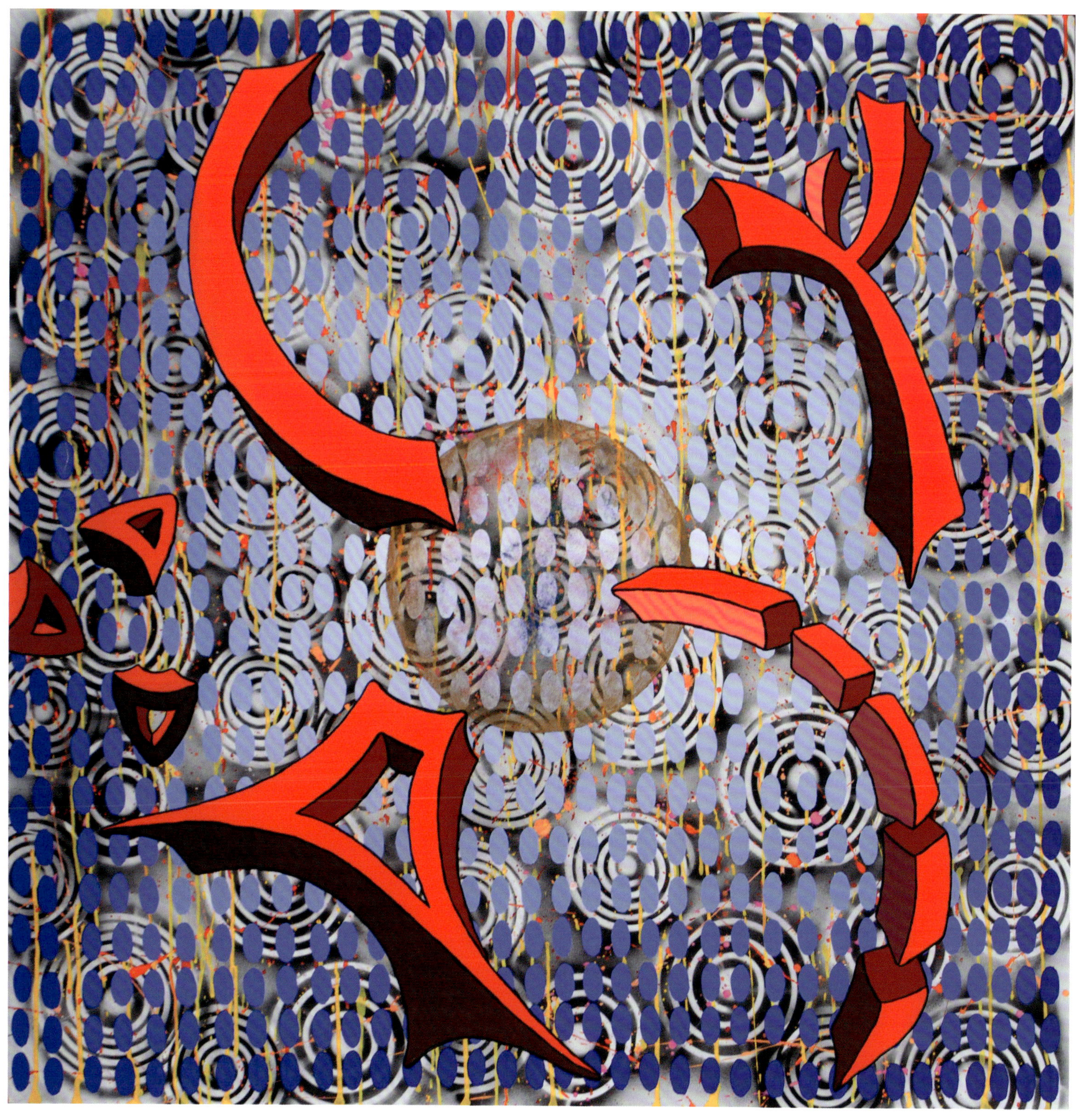

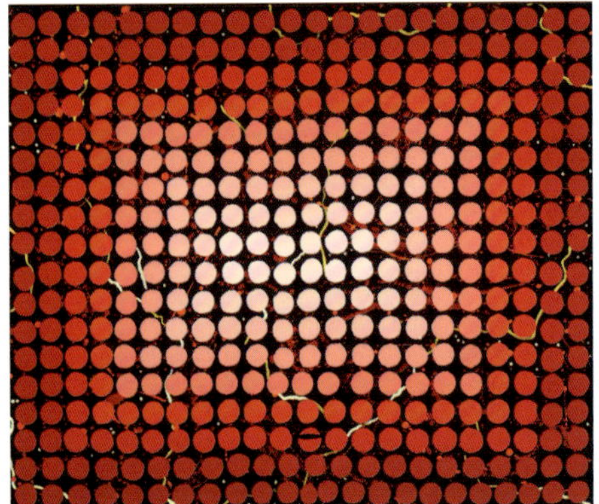

My Father's Ruby, 2005
Acrylic on canvas
36" x 48"

primary creativity, indeed, turns creativity into submissive compliance rather than transformative transcendence of their materiality, thus inducing self-falsification.

Uncanny auratic, spiritual, soulful, transfigurative, numinous[15] effect is primary creativity at its most explicit. Numinous aura is the soul as nominal body. It is the point of the Transfiguration: the body transfigured—the body experienced as simultaneously material and immaterial, solid and transparent, visible and invisible, tangible and intangible (and thus satisfies the Doubting Thomas as well as the visionary mystic)—is the soul made manifest. The soul remains hidden in the inner sanctum of the self even as it makes itself intensely felt through aura. Revealed through sacred aura, the soul is primary creativity purified. The circular halo that traditionally symbolizes aura, containing it in a simple geometrical form comprehensible to everyone—all the more so because the self-contained circle symbolizes the self-contained cosmos (it unconsciously acknowledges that space is curved)—is the abstract essence of the core soul. If to abstract is to concentrate in pure form and thus absolutize, then the auratic halo is creativity concentrated and absolutized. To have an aura is to be centered in creativity—to have creative power, and thus to be divine. Indeed, crowned with an auratic halo a person becomes as sacred as the Creator. The halo confers creative authority—the authority at the center of the cosmos, indeed, the authority to create a center for the universe. Goldberg's new abstract paintings assert the power of the center,[16] and their auratic center is implicitly a halo. She has released the creative energy stored in the finite circular halo, and let it radiate freely through infinite space.

Here is my answer to Hobsbawm: convincing abstract painting communicates consciousness of the implicate order of being through the numinous aura of creative art. Numinous aura is a sign of artistic perception of the implicate order. It is the spiritual order of factual being, and can only be perceived by spiritually conscious art—art that, as Kandinsky said, belongs to the spiritual life and is "one of its most powerful agents."[17] For Kandinsky, spiritual consciousness was enriched by scientific consciousness, and Goldberg makes it clear that they are inseparable—similar differences and different similarities, to refer again to the first Bohm epigraph. Convincing art "communicate[s] feeling directly from mind to mind, with no intent to explain why the impact occurs," the sociobiologist Edward O. Wilson writes,[18] and convincing abstract art communicates spiritual feeling directly. It has a direct spiritual impact that seems inexplicable—enigmatic. It radically alters consciousness of particular facts, showing that they imply cosmic order.

Aura was the great discovery of the pioneering abstractionists. Both Kandinsky and Malevich called it non-objective sensation and feeling. They struggled to present it as a presence in and for itself, but they could only suggest it—offer an impression of it or convey it through a mood, to use Kandinsky's words. These days, abstraction rarely does that. It has become almost completely "positivist," to use Greenberg's word. That is, colors and forms became reified matter of simple fact. Losing evocative power and symbolic meaning, they no longer offered an insightful glimmer let alone soulful hint of the implicate order and the primary creativity informing it. Albers's *Homage to the Square* paintings achieve a certain aura by way of geometry, and Pollock's all-over paintings achieve a certain aura by way of gesture, but similar achievements since theirs have been rare (with the notable exception of Sean Scullly's *Wall of Light* paintings).

But the aura in their abstract paintings seems subdued and superficial compared to the insistent auratic—radically numinous—character of Goldberg's abstract paintings. She achieves it in part by dialectically integrating gesture and geometry, transfiguring them in the process. Goldberg reinvents aura by reconciling the opposites that have tended to develop separately in abstract painting. (Each finally becomes an empty extreme.) The esthetic result has more spiritual effect—greater auratic authority—than each is capable of achieving by itself. If esthetic experience is immature spiritual experience, then spiritual experience is mature experience of the implicate order. The esthetically convincing abstract painting becomes spontaneously spiritual, but an exclusively geometrical or gestural esthetic is nowhere near as spiritually convincing—conveys much less cosmic feeling, to use Roger Fry's term—than a "cosmically" inclusive dialectic.

Goldberg's abstract paintings offer much more than a shallow impression of aura, as Albers do, or an unstable mood of aura, as Pollock's do. For her aura is not inarticulate and indefinite—problematic and vague—but an epitomizing expression of the implicate order. Goldberg's aura conveys its intense definiteness—the relentless process of creative enfoldment that is the holomovement. Her aura has ontological presence: it is unequivocally given—substantially real—rather than an epistemological myth or elusive feeling. In her works mysticism and science seem to fuse, but they are ultimately more scientific than mystical: scientific icons of spiritual consciousness—the spiritual physics of the implicate order esthetically perceived in all its abstract concreteness. If science is mysticism satisfied—what seems beyond comprehension made comprehensible—then Goldberg's abstract paintings show that the seemingly mystical, incomprehensible implicate order is scientifically comprehensible. And that pure science involves a mystical yearning, however unconscious—but implicit in wonder (no esthetic perception without it)—to become enfolded in it, that is, to be "mystified."

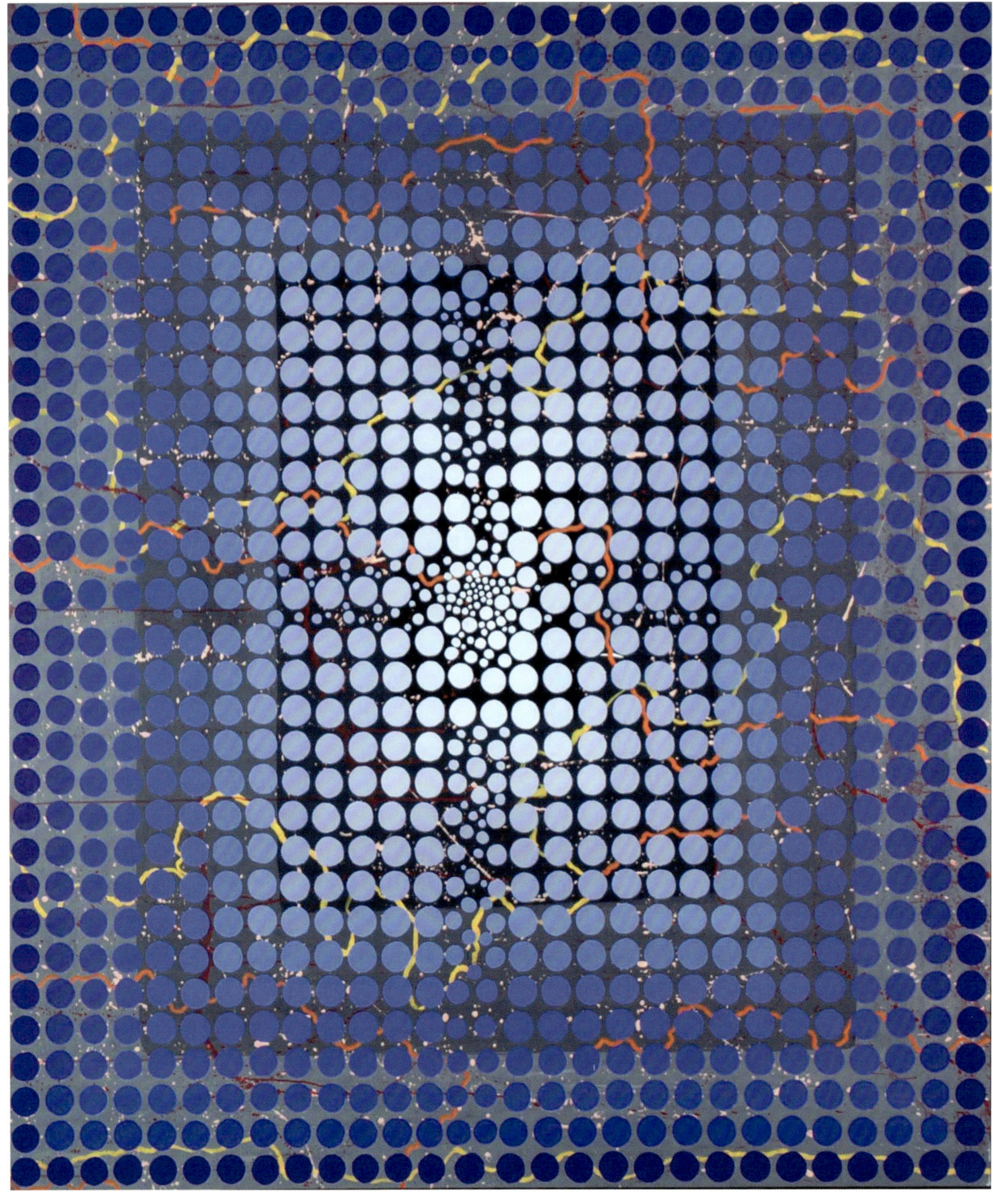

Listening to Ivy; Rushing Toward Blue, 2005
Acrylic on canvas
84" x 72"

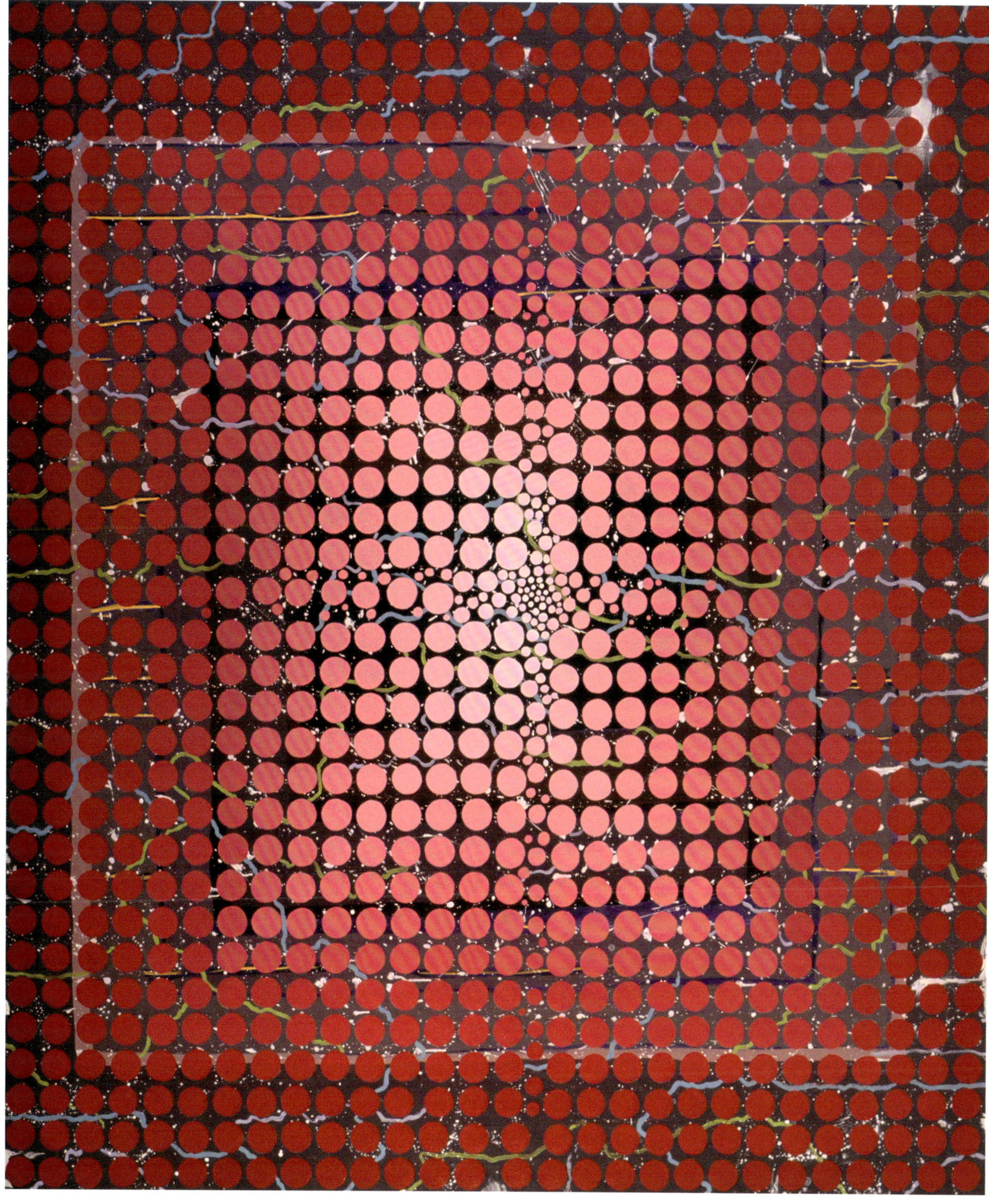

Listening to Ivy; Rushing Toward Red, 2005
Acrylic on canvas
84" x 72"

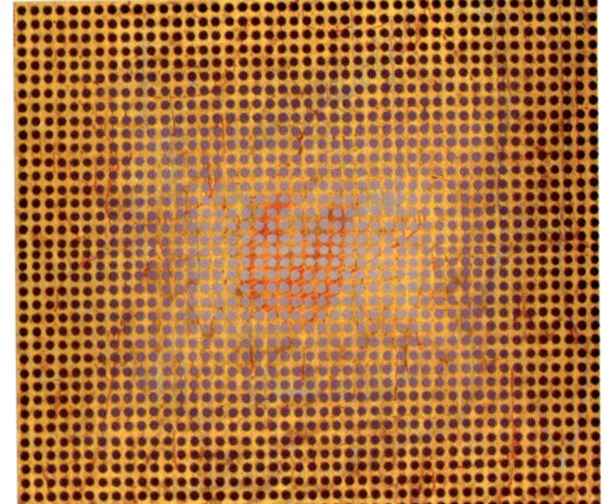

September at Garrison Boulevard, 2007
Acrylic on canvas with reflective chips
72" x 84"

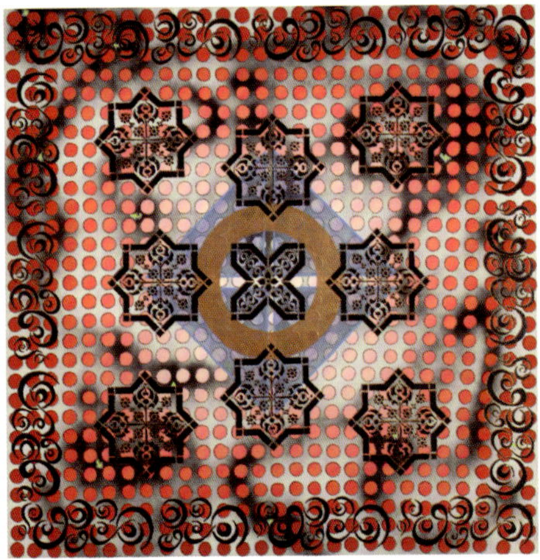

Dinner on Bancroft Road, 2005
Acrylic on canvas
36" x 36"

2

Goldberg is a modernist painter, but she is a modernist painter with a difference: she recapitulates the history of modernist abstract painting while giving it a new kind of transcendence—the transcendence of the implicate order, more particularly, transcendence of the formal facts of the painting by showing them to be meaningless apart from the implicate order. Completely contained by it, they become instances of it, even as the illusion of their independence is maintained by the intensity—increased exhibition power, one might say—they acquire by being recognized as its constitutive details. "Modernist painting calls attention to the physical properties of the medium, but only in order to have these transcend themselves," Greenberg said.[19] "The great masters of the past achieved their art by virtue of combinations of pigments whose real effectiveness was 'abstract'." Their "greatness is not owed to the spirituality with which they conceived the things they illustrated so much as it is to the success with which they ennobled raw matter to the point where it could function as art."[20] For Greenberg, "art explains to us what we already feel, but it does not do so discursively or rationally; rather, it acts out an explanation in the sense of working on our feelings at a remove."[21]

Greenberg neglects to say that to ennoble is to spiritualize—to create the auratic effect of feeling by giving the pigments esthetic resonance. Aura is not a socio-culturally contingent phenomenon, as Walter Benjamin and other advocates of mechanical reproduction (including Hobsbawm) think, but a creative manifestation of profound feeling that can appear in any culture, and has appeared in every culture. Works of art bear universal witness to this. What Goldberg achieves is an auratic effect of spiritual feeling—an esthetic experience of spiritual depth and the holomovement of primary creativity—in a sophisticated form suited to modern scientific culture. Rudimentary consciousness of the implicate order—belief in the formless Beyond—appears in traditional religion, but modern science shows that the Beyond has form. Goldberg offers us an artistic perception of it.

As I have mentioned, a consistent feature of Goldberg's abstract paintings is their auratic center. A chaotic matrix can spontaneously generate structured crystal, suggesting that order is implicit in chaos, and Goldberg's oddly crystalline center—a sort of geometrical diamond in the rough—seems to spontaneously generate from the chaotic matrix of her gestures, that is, their holomovement, which looks chaotic to the positivistic eye. The inarticulate matrix is vividly articulate in many paintings, but in many others the "Brownian movement"—trajectories of “sensational” particles stochastically appearing “out of the blue”— enfold themselves into a crystal-clear grid, evoking and symbolizing the implicate order. At the center of almost every grid is a luminous aura, quintessentializing its geometry while radiating beyond it. The abstract grid seems hermetically sealed, but it is an infinitely expansive order, a sort of electromagnetic field in which every particle of sensation is implicated. It vibrates in singular place, even as it belongs to the whole beyond it.

Sometimes an individual particle seems imbued with all-consuming radiance, as in *Gwynn Oak* (this page), where one particle marks the center of the grid, and sometimes the radiance floods the grid, dematerializing the particles, as in *The Passion of Winter* (p. 30). The grid may be luminous and the center dark, as in *Jackie Takes Me to the Movies* (p. 8) and *September at Garrison Boulevard* (opposite page), and the center may be marked by a cross, as in *Listening to Ivy: Rushing Toward Blue* (p. 24) and *The Night of Mu Sig's June Week* (p. 19). “X” marks the center in *Dinner on Bancroft Road* (opposite page), and the iconic geometrical form in the center of *The Summer Parade* (p. 18) and *Listening to Ivy: Rushing Toward Red* (p. 25) is transfixed by an “X.” Sometimes the geometrical center is composed of luminous particles, as in *Gwynn Oak*, *My Father's Ruby* (p. 22), *Miss Blue Newton Calls the Role* (this page), and *Listening to Ivy #1* (p. 31). Sometimes the luminosity of the geometrical center is so intense that it dissolves the particles that constitute it, as in *Listening to Ivy: Remembering Brookville* (p. 10). Sometimes the geometrical center is golden, as *Bobby Bloom on the Boardwalk* (p. 29) and *2pm at Hanlon Park* (p. 17), and sometimes pitch black, as in *The Carnival at Our Lady of Lourdes* (p. 14) and *Duvall Pharmacy* (p. 28). The center seems to emerge from the grid even as it remains embedded in the grid. Sometimes it seems to be an abysmal depth—a kind of black hole—and at other times a beacon in the void.

Sometimes there are geometrically eccentric fragments which seem suspended in space, as in *Saturday Morning at the Hippodrome* (p. 21), *SK's Car* (p. 29), and *Three Towers* (p. 13). They have a kind of ornamental presence. They seem like finite fragments of the infinite implicate order—unpredictable crystallizations of its holomovement. Seemingly independent, each is the germ of a possible explicate order. They have a certain affinity, and sometimes are in mirror relationship to each other, but they never combine, suggesting the inadequacy of the explicate order as an explanation and mirror of the implicate order. In a sense, they are the spatialized and temporalized holomovement—they are highly specific—which lacks any specific space and time. *A Night in Carlin's Park* (p. 32) seems derived from Albers's *Homage to the Square*, but

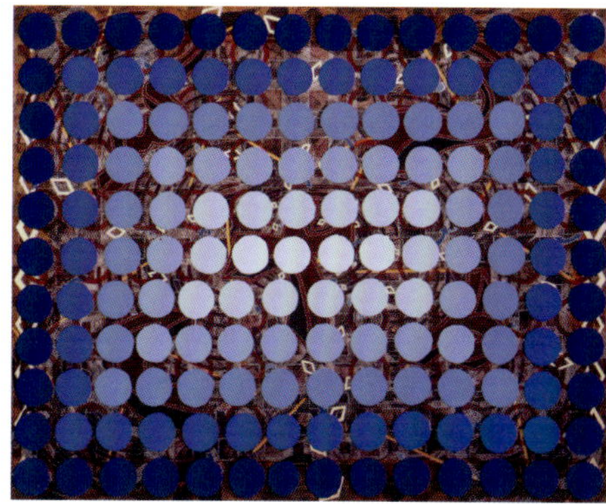

Miss Blue Newton Calls the Role, 2005
Acrylic on paper
15" x 20"

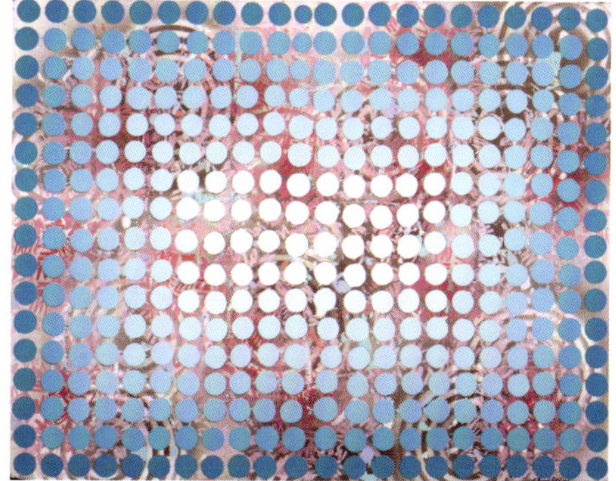

Gwynn Oak, 2005
Acrylic on canvas
12" x 18"

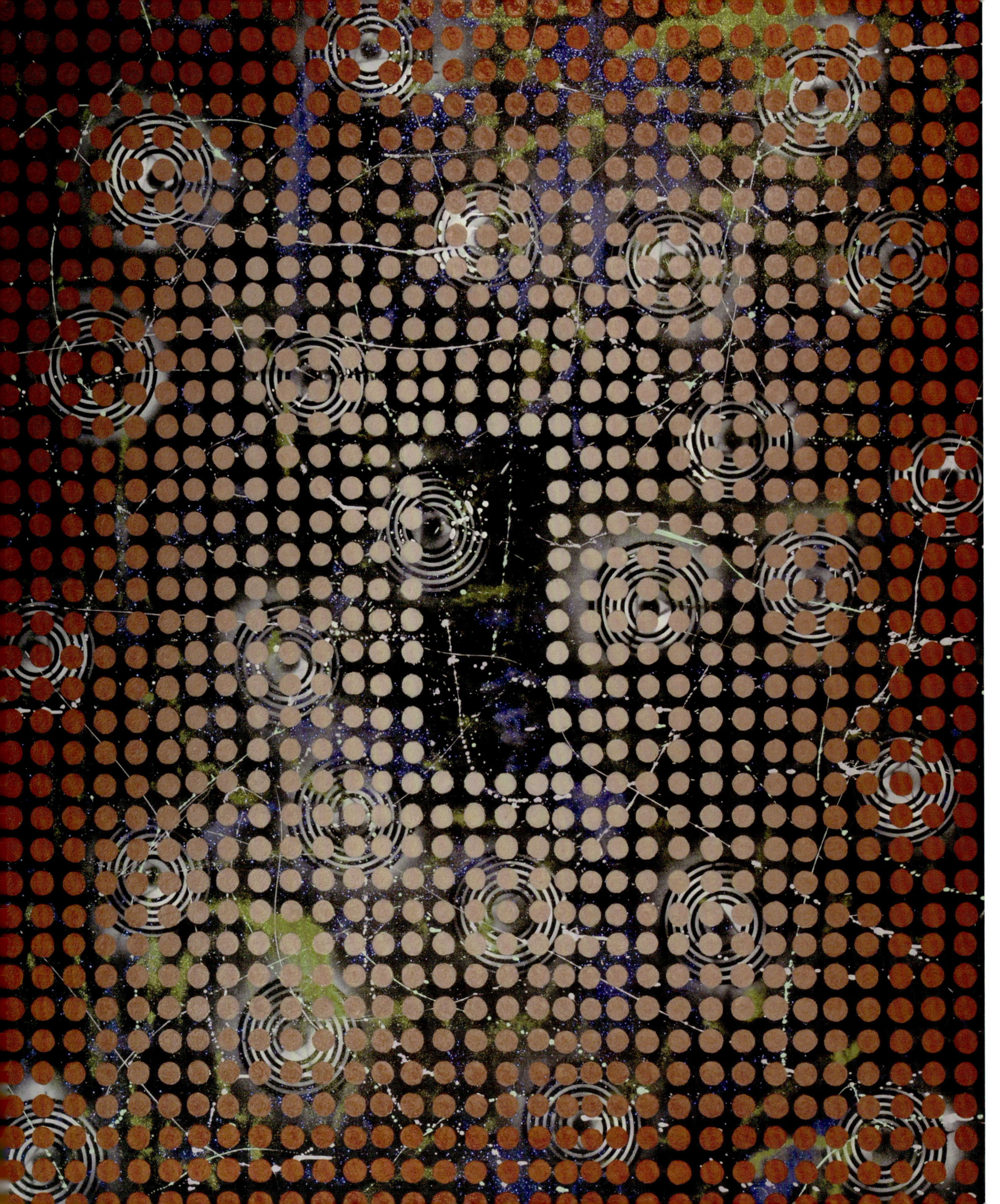

Goldberg's auratic light is much more brilliant, and the contrast between illuminated transparency and opaque darkness much more dramatic and complex. More is at stake in her grid than in Alber's square. Her geometry has greater spiritual quality than his. His abstractions illustrate the "interaction of colors," to refer to the title of his book. It legitimated the de-transcendentalization of abstract painting and its anti-auratic reduction to mechanical positivism. One might say that Albers remains bound by the explicate order, while Goldberg adventures in the implicate order, with quantum theory as her guide. She shows that the implicate order is not the terra incognita traditional religion thought it was, but a peculiarly modern music.

Goldberg's abstract paintings are in fact a very original musical painting, to refer to Kandinsky's influential idea. (It derives from Walter Pater's view that music is the highest art.[22]) Her "Compositions" of color are quite different—a more advanced and complicated visual music—than his, to use the term he did for the paintings he regarded as most musically consummate. He thought they were visual symphonies—orchestrations of color—that could hold their own against auditory symphonies. Indeed, he meant them to be directly comparable to literal music, especially Wagner's romantic music, which was among the inspirations that led him to paint abstractly. For Kandinsky, Wagner painted with music, and his compositions were "painterly." Later, Schönberg's explicitly abstract and more austere atonal compositions confirmed that Kandinsky had been esthetically correct in making completely abstract compositions. He was in tune with the times, above all the leading music of modern times—times defined by the new dynamics of nature uncovered by modern science, as he noted. (It is worth adding that Schönberg wrote for Kandinsky's *Blue Rider Almanac* [1914], and that Schönberg painted, if not entirely abstractly. My point is that he agreed with Kandinsky—they became friends—that painting was in fact a kind of music and that music was a kind of painting.)

For Goldberg, abstract paintings are also pure music, but her pure music synthesizes Wagner's painterly "maximalist" music, with its romantic intensity and dramatic harmonies—its seemingly overflowing excesses (certainly sense of uncontainable abundance)—and Schönberg's dissonant music (as Kandinsky called it, in acknowledgement of the dissonance of his own music), with its stochastic minimalism (certainly concentrated compared to Wagner's music, which has the melodic motif rather than discreet note as its basic unit). Goldberg's grid paintings also have a peculiar affinity with Philip Glass's minimalist compositions. She also repeats minimalist modules (her particles), and also implicitly ad infinitum. Goldberg fuses coloristic intensity and sensual intimacy—an uncanny inner voluptuousness—with minimalist or systemic

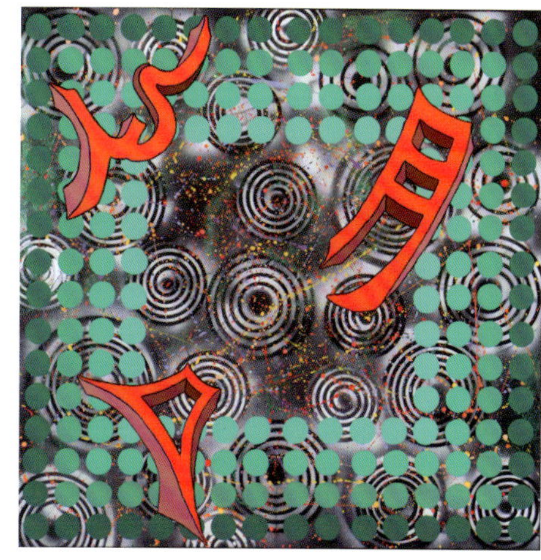

SK's Car, 2006
Acrylic on canvas with reflective chips
36" x 36"

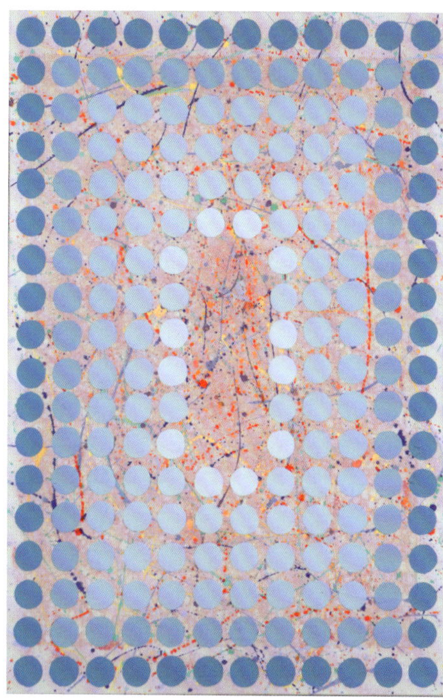

Bobby Bloom on the Boardwalk, 2006
Acrylic, reflective chips, Japanese rice paper on canvas
36" x 24"
Private Collection

Duvall Pharmacy, 2006
Acrylic on canvas with reflective chips
72" x 60"

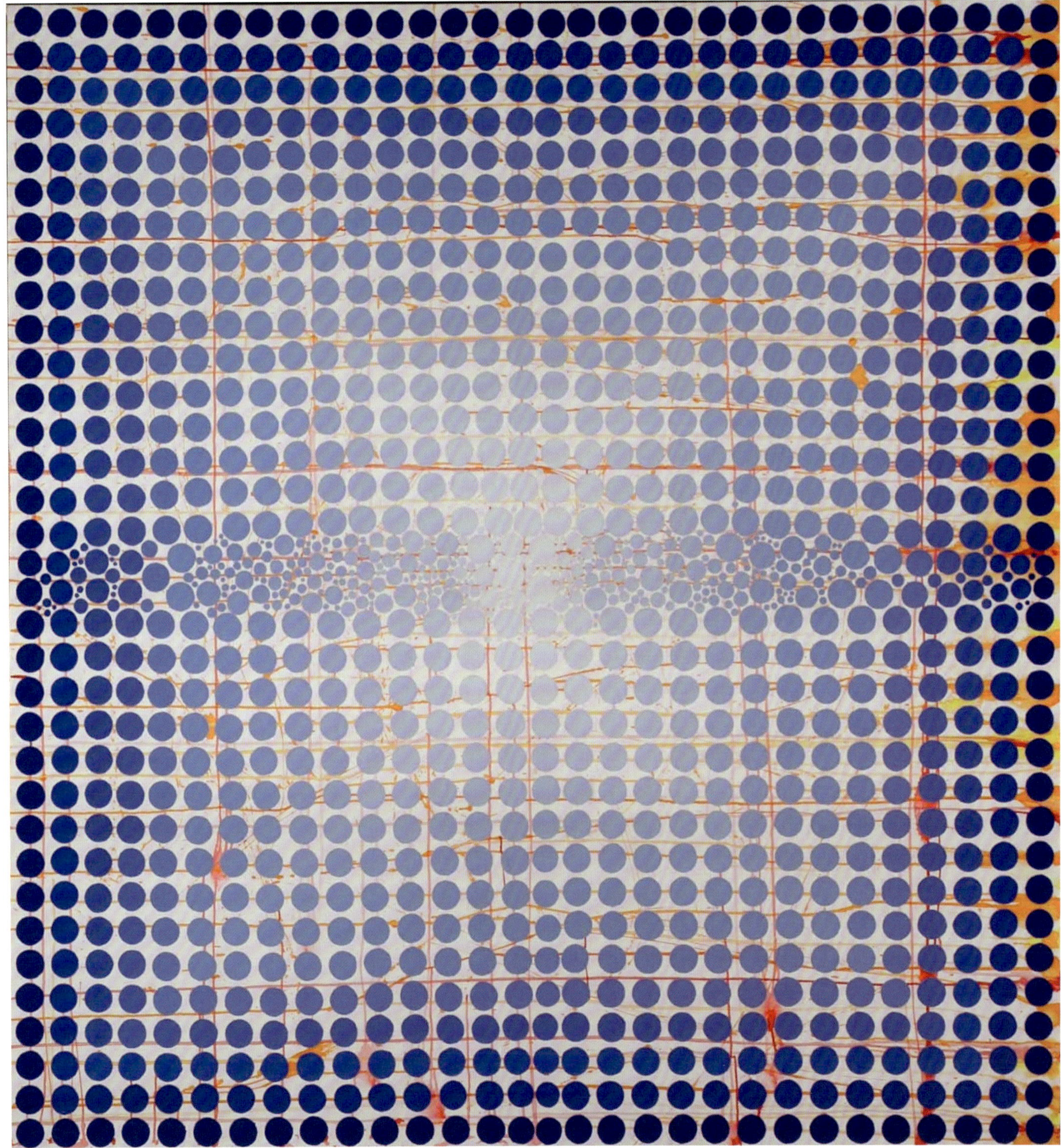

The Passion of Winter, 2005
Acrylic on canvas
72" x 84"

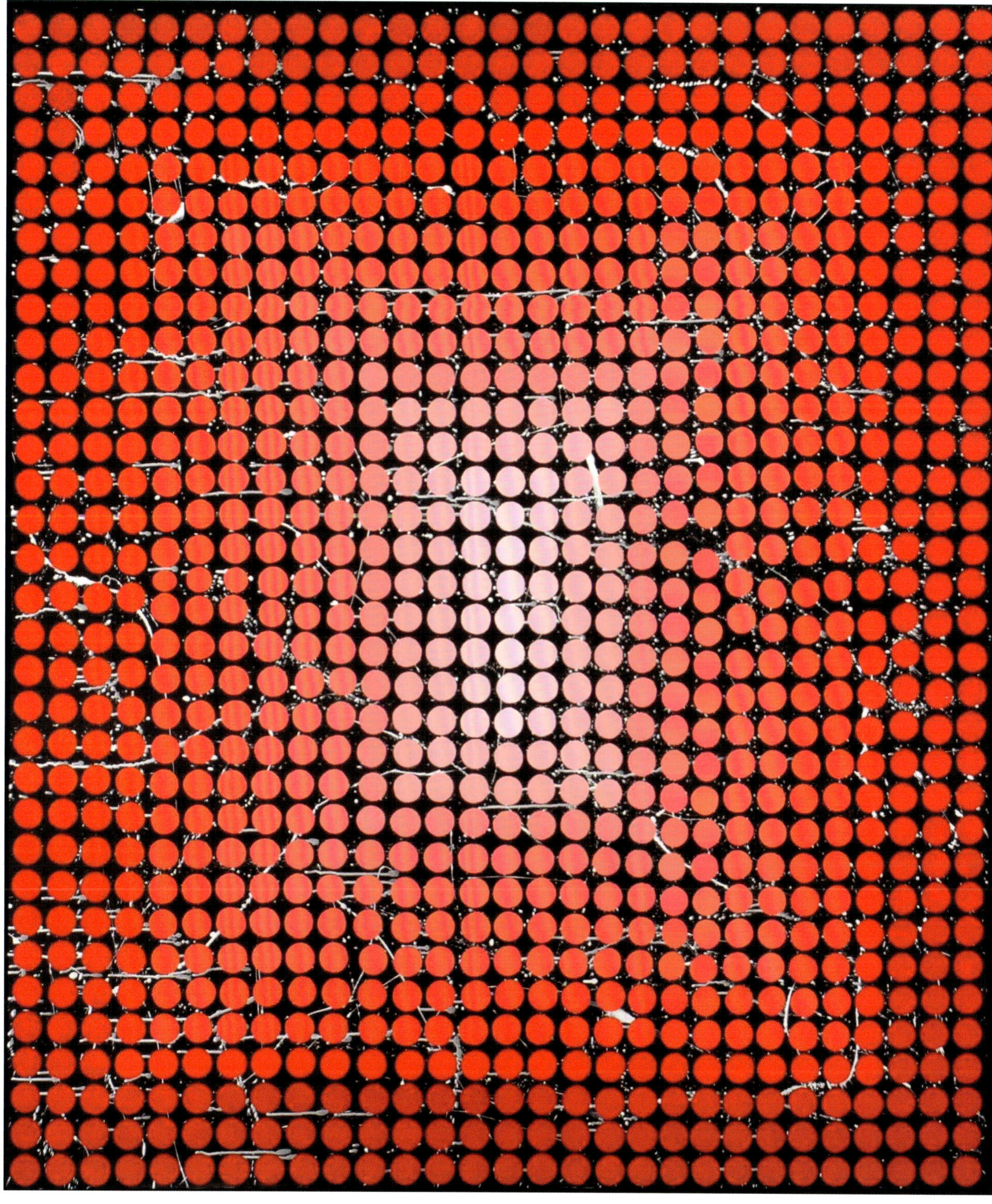

Listening to Ivy #1, 2005
Acrylic on canvas
84" x 72"

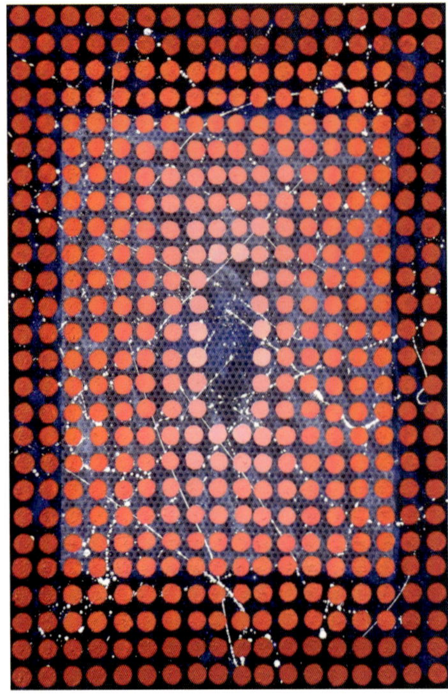

A Night in Carlin's Park, 2007
Acrylic, reflective chips, Japanese rice paper on canvas
36" x 24"

painting (as Lawrence Alloway called it) and atonal "agitation," an uncanny side effect of the random "sequencing" of notes. I am arguing that Goldberg's musical paintings reconcile musical opposites, just as they reconciled geometrical form and gestural energy. One might say that her gestural particles—pointillist "bursts" of luminous color—spontaneously form an infinite grid, even as the seemingly homogeneous grid makes their heterogeneity aesthetically shocking. Thus, her musical paintings show that aesthetic perception is what the psychoanalyst D. W. Winnicott called creative perception, which he thought alone made life worth living, no doubt because it showed that it was rooted in primary creativity. A sort of austere romantic, dissonant and harmonious at once, Goldberg shows that excess and discipline are the core of creativity.

Looking at Goldberg's abstract paintings, one seems to be watching a ceaseless stream of cosmic consciousness—a consciousness available only through aesthetic perception and the profoundest consciousness human beings are capable of (the kind of consciousness mystics struggle to achieve)—and listening to music, which seems to mirror and track human consciousness, "with its constant flow of evanescent thoughts, feelings, desires, urges and impulses," all "flow[ing] into and...enfold[ing] each other," that is, implicit in each other, as Bohm and Hiley write.[23] They think that listening to music—even more, seeing music as gesture and geometry, as particles of sensation and axiomatic structure, which is what we see when we are esthetically shocked and spiritually aroused by Goldberg's paintings—is an especially clear example of enfoldment. That is, musical composition comes closest to communicating the implicate order.

"At a given moment, a certain note [think of Goldberg's particles of color as notes] is being played, but a number of the previous notes are still 'reverberating' in consciousness. Close attention will show that it is the simultaneous presence and activity of all these related reverberations that is responsible for the direct and immediately felt sense of movement, flow and continuity, as well as for the general meaning [spiritual purpose] of the music. To hear a set of notes so far apart in time [the grid keeps them close together] that there is no consciousness of such reverberation will destroy altogether the sense of a whole unbroken living movement that gives meaning and force to what is being heard [or seen]."[24] Such reverberation is the aura in creative action. ●

Notes

[1] Hilla Rebay, "The Beauty of Non-Objectivity" (1937), Francesca Frascina and Charles Harrison, eds. *Modern Art and Modernism: A Critical Anthology* (London and New York: Harper and Row, 1982), 148

[2] David Bohm and Basil Hiley, *The Undivided Universe: An Ontological Interpretation of Quantum Theory* (London and New York: Routledge, 1995), 363

[3] Ibid., 381-82

[4] David Bohm, *Wholeness and the Implicate Order* (London and Boston: Routledge & Kegan Paul, 1983), 141

[5] Max Horkheimer, *Critique of Instrumental Reason* (New York: Continuum, 1974), 99

[6] Barr's diagram appeared on the cover of the exhibition catalogue *Cubism and Abstract Art* (New York: Museum of Modern Art, 1936). It "argues" that "non-geometrical abstract art" and "geometrical abstract art" are the simultaneous climaxes of modern art. Barr traces the development of the former through "(Abstract) Expressionism," "(Abstract) Dadaism," and "(Abstract) Surrealism," thus disregarding the fact that all three movements are incomprehensible apart from their intention to make us artistically conscious of the unconscious. Similarly, he traces the development of the latter through Cubism, Suprematism, Constructivism, Purism, and Neo-Plasticism, disregarding the social critical aspect of their abstraction.

[7] Ananda Coomaraswamy, *Samvega: Aesthetic Shock*, Collected Papers, vol. I (Princeton: Princeton University Press, 1977), 182, writes: "It will not, then, surprise us to find that it is not only in connection with natural objects (such as the dewdrop) or events (such as death) but also in connection with works of art, and in fact whenever or wherever perception (aesthesis) leads to a serious experience, that we are really shaken." See also Donald Kuspit, "The Emotional Gains of Aesthetic Shock," *Psychoanalytic Inquiry*, 26 (June-July 2006), 344-361

[8] Kandinsky: *Complete Writings on Art*, Kenneth C. Lindsay and Peter Vergo, eds. (New York: Da Capo Press, 1994), 142

[9] Clement Greenberg, "The Role of Nature in Modern Painting," *Partisan Review*, 16 (January 1949), 79, writes: "The process by which Cubism, in pushing naturalism to its ultimate limits and over-emphasizing modeling–which is perhaps the most important means of naturalism in painting–arrived at the antithesis of naturalism, flat abstract art, might be considered a case of 'dialectical conversion'." In "Art" (Gustave Courbet), *Nation,* 168 (January 8, 1949), 51, writes: "We see once again that by driving a tendency to its farthest extreme–in this case the illusion of the third dimension–one finds oneself abruptly going in the opposite direction." Goldberg, like the best artists, pushes a tendency–flat, abstract painting–to its extreme, resulting in the illusion–a sort of spontaneous vision–of "round" cosmic space, that is, four-dimensional space.

[10] Eric Hobsbawm, *Behind the Times: The Decline and Fall of the Twentieth-Century Avant-Gardes* (London: Thames and Hudson, 1998), 24

[11] Ibid.

[12] I am alluding to D. W. Winnicott's theories of playing and creativity, particularly his view that "It is creative apperception more than anything else that makes the individual feel that life is worth living. Contrasted with this is a relationship to external reality which is one of compliance, the world and its details being recognized but only as something to be fitted in with or demanding adaptation." "Creativity and Its Origins," *Playing and Reality* (London and New York: Tavistock and Methuen, 1982), 65. I am suggesting that Goldberg's abstract painting embodies her creative apperception of the implicate order, and as such is non-compliant with traditional abstraction and everyday perception in the explicate order.

Creative apperception conveys a zest for life, even joie de vivre–the sense of inexhaustible aliveness in the linear dynamics of the particle trajectories, streaking across the canvas like falling stars, and the saturated colors giving voluptuous substance to cosmic inner/outer space, and the sense of all dynamically in all conveyed by their "interpenetrating intermixture," of Goldberg's self-empowering abstract paintings.

[13] Otto Rank, *Art and Artist: Creative Urge and Personality Development* (New York and London: Norton, 1982), 355

[14] Ibid.

[15] Rudolf Otto, *The Idea of the Holy* (New York: Oxford University Press, 1958), chapter IV regards the numinous as the core "religious emotion." It involves consciousness of the "mysterium tremendum," bringing with it "the peculiar quality of the 'uncanny' and 'aweful' 'awful'," often conveyed through "exaltedness and sublimity"; a sense of "absolute overpoweringness" conveyed through "majesty" and an "element of 'energy' or urgency." One experiences all of these in Goldberg's abstract paintings. Aura is "the 'numen'... experienced as present," (12) and through Goldberg's artistic realization of it–her articulation of its innate esthetics–the numen shines forth in pure presence, that is, unadulterated by subjective impression and mood.

[16] Goldberg's "centering" is a remarkable demonstration of what Rudoph Arnheim in *The Power of the Center* (Berkeley and London: University of California, 1982), 5, calls "a center in the dynamic sense," that is, "a focus from which energy radiates into the environment." At the same time, the center gathers up the energy of the field, concentrating and balancing the forces at odds in it, making for what Arnheim calls a "balancing center" that is a "vortex of forces."

[17] Kandinsky, 131

[18] Edward O. Wilson, *Consilience* (New York: Vintage Books, 1999), 238

[19] Clement Greenberg, *Modernism with a Vengeance*, 1957-1969, Collected Essays and Criticism (Chicago and London: University of Chicago Press, 1993), vol. 4, 33

[20] Clement Greenberg, *Arrogant Purpose*, 1945-1949, Collected Essays and Criticism (Chicago and London: University of Chicago Press, 1988), vol. 2, 233

[21] Clement Greenberg, *Affirmations and Refusals*, 1950-1956, Collected Essays and Criticism (Chicago and London: University of Chicago Press, 1993), vol. 3, 216

[22] Pater famously stated: "It is the art of music which most completely realizes this artistic ideal, this perfect identification of matter and form. In its consummate moments, the end is not distinct from the means, the form from the matter, the subject from the expression; they inhere in and completely saturate each other; and to it, therefore, to the condition of its perfect moments, all the arts may be supposed constantly to tend and aspire." "The School of Giorgione," *The Renaissance* (New York: Modern Library, n. d. [1873], 114. The argument of this essay is that a remarkable number of Goldberg's abstract paintings are such "perfect [musical] moments."

[23] Bohm and Hiley, 382

[24] Ibid.

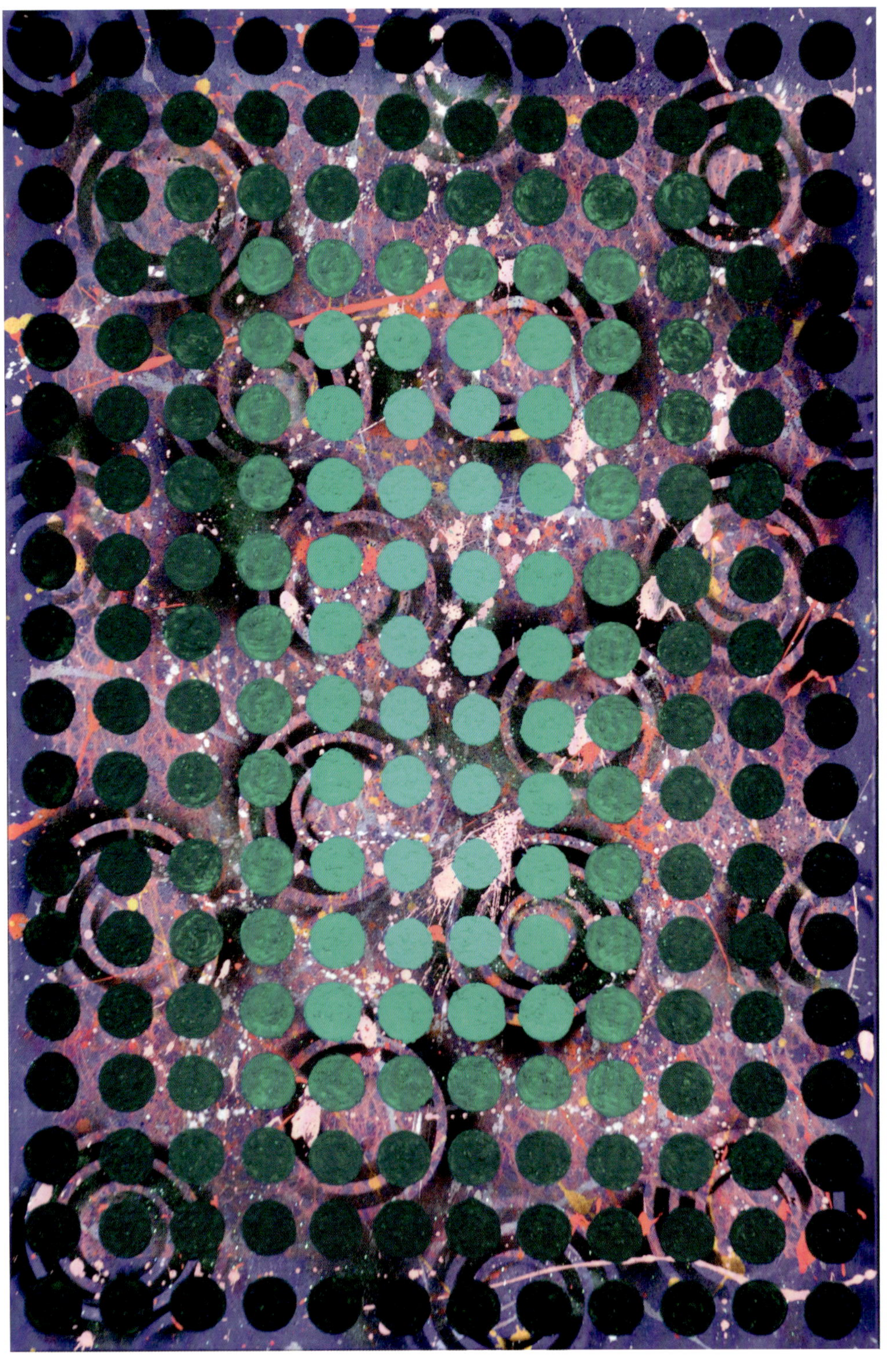

Sunset Over Saturn, 2006
Acrylic on canvas with reflective chips
36" x 24"

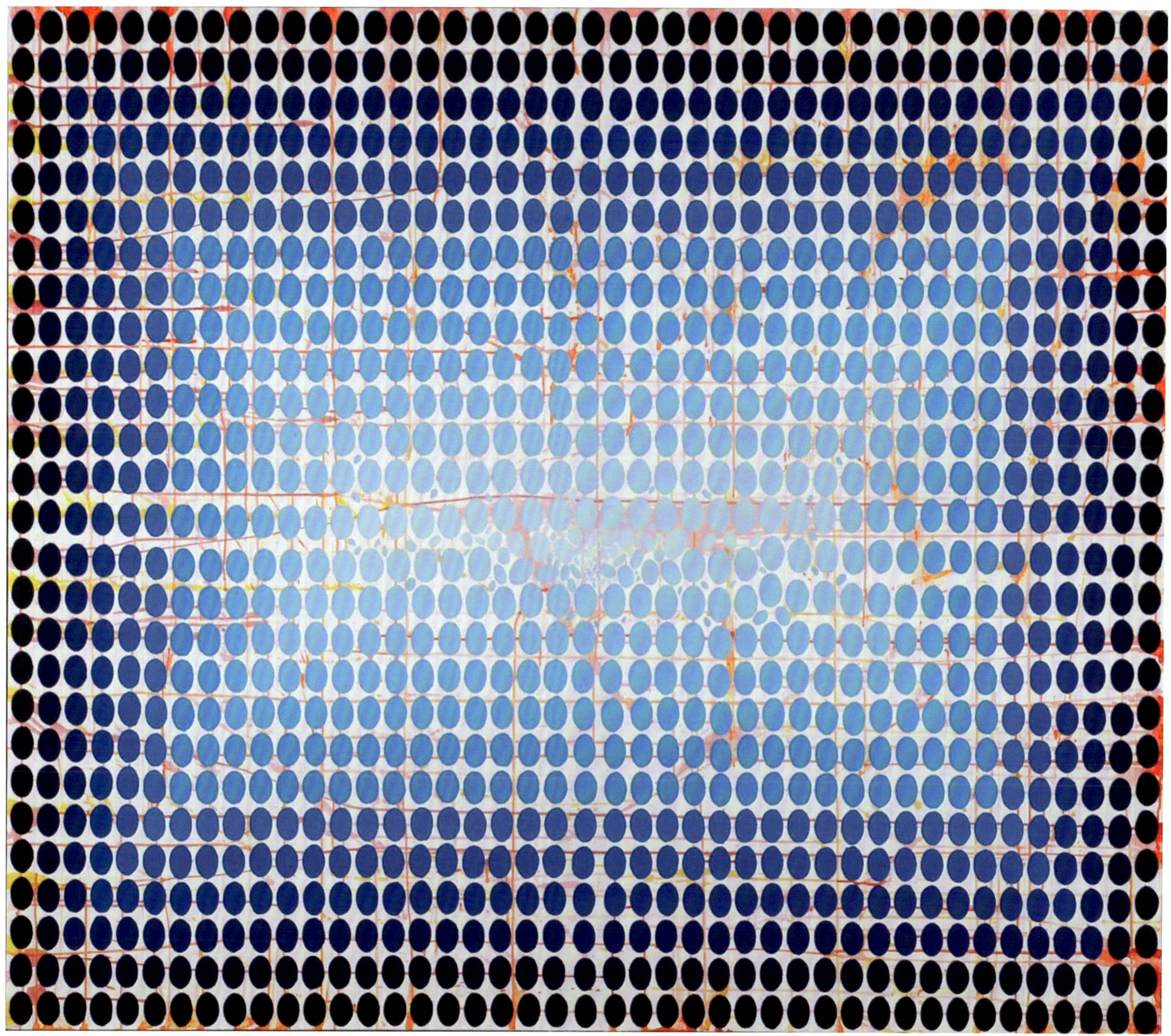

Listening to Ivy; Tuning into Blackbox Recorder, 2005
Acrylic on canvas
60" x 70"

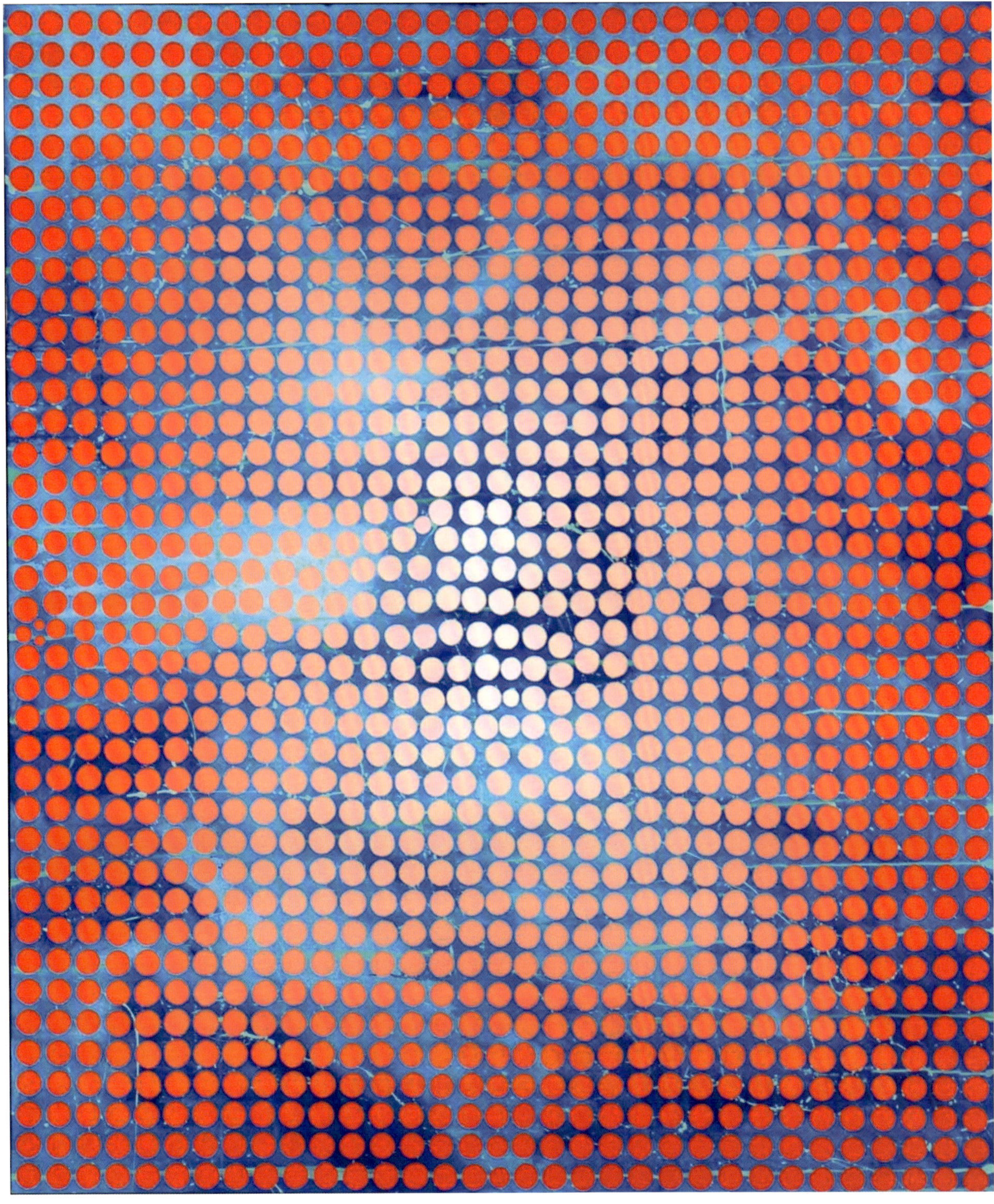

Listening to Ivy; Waiting for August, 2005
Acrylic on canvas
72" x 68"

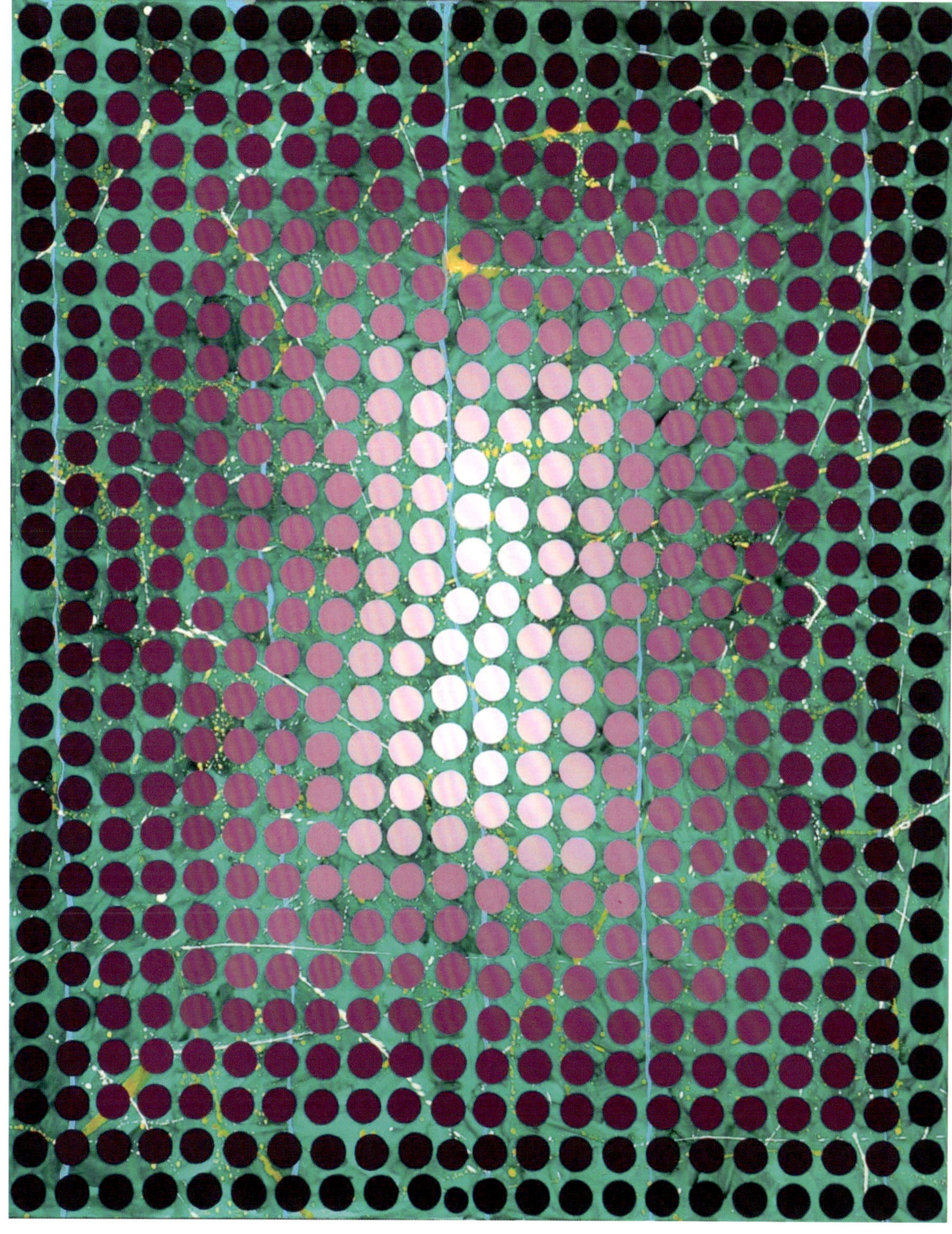

The Light of Late August, 2005
Acrylic on canvas
60" x 48"

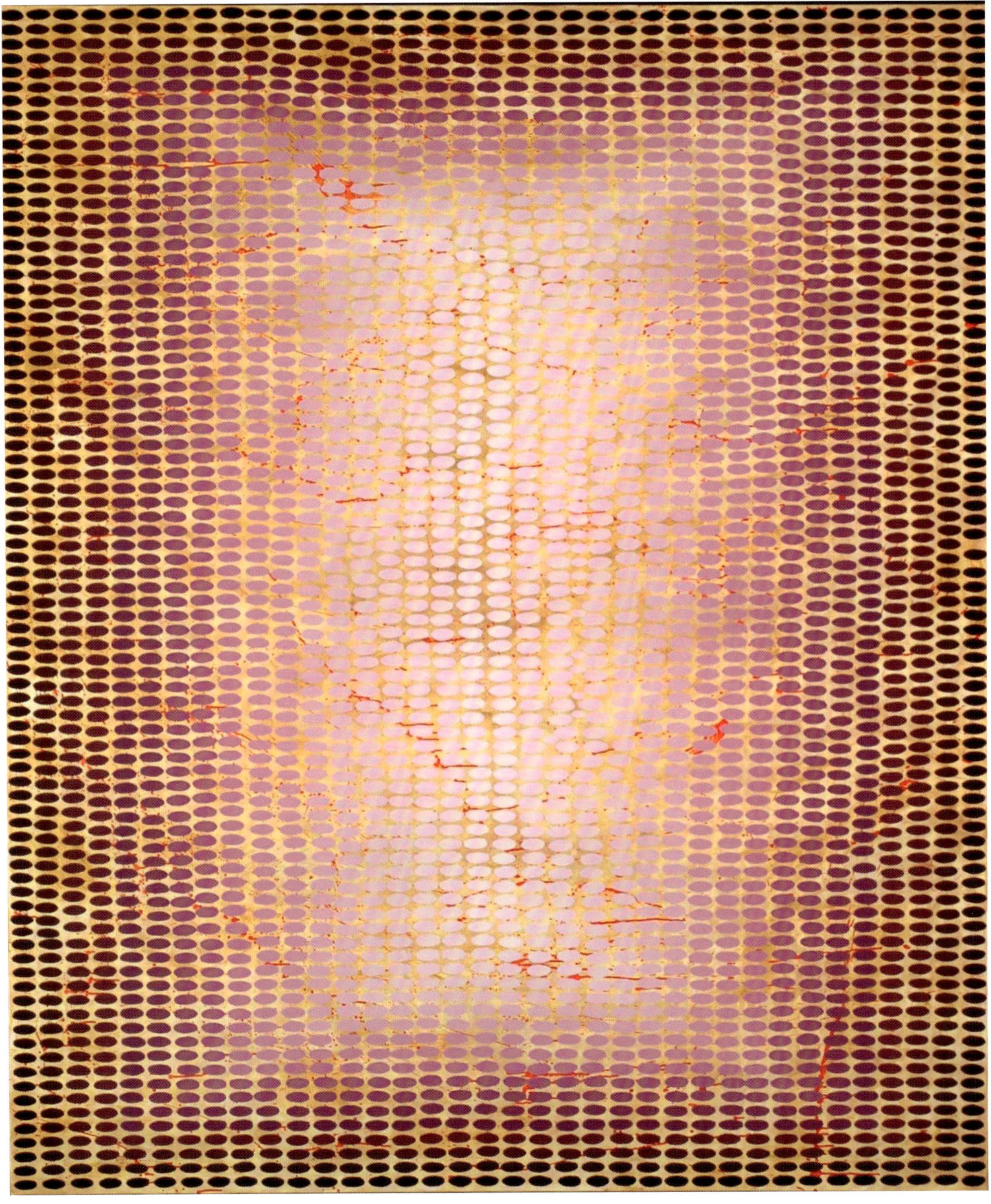

Purple Snow, 2005
Acrylic on canvas
84" x 72"

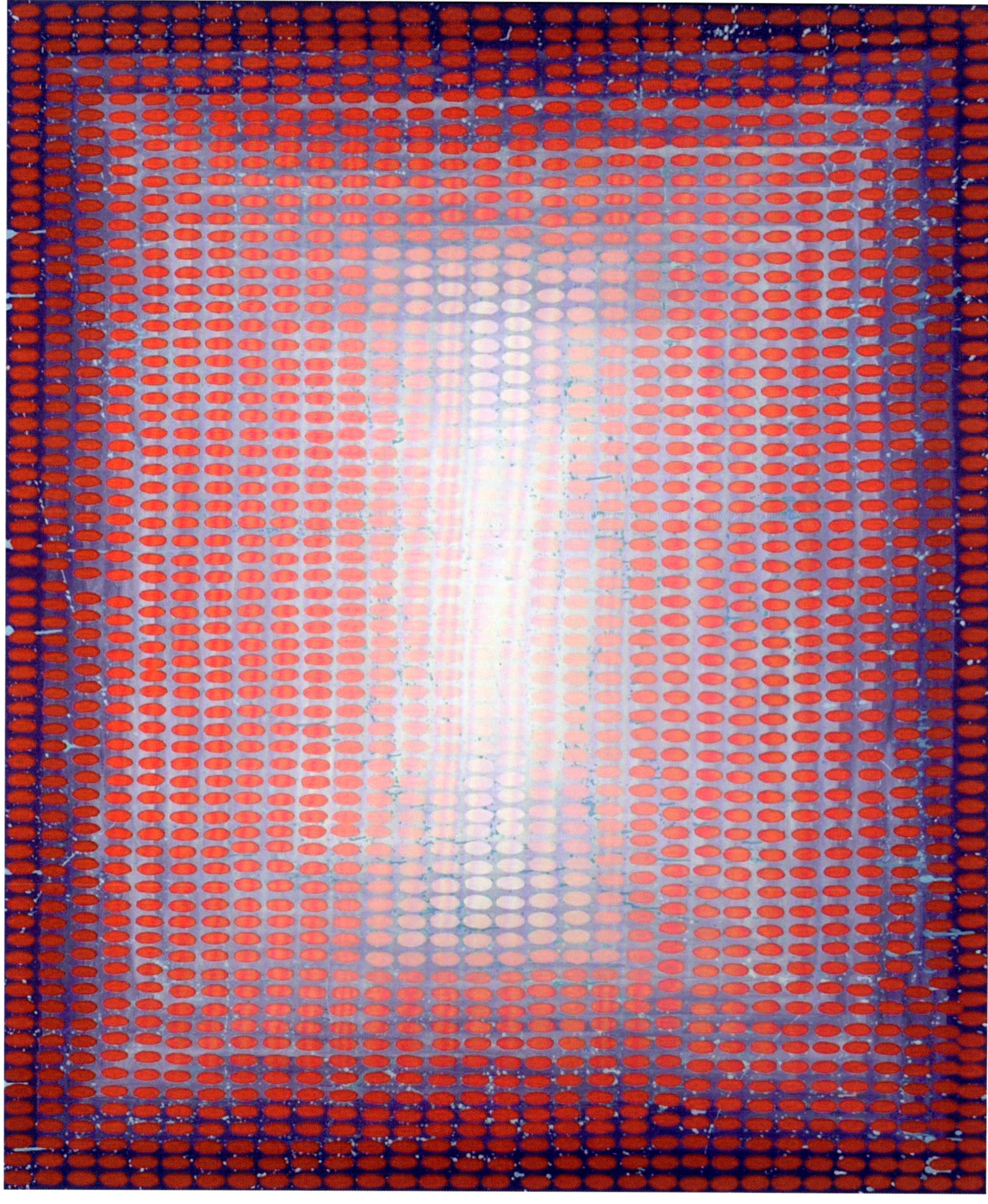

In Spite of it All, 2005
Acrylic on canvas
84" x 72"

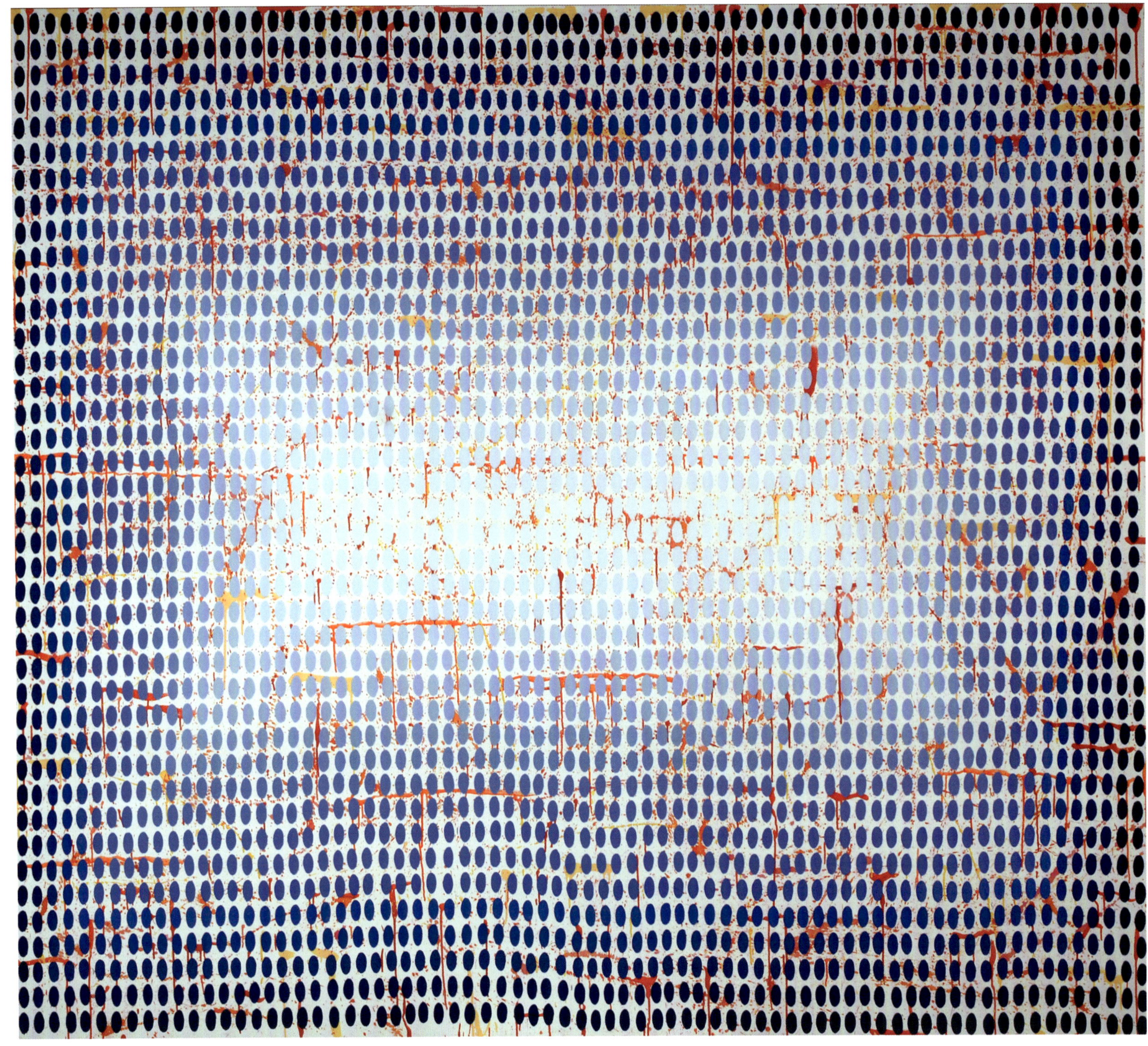

The Big Five at Forest Park Crosswalk, 2006
Acrylic on canvas
96" x 108"

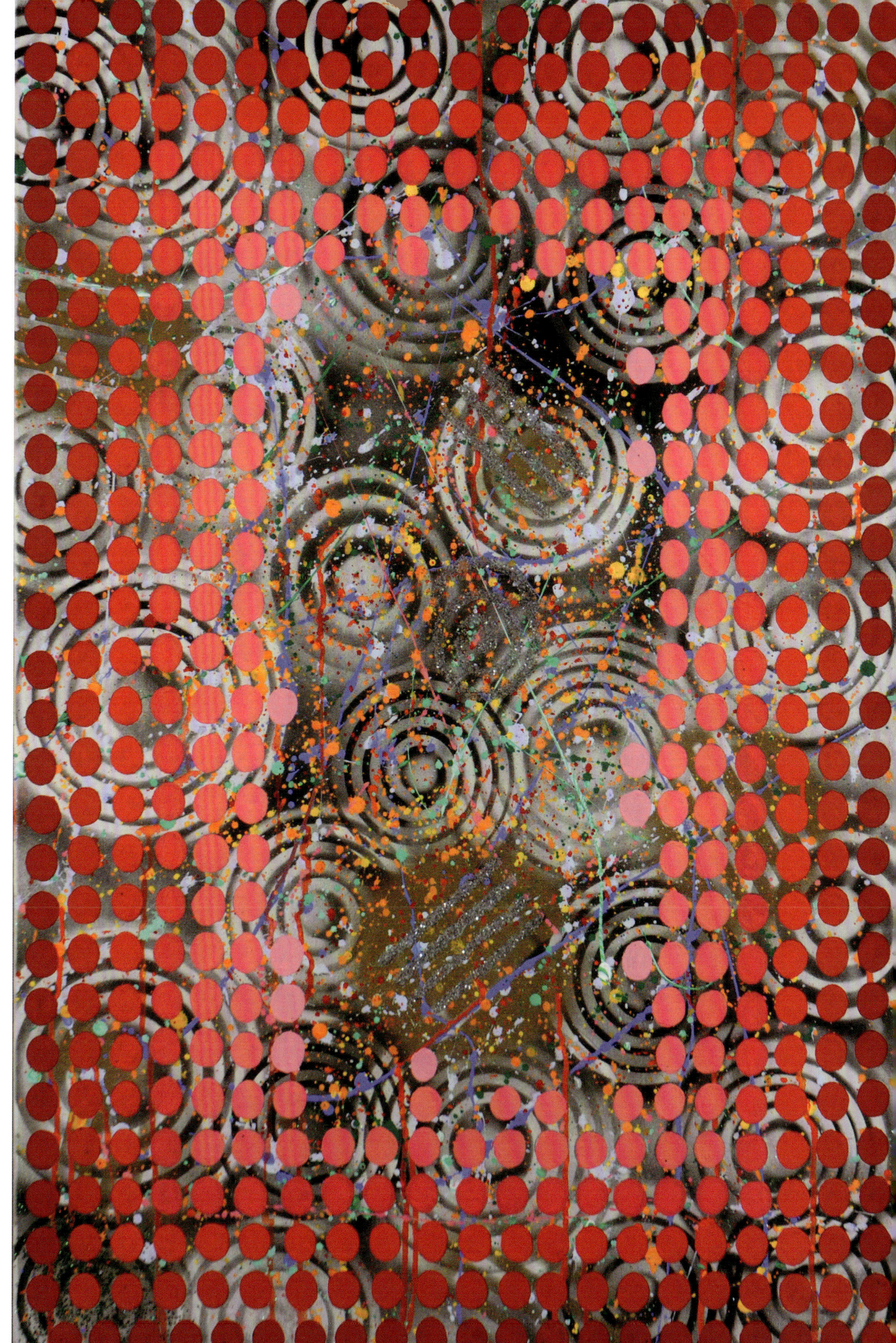

Ray and Ellinor Love Each Other, 2006
Acrylic on canvas with reflective chips
36" x 24"

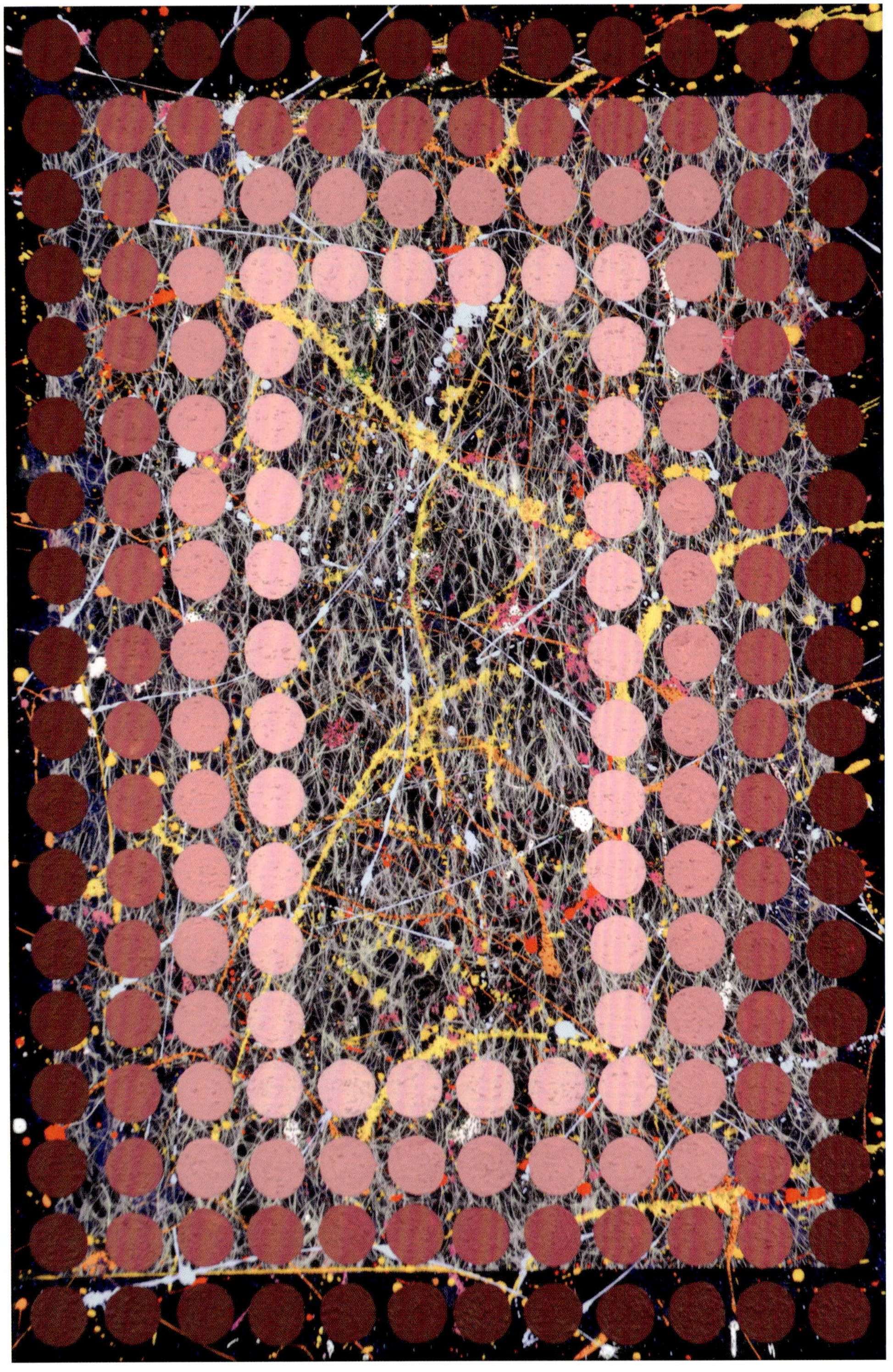

Ode to Maggie, 2006
Acrylic, reflective chips, Japanese rice paper on canvas
36" x 24"

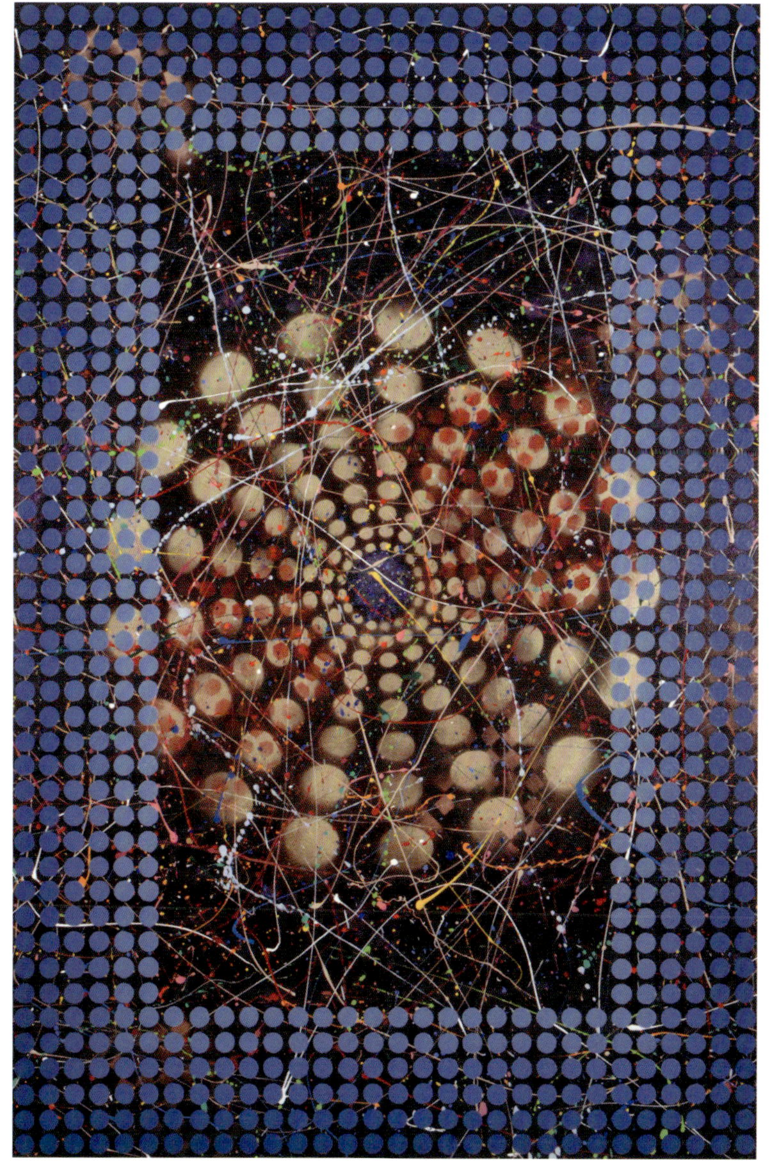

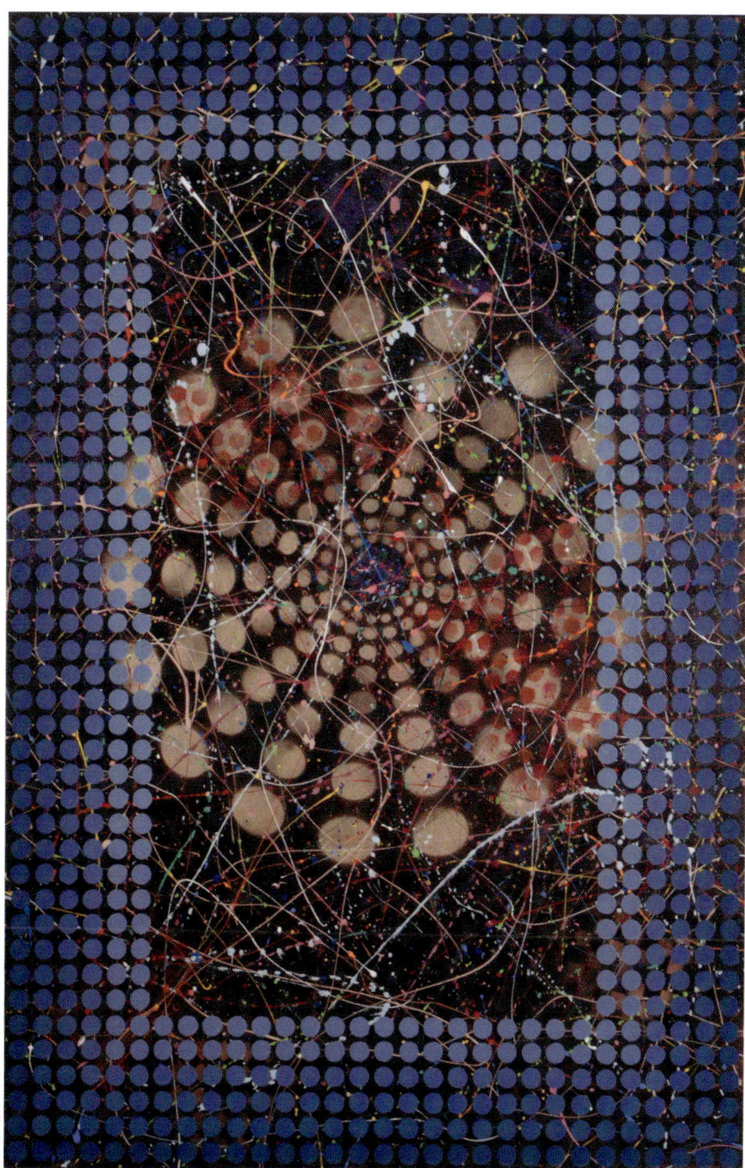

The Serenade of STP, 2007, Diptych
Acrylic on canvas
48" x 72" each

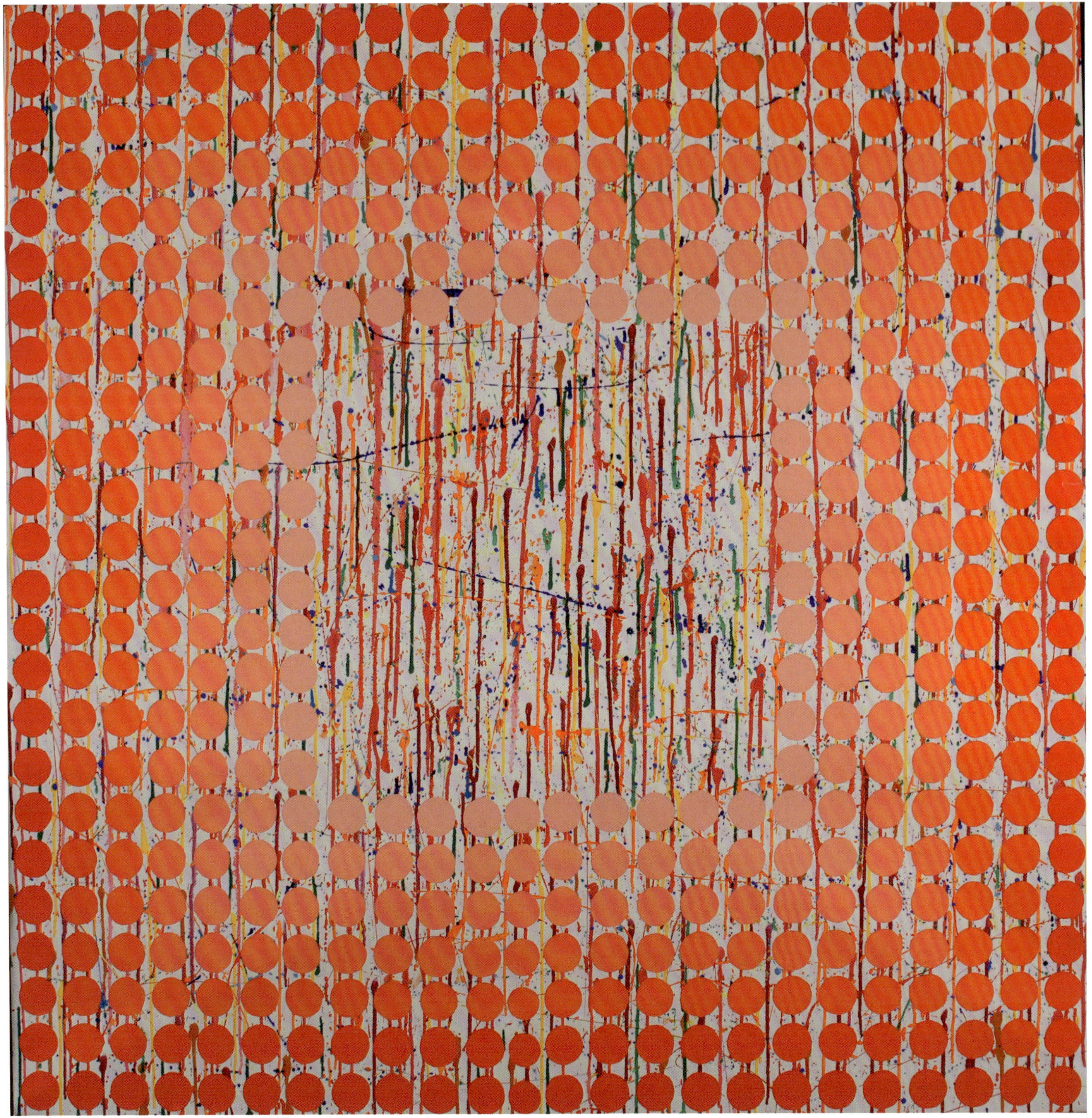

Mr. Healey Reads His Script, 2006
Acrylic on canvas
48" x 48"

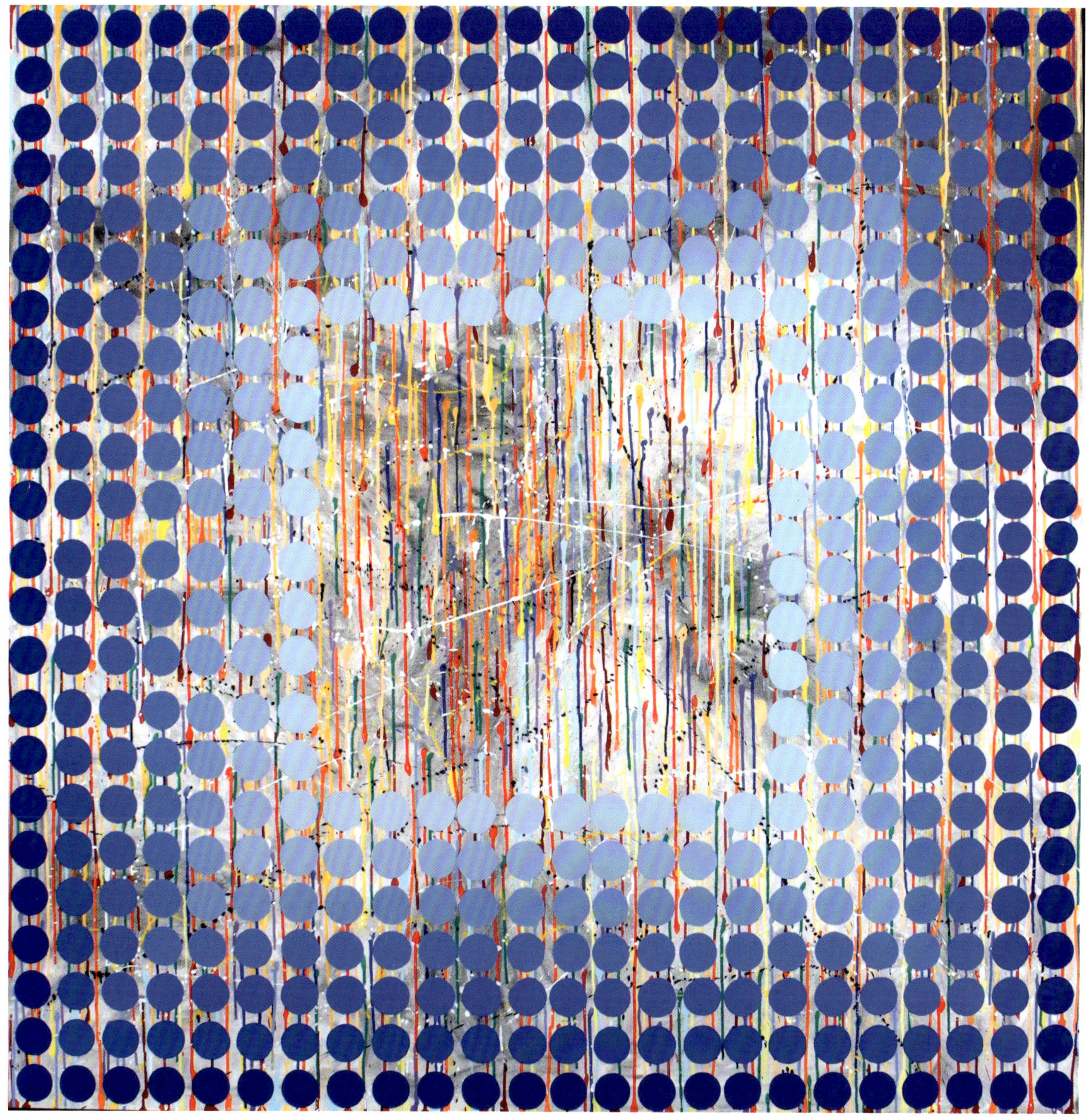

Missing Feryal, 2006
Acrylic on canvas
48" x 48"

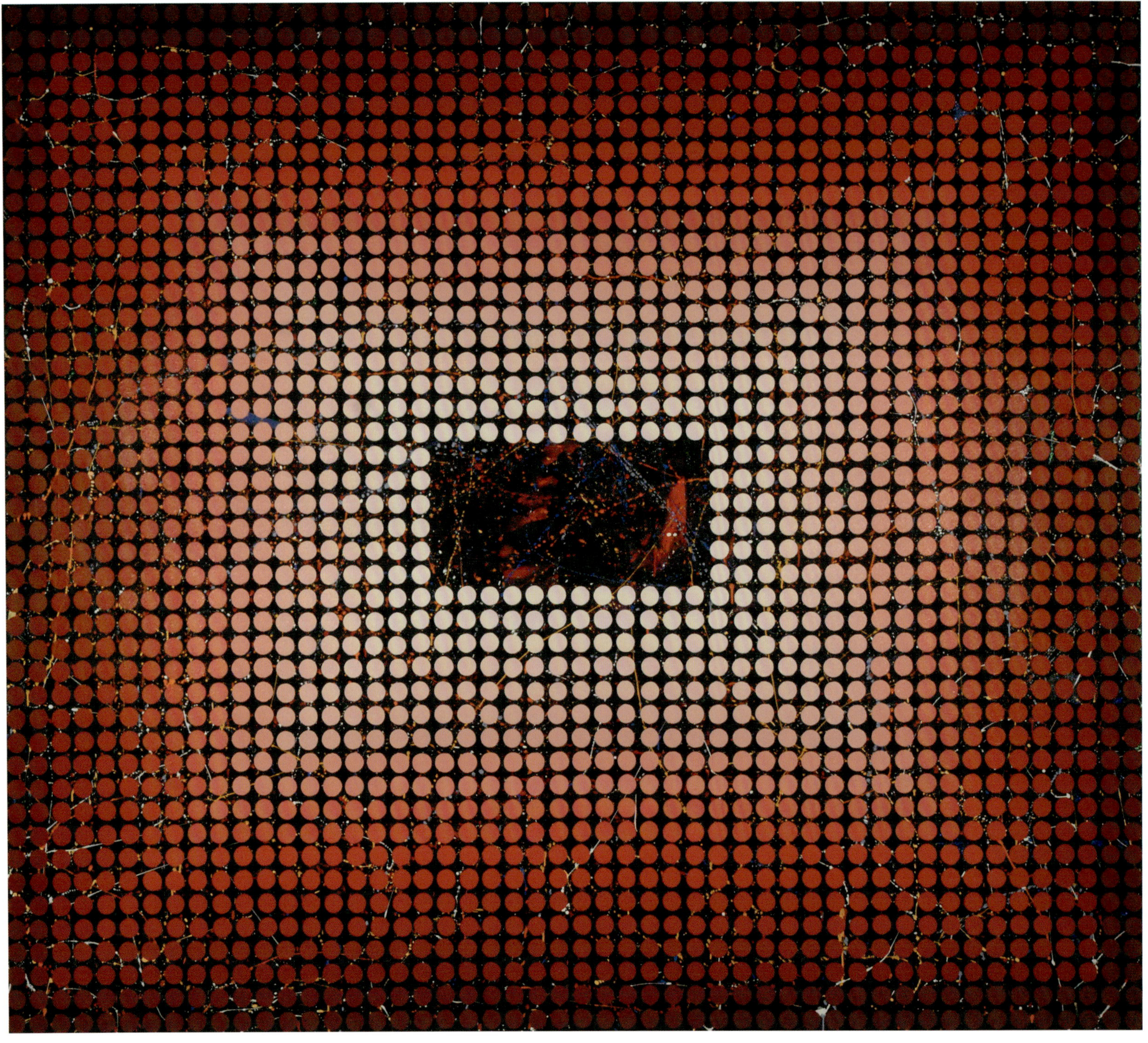

What's the Fastest Elevator in the World?, 2006
Acrylic on canvas with reflective chips
96" x 108"

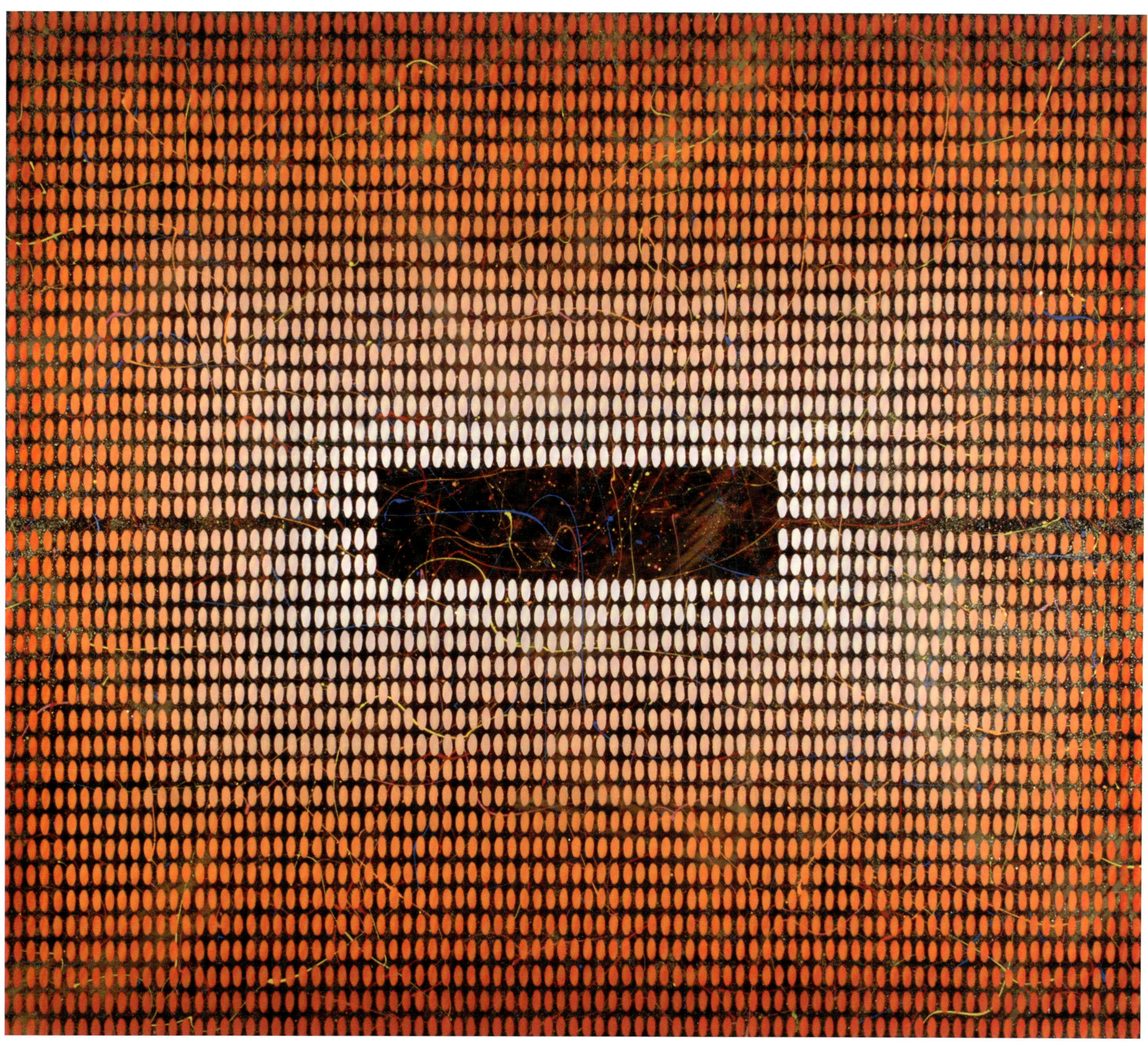

Mister Velder's English Class, 2007
Acrylic on canvas with reflective chips
84" x 96"

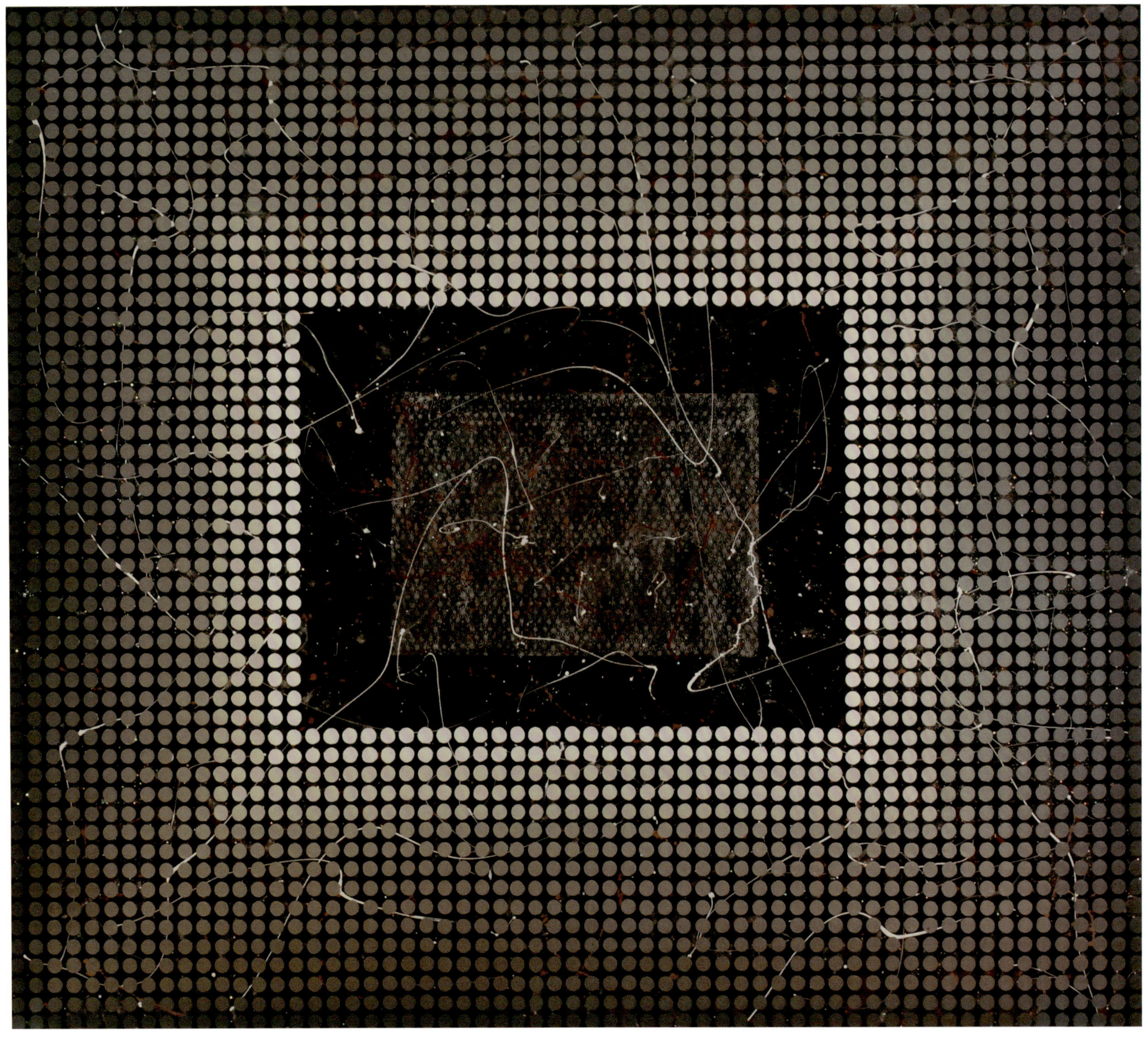

Bertrand Russell Visits Bancroft Road, 2007
Acrylic on canvas with reflective chips and Japanese rice paper
84" x 96"

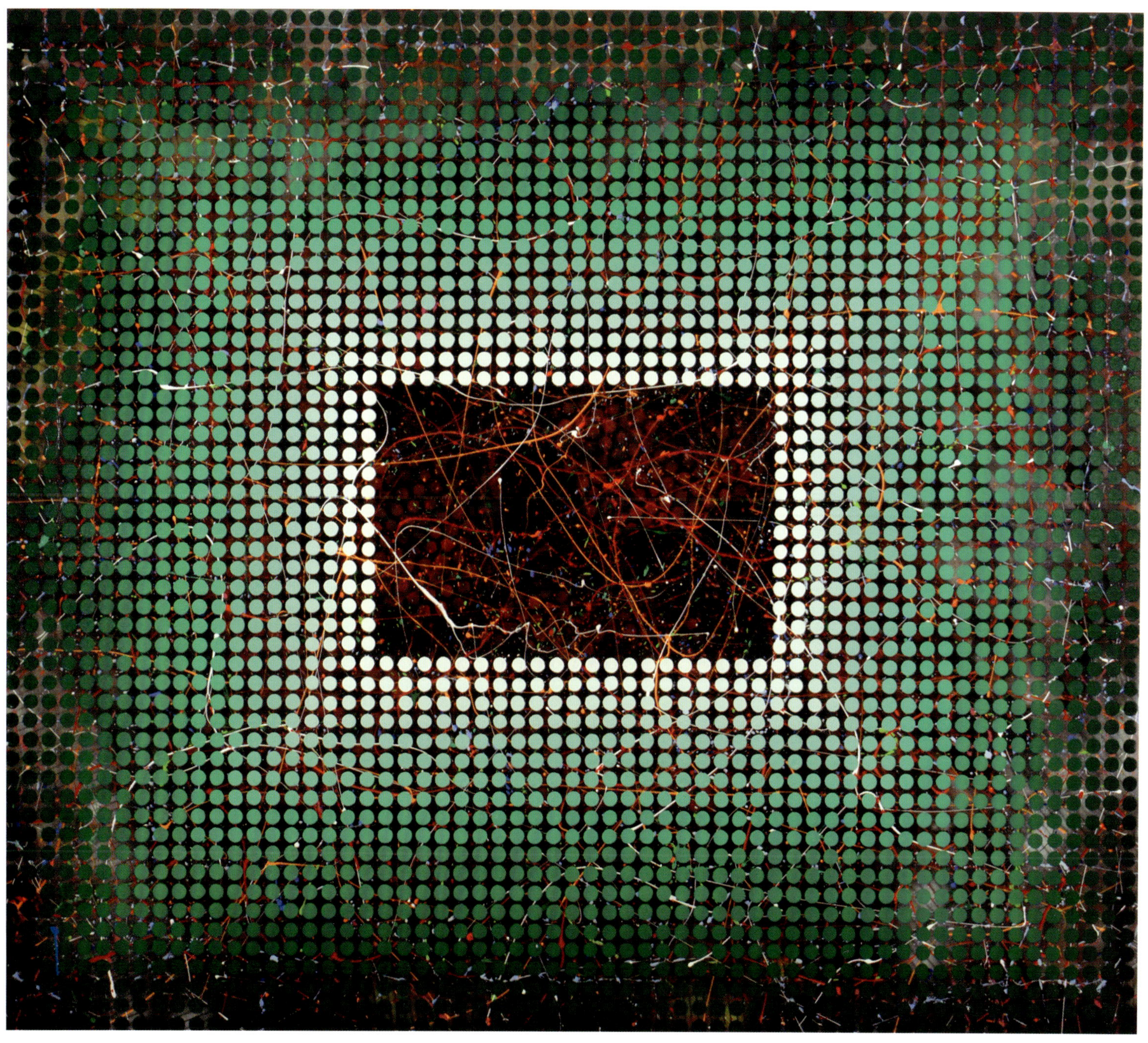

The June Joyance, 2007
Acrylic on canvas with reflective chips
84" x 96"

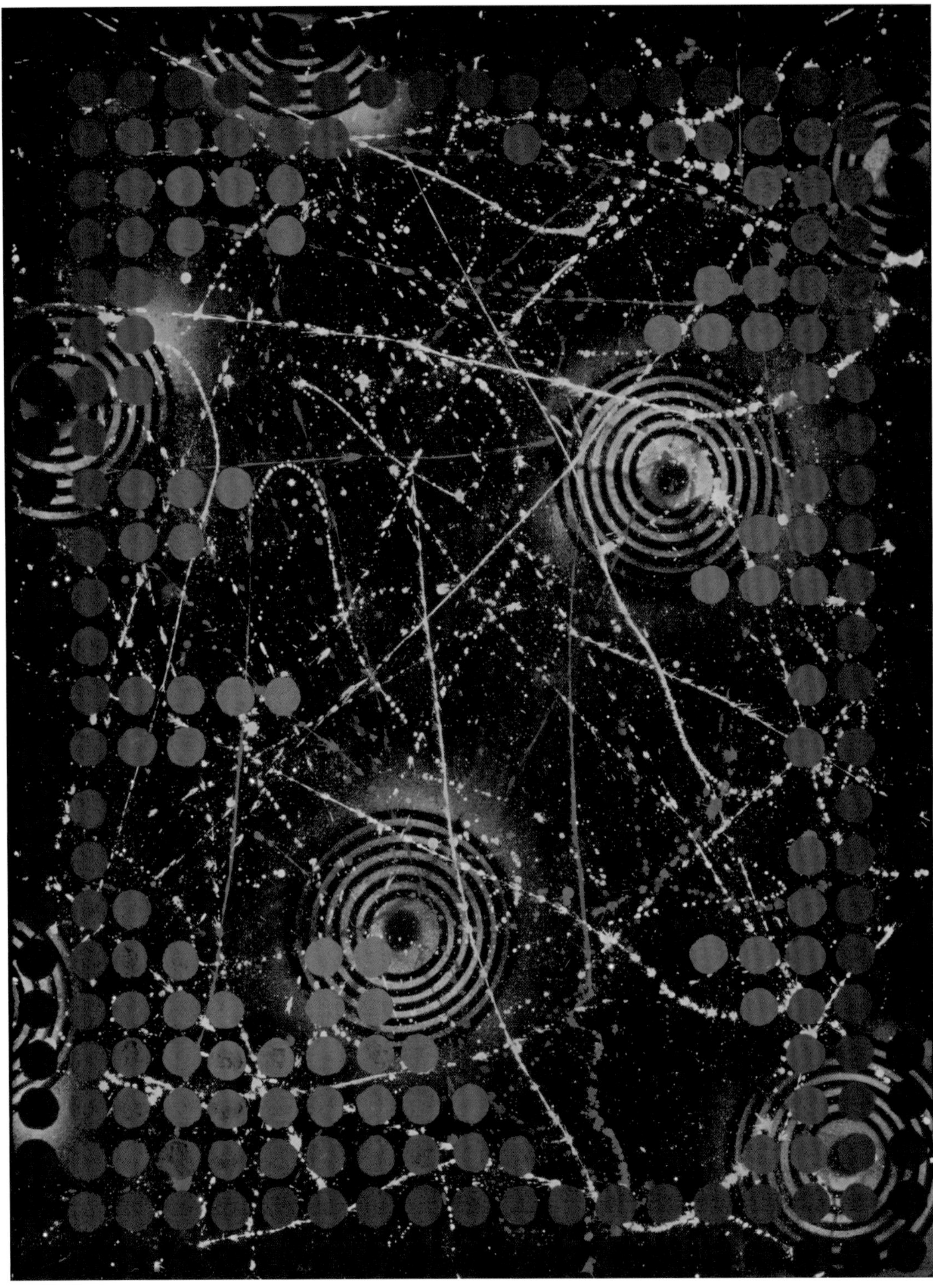

Lucid Dreams of Purple Snow, 2007
Acrylic on canvas with reflective chips
30" x 40"

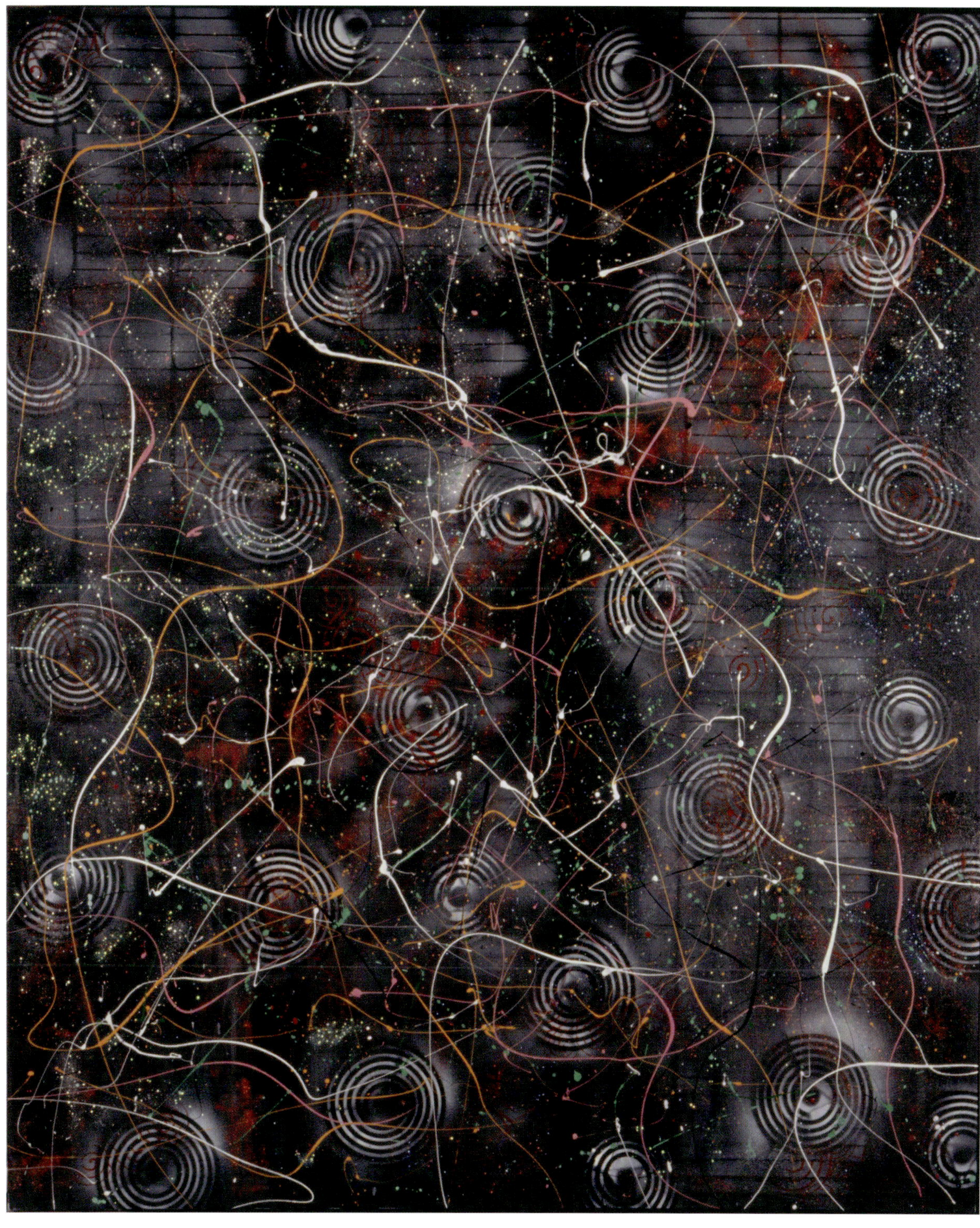

BP#4, 2007
Acrylic on canvas with reflective chips
60” x 72”

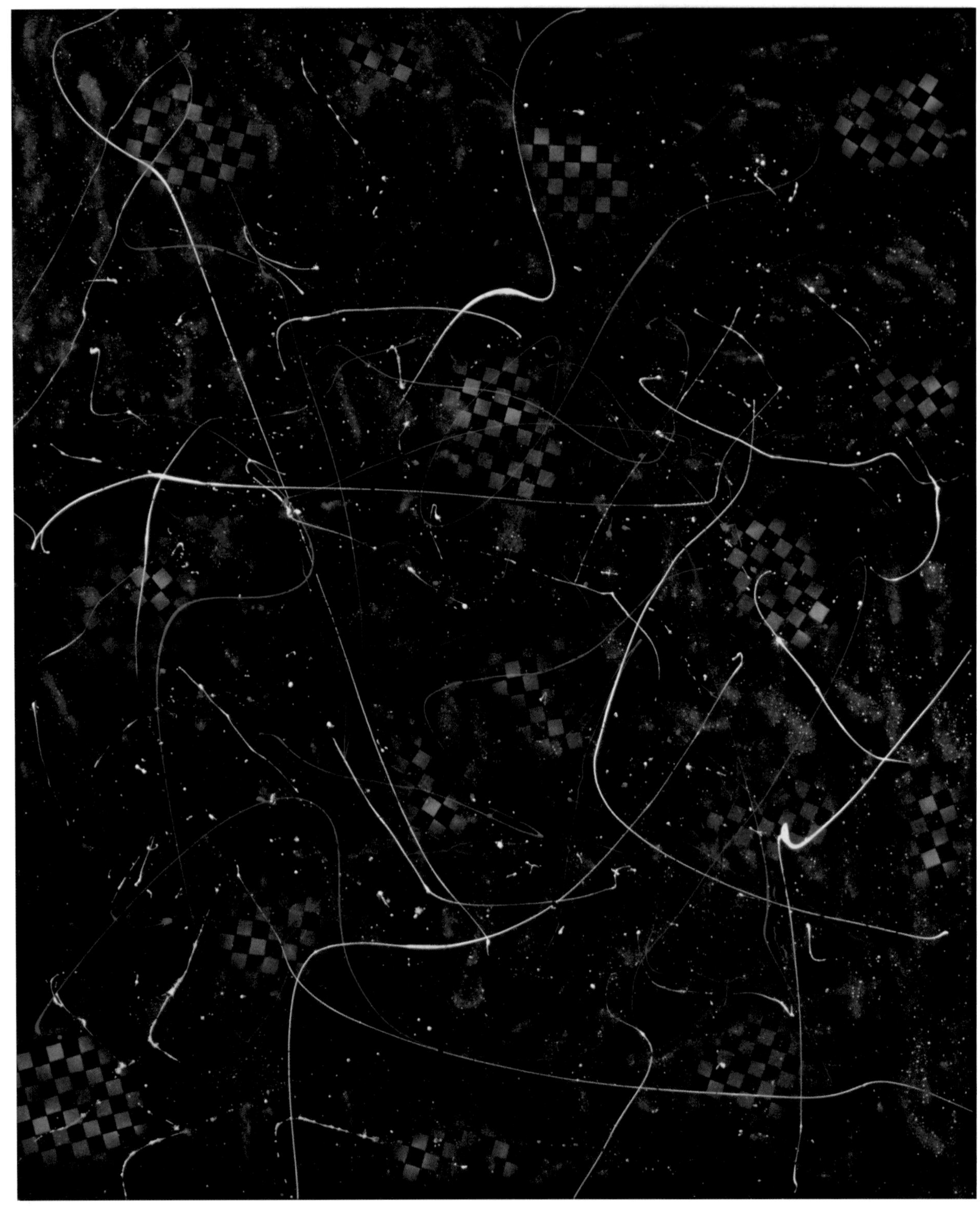

BP#2, 2007
Acrylic on canvas with reflective chips
72" x 60"

BP#0, 2007 ▶
Acrylic on canvas with reflective chips
36" x 36"

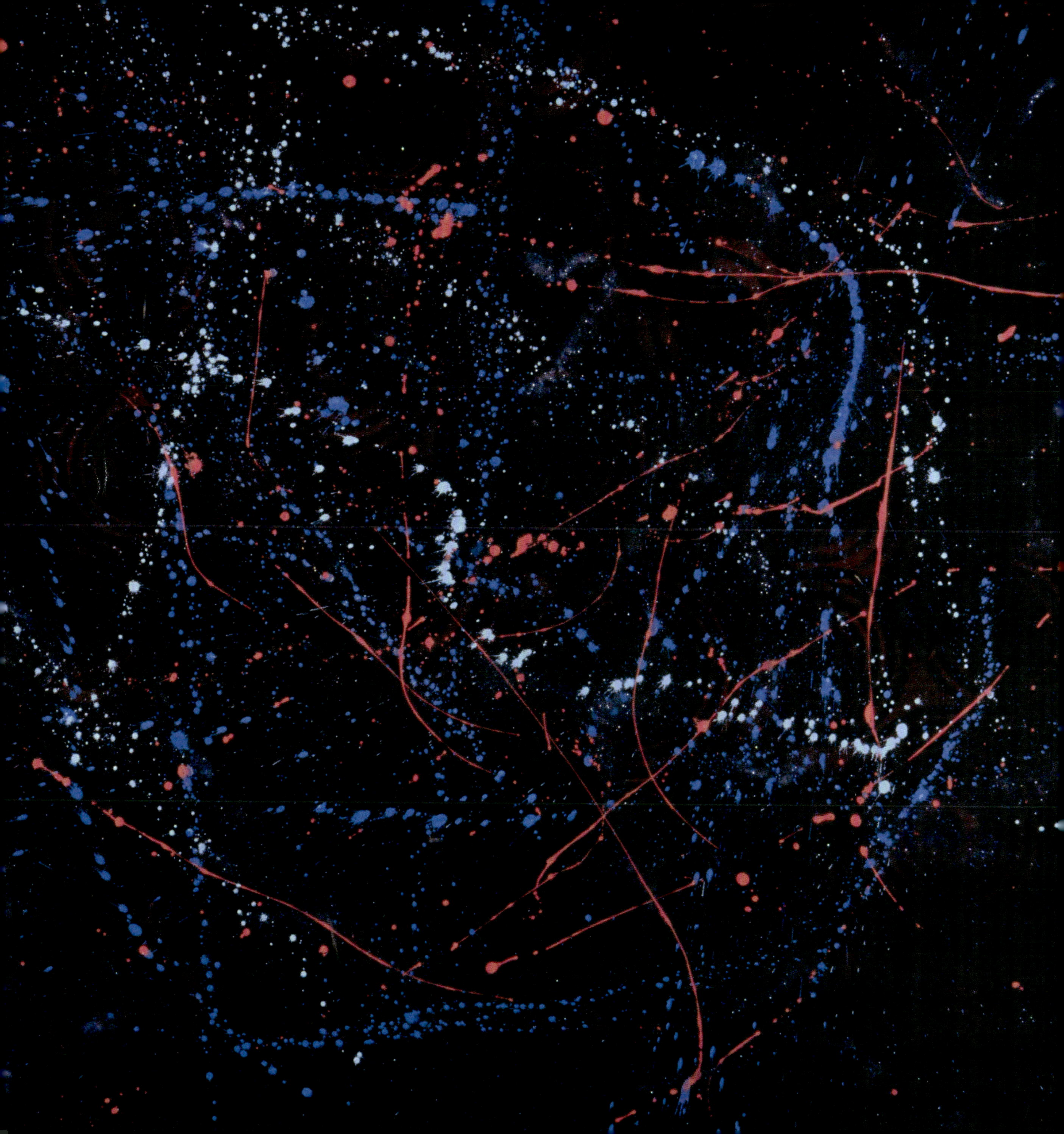

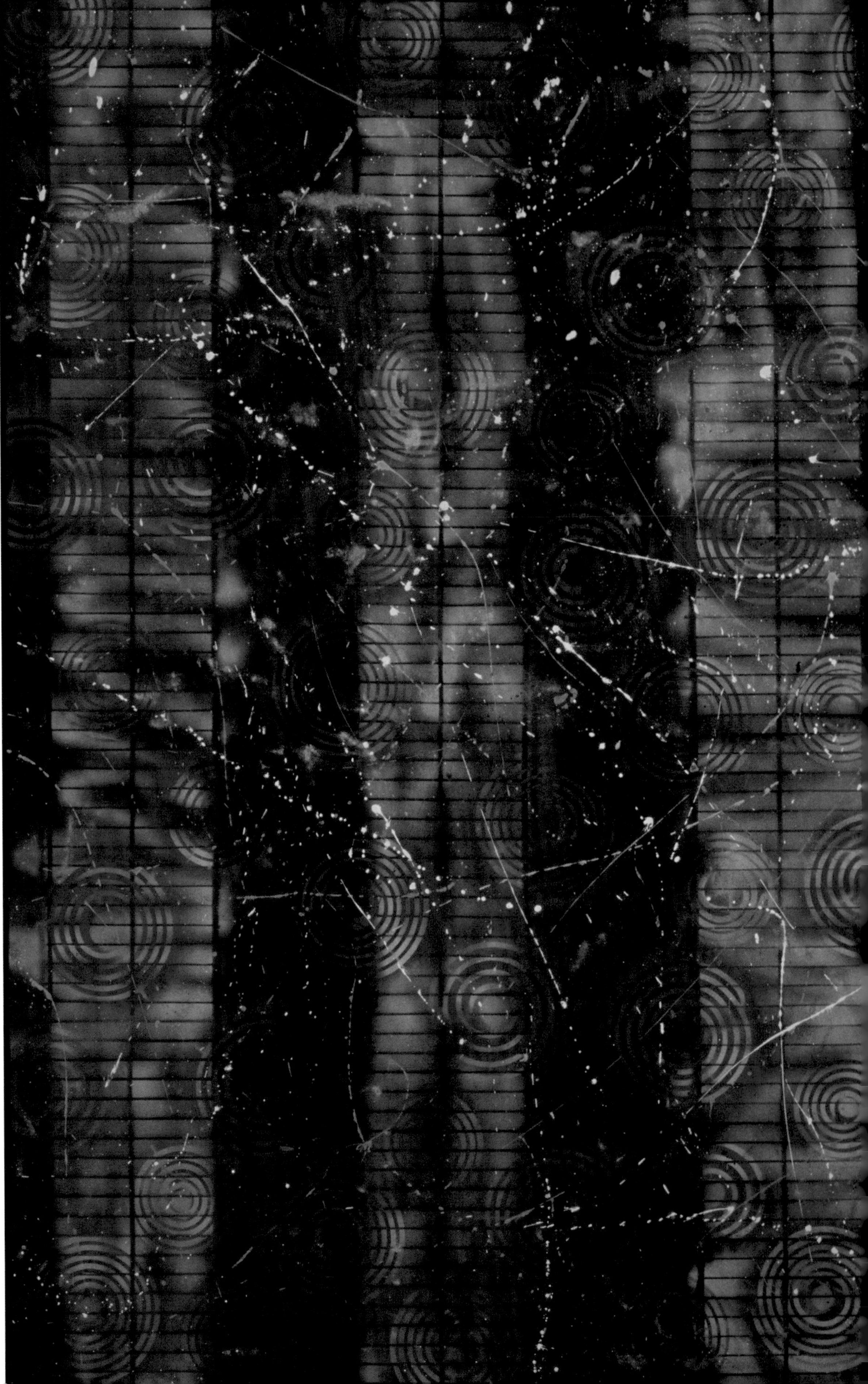

BP#3, 2007
Acrylic on canvas with reflective chips
48" x 72"

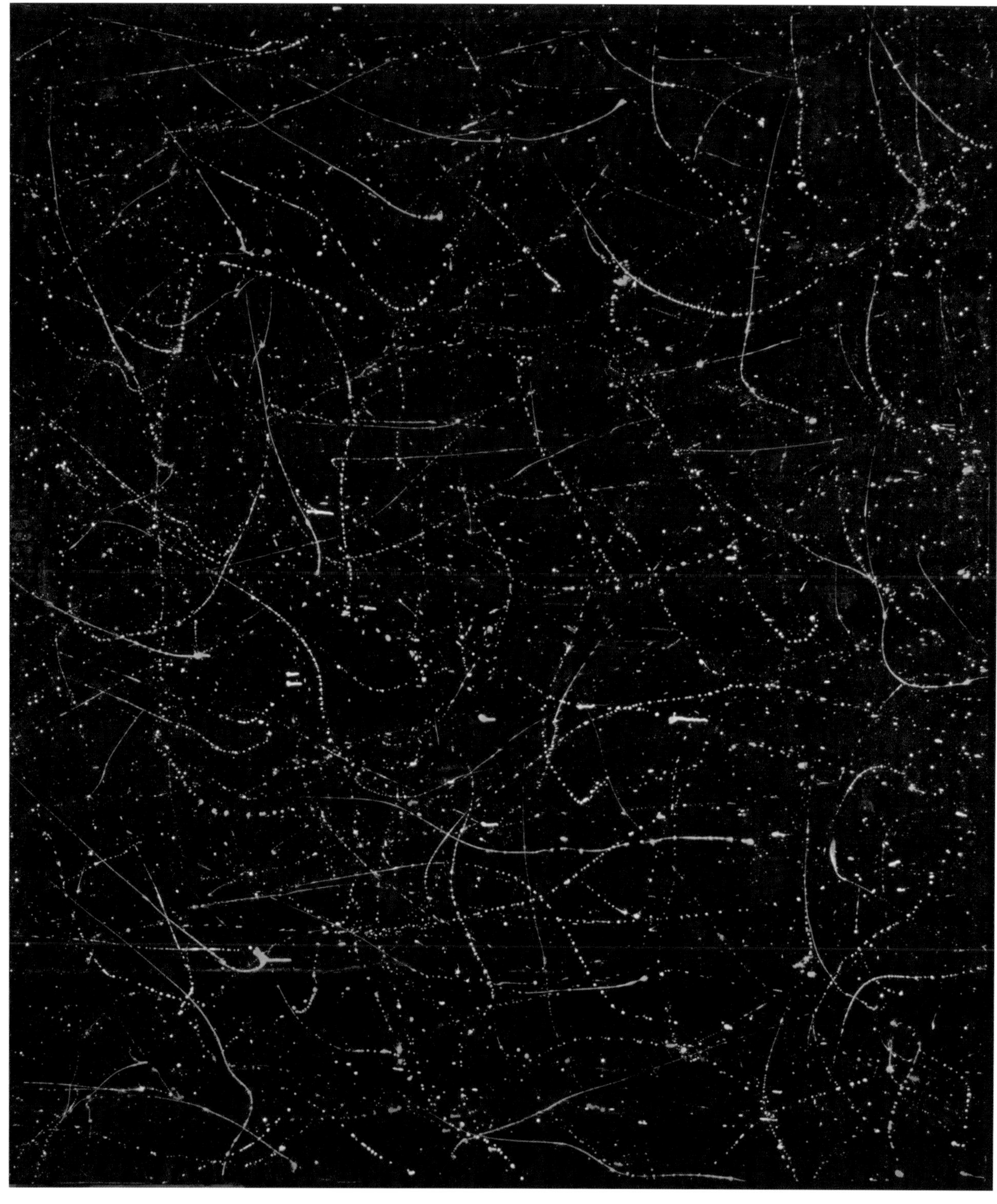

BP#1, 2007
Acrylic on canvas with reflective chips
72" x 84"

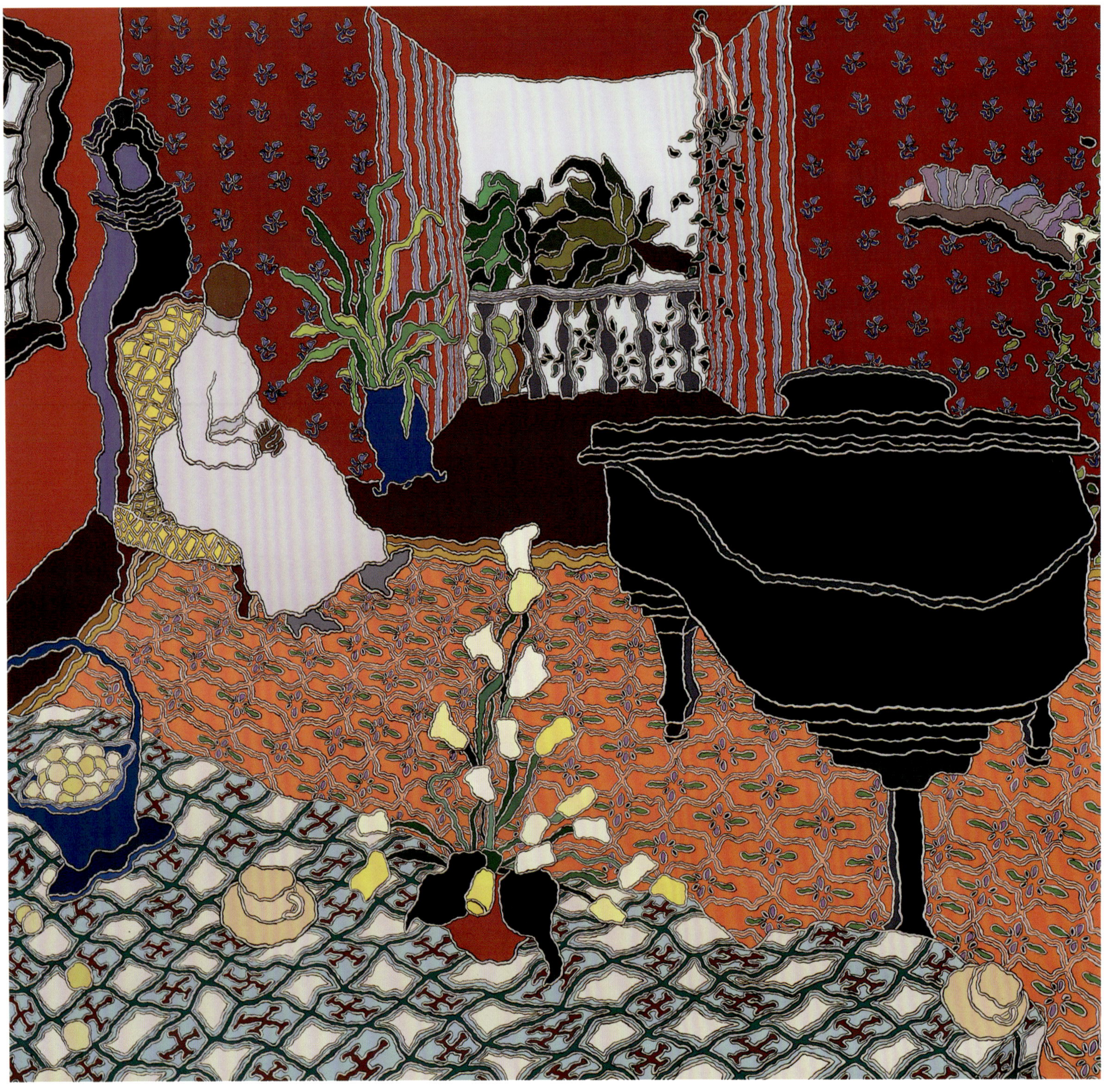

The Music Room, 1982
Acrylic on canvas
60" x 64"
Private collection

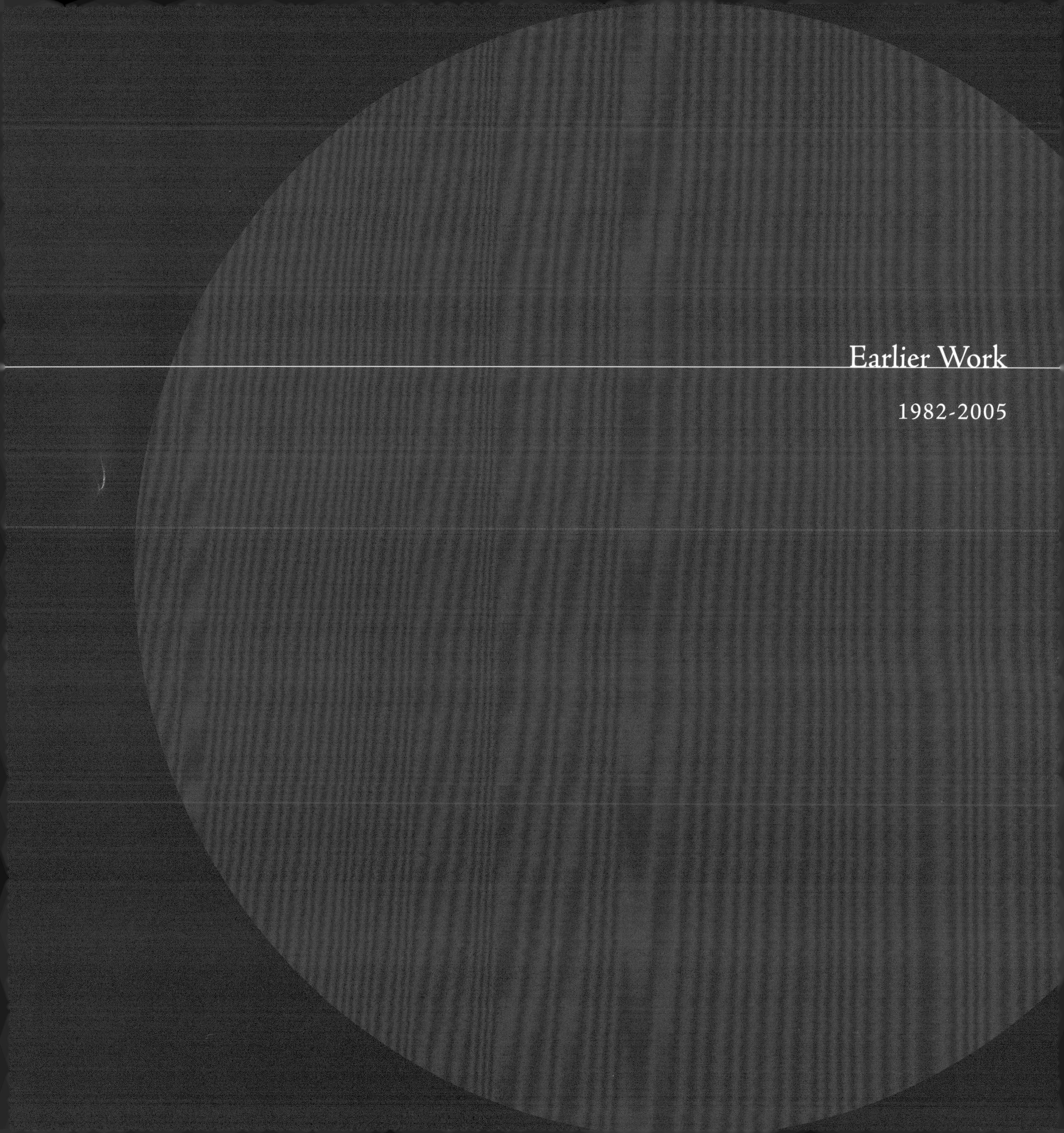

Earlier Work

1982-2005

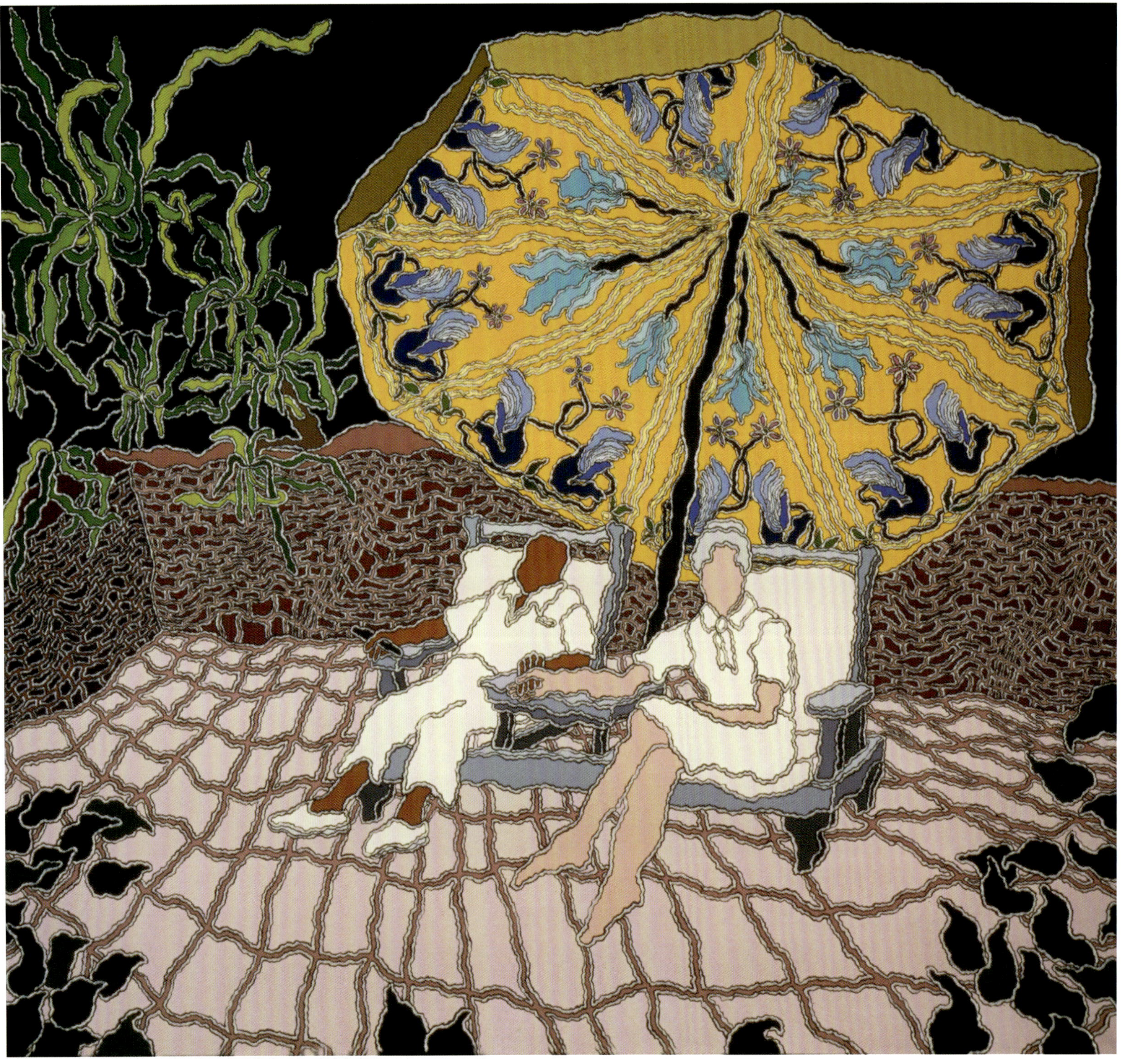

Uncle Jack and Aunt Florence Love Each Other, 1982
Acrylic on canvas
58" x 64"
Private collection

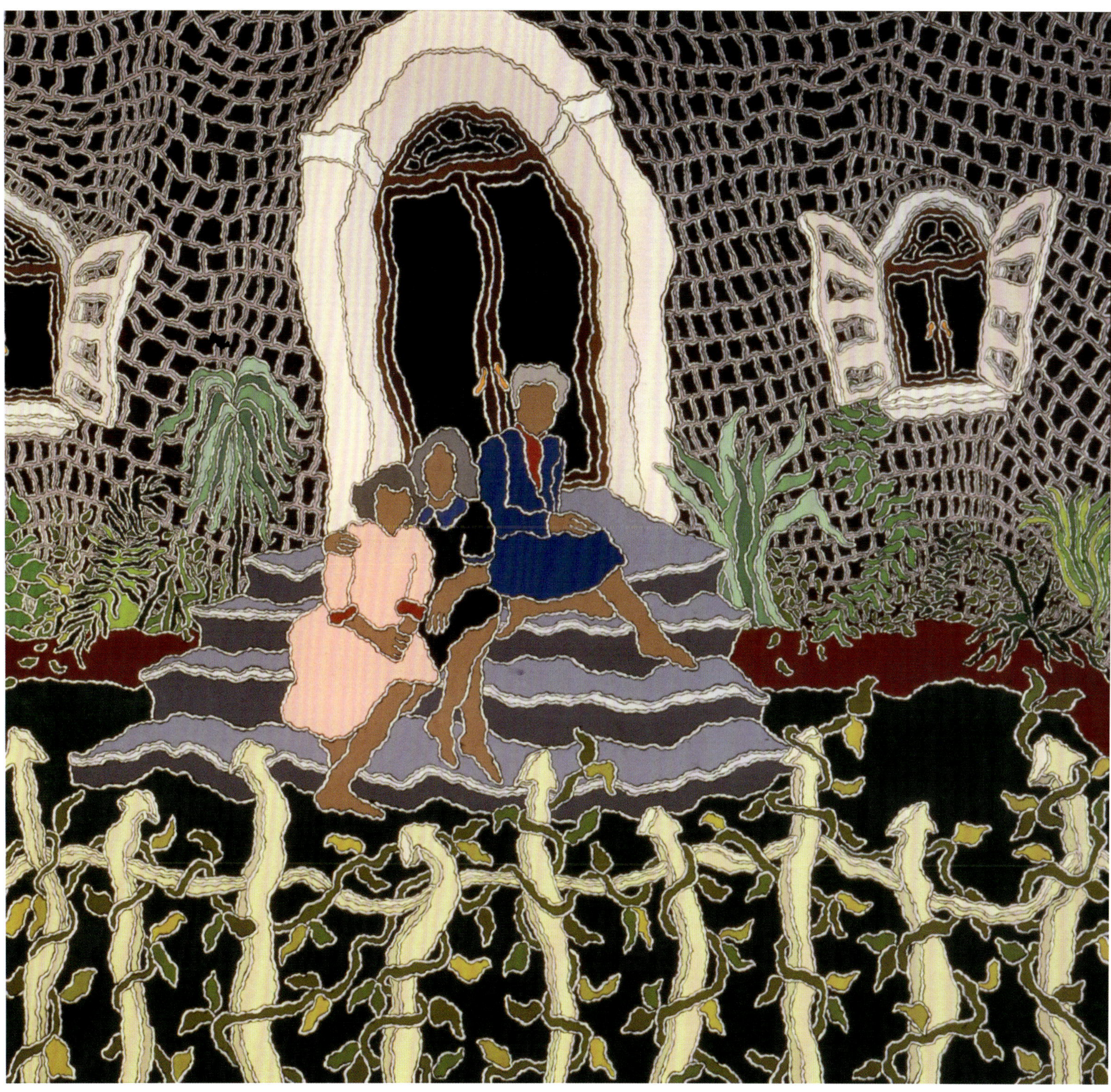

Powhattan Avenue, 1983
Acrylic on canvas
58" x 62"
Private collection

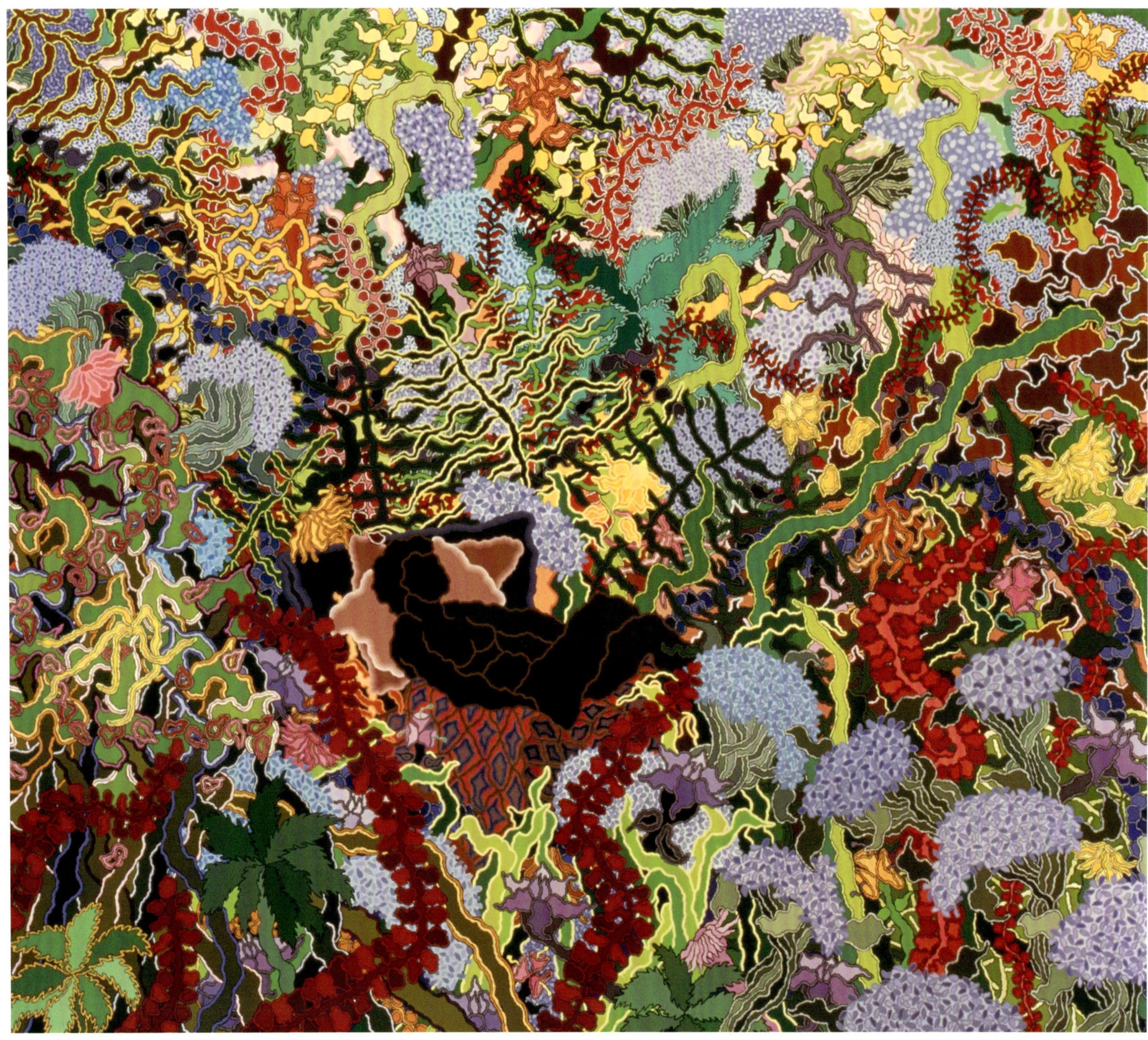

Ya-Ya Decides to Go with America, 1984
Acrylic on canvas
58" x 62"
Collection of Mr. and Mrs. Ben Huberman

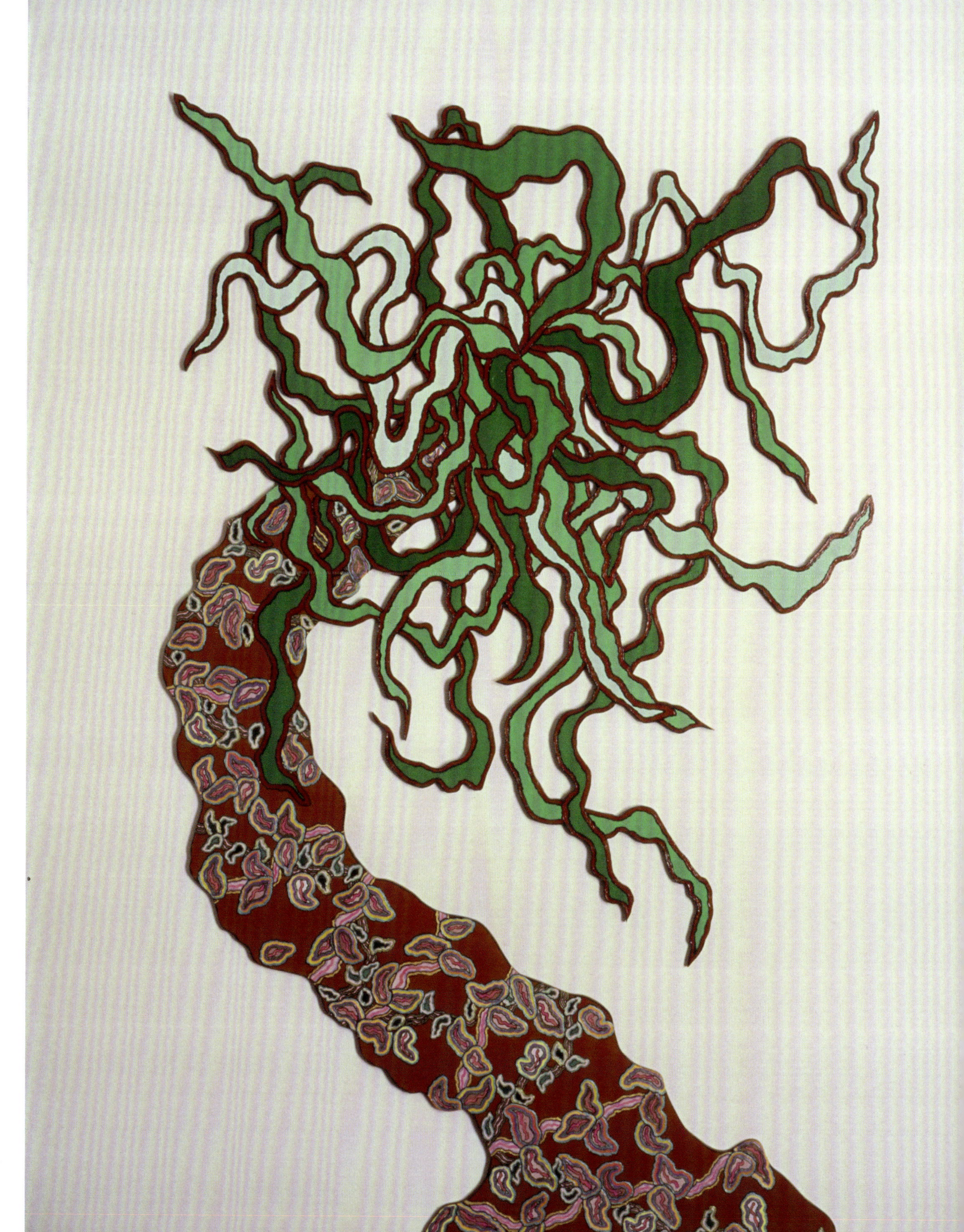

Palm Tree, 1984
Acrylic on wood
60" x 96"
Collection of Mr. and Mrs.
Ben Huberman

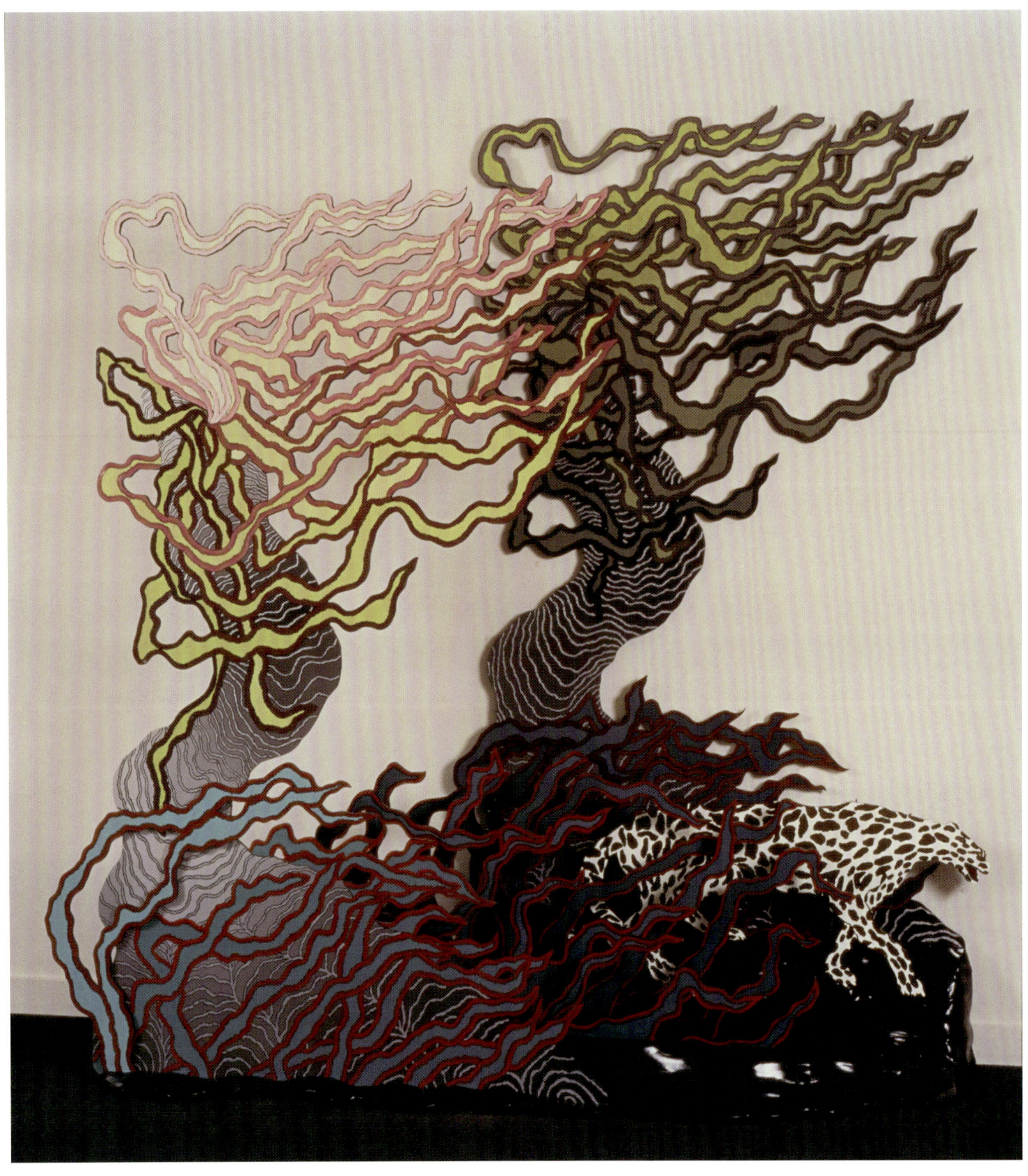

Leopard, 1985-86
Acrylic on wood
108" x 96" x 23"

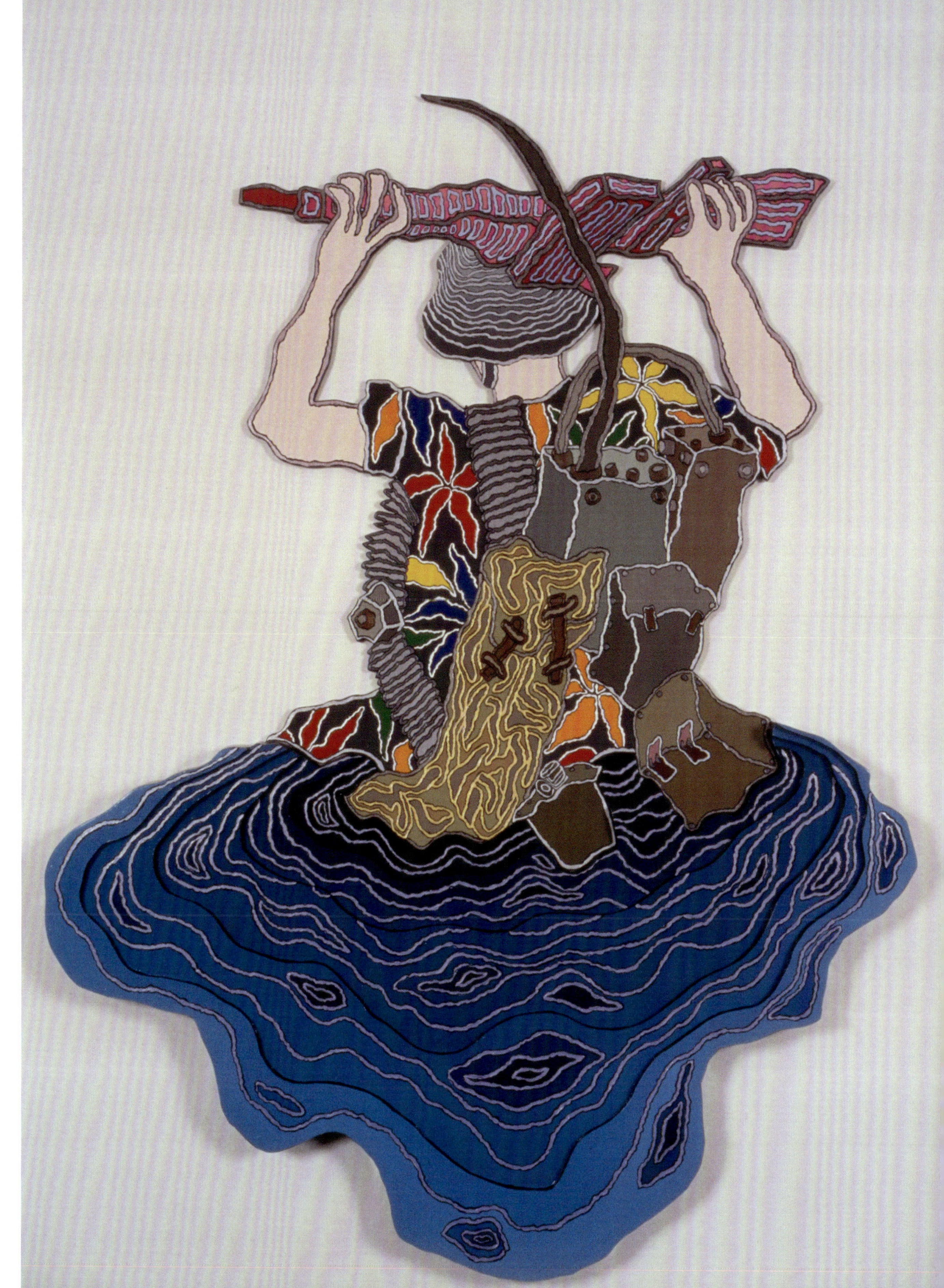

The Wade, 1985-86
Acrylic on wood
84" x 72" x 7"
Collection of Mr. and Mrs.
Ben Huberman

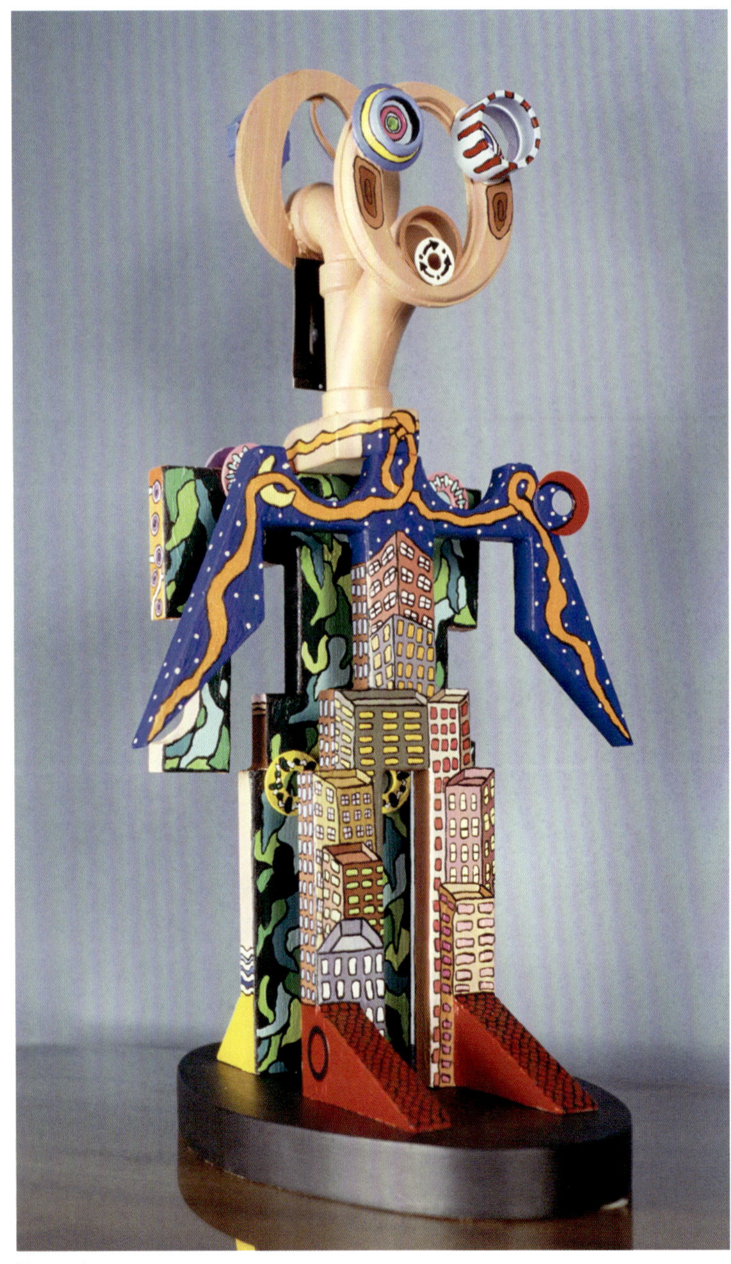

Front view

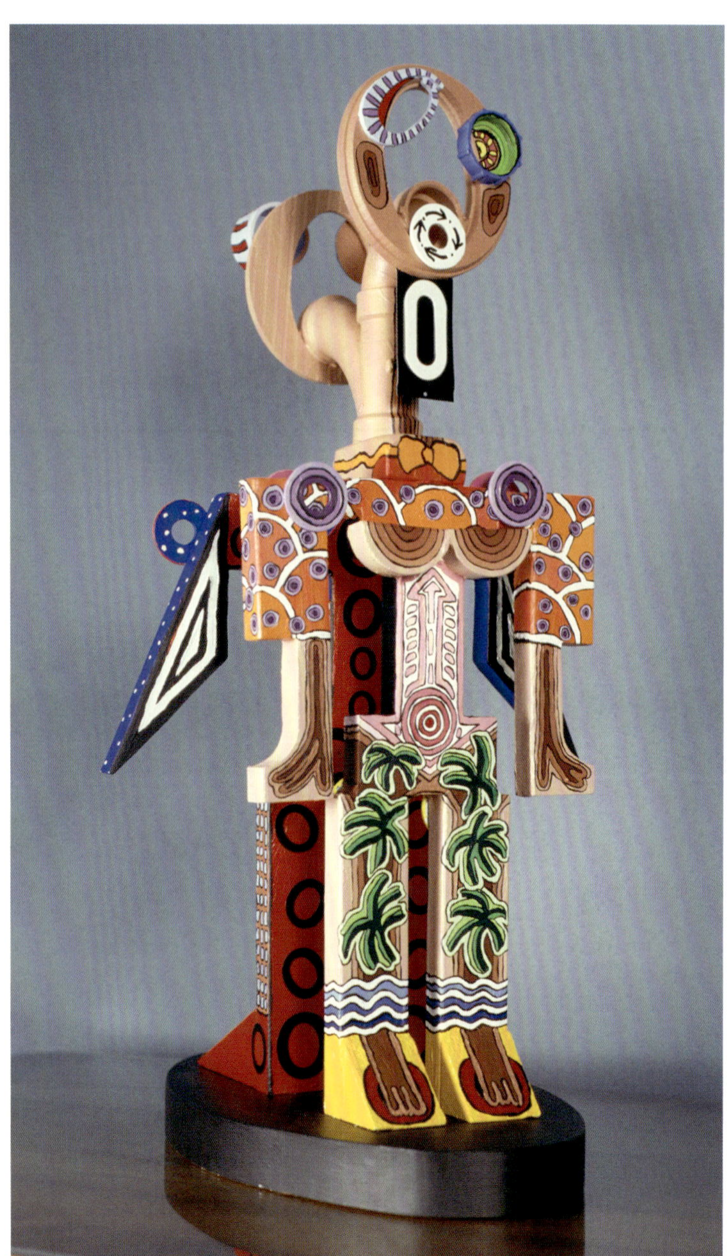

Back view

Honoring the Zero, 1986-87
Acrylic on wood
18" x 5" x 5"
Private collection

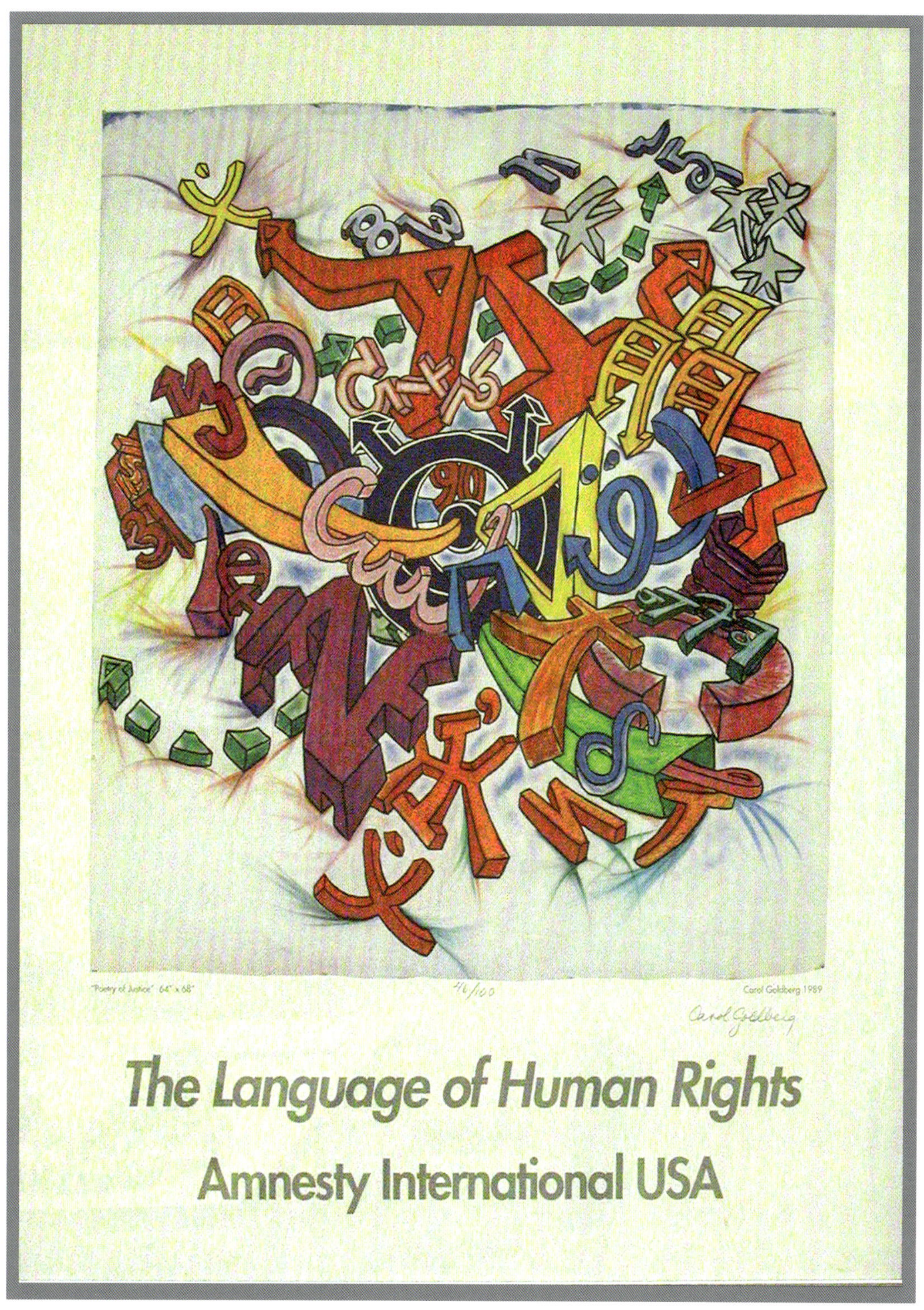

The Language of Human Rights, Amnesty International USA, framed poster, 1990
Original: pastel on Arches paper
60" x 72"
Collection of Amnesty International

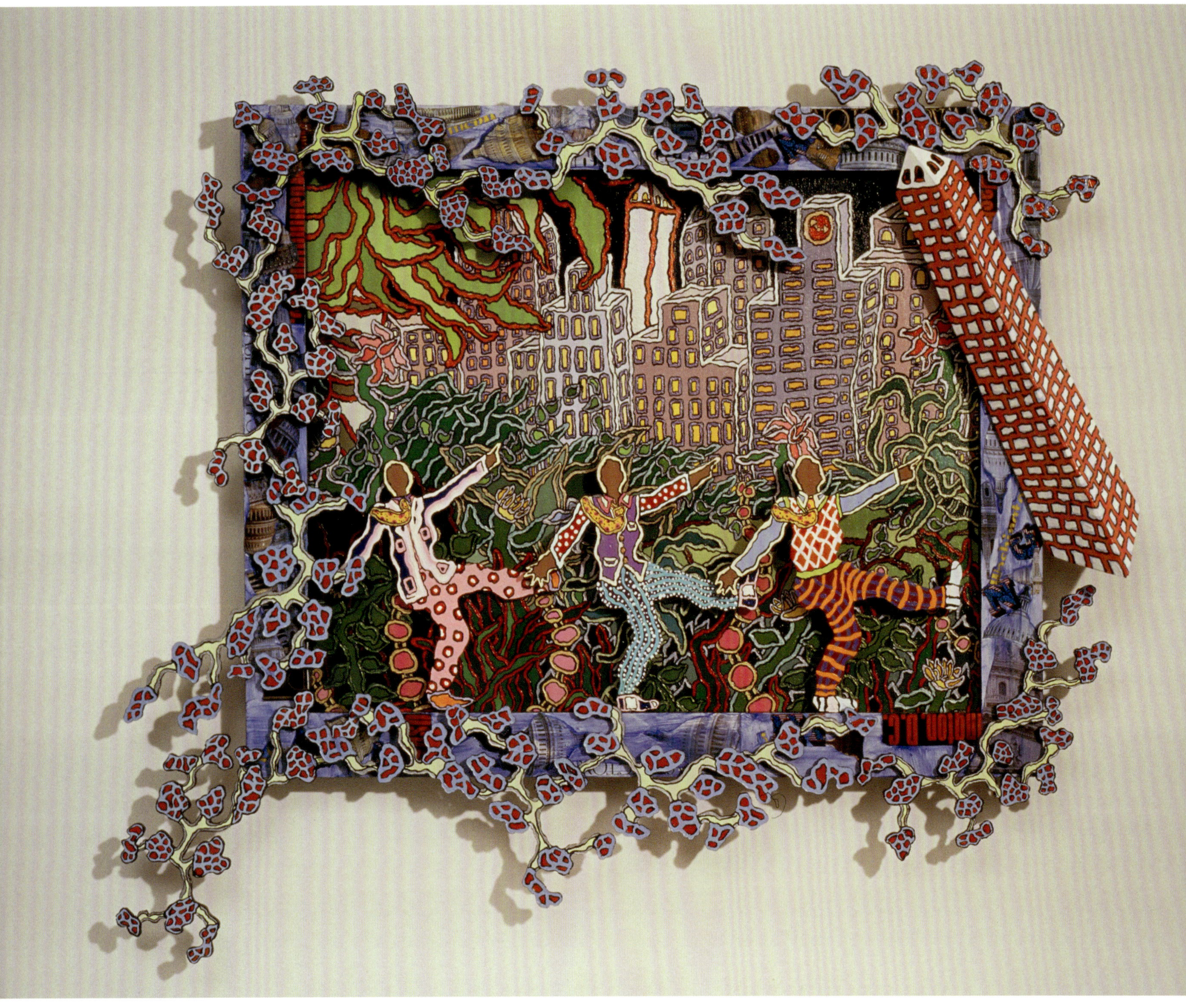

Dancing in DC, 1987
Acrylic on canvas and wood
24" x 36"
Private collection

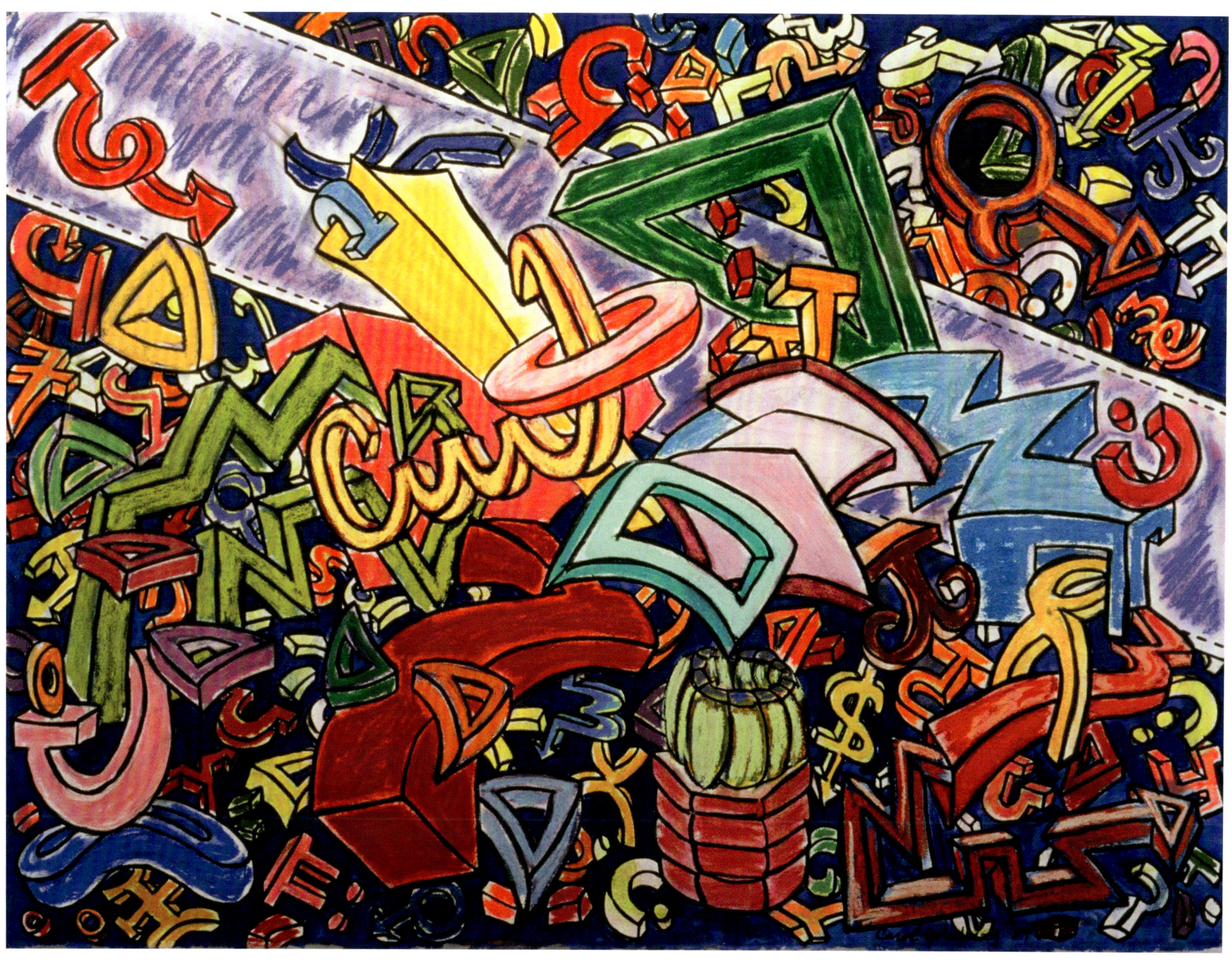

Untitled, 1989
Mixed media
18" x 24"
Private collection

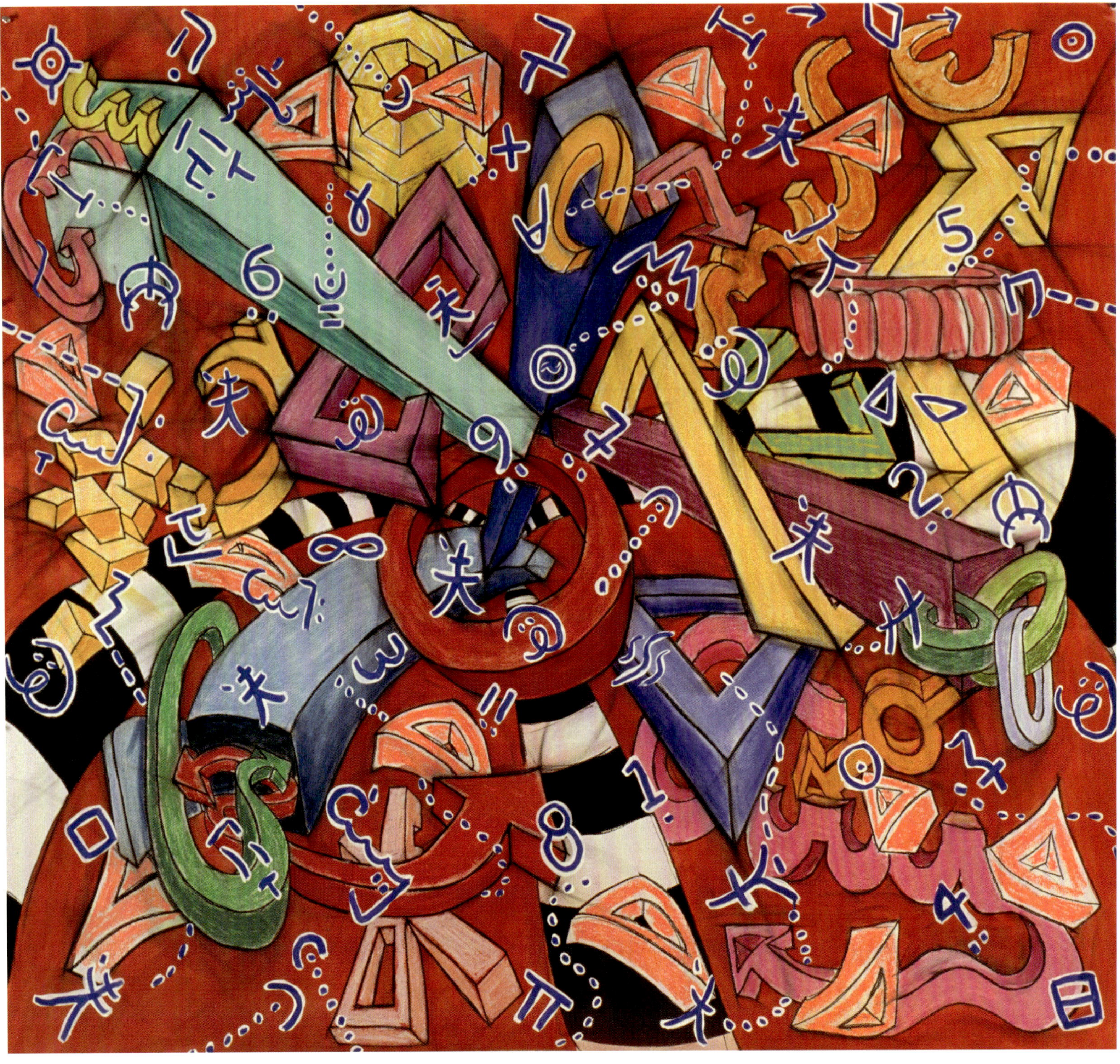

Mr. Hadron Goes to Washington, 1989
Mixed media
53" x 60"
Private collection

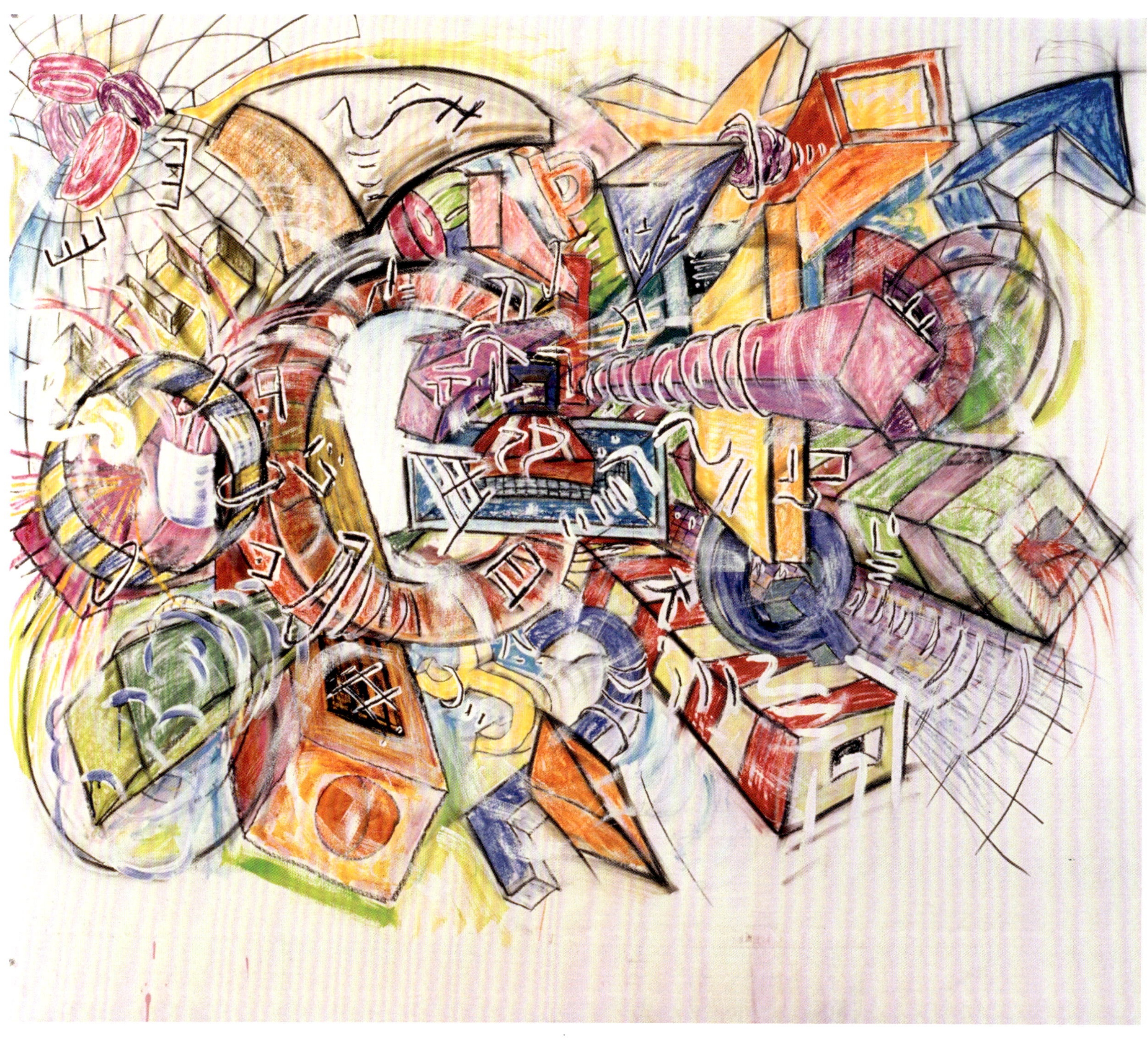

Time Forest, 1989
Mixed media
47½" x 60"
Collection of Carolyn and Warren Kaplan

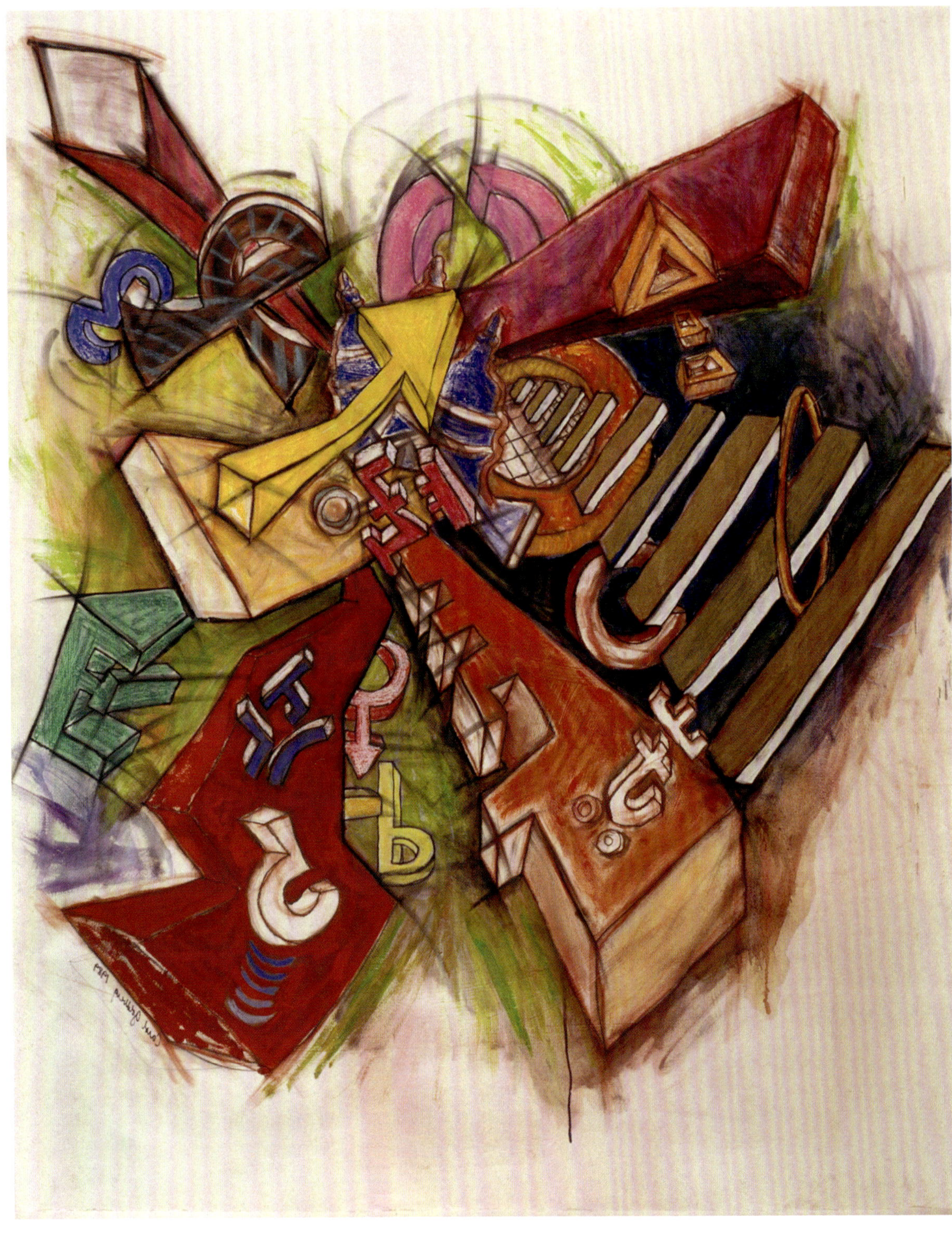

Borrowing from Bosons, 1989
Mixed media
48" x 60"
Private collection

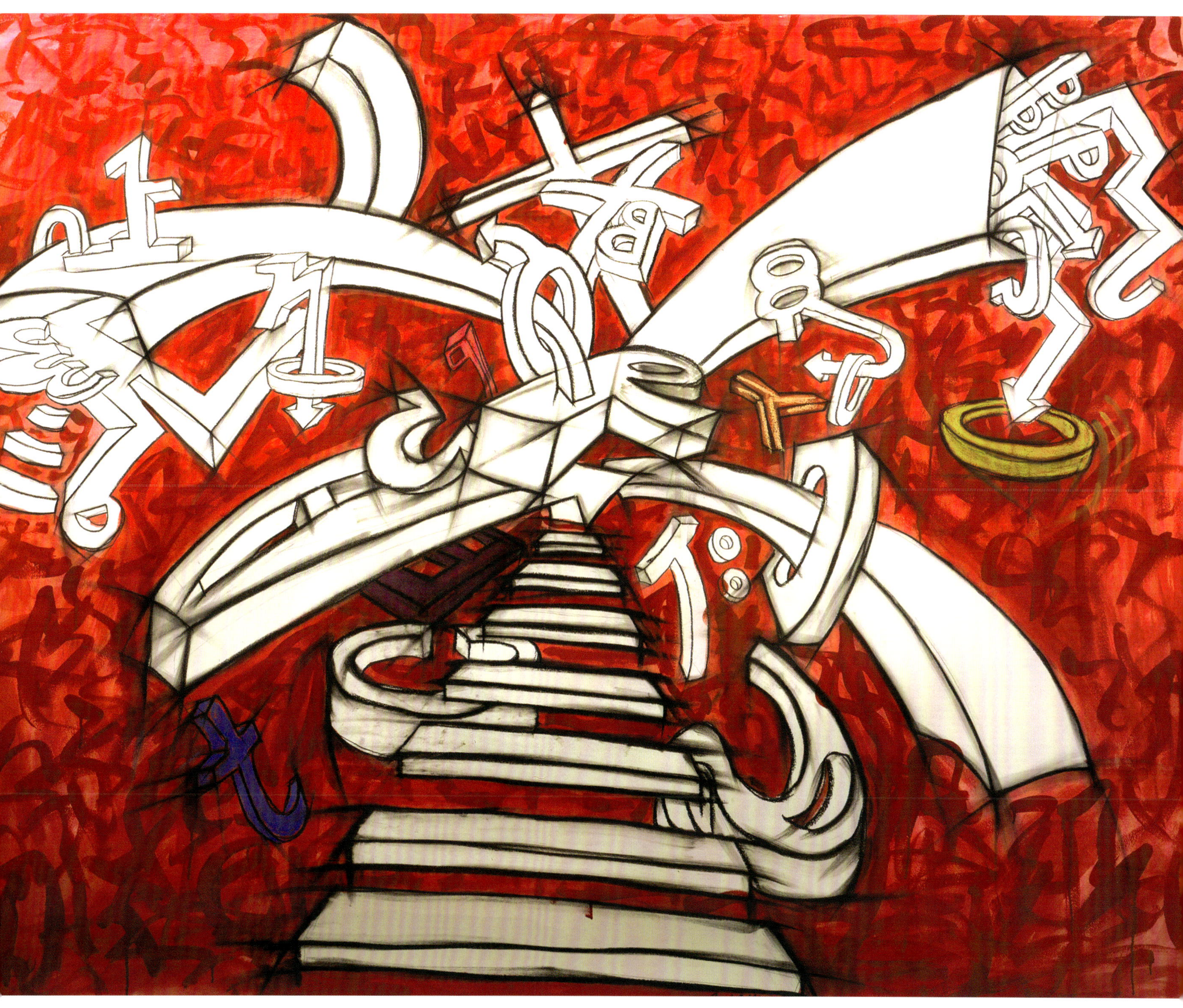

Red Shift, 1989
Mixed media
46½" x 60"
Collection of Mr. and Mrs. Ben Huberman

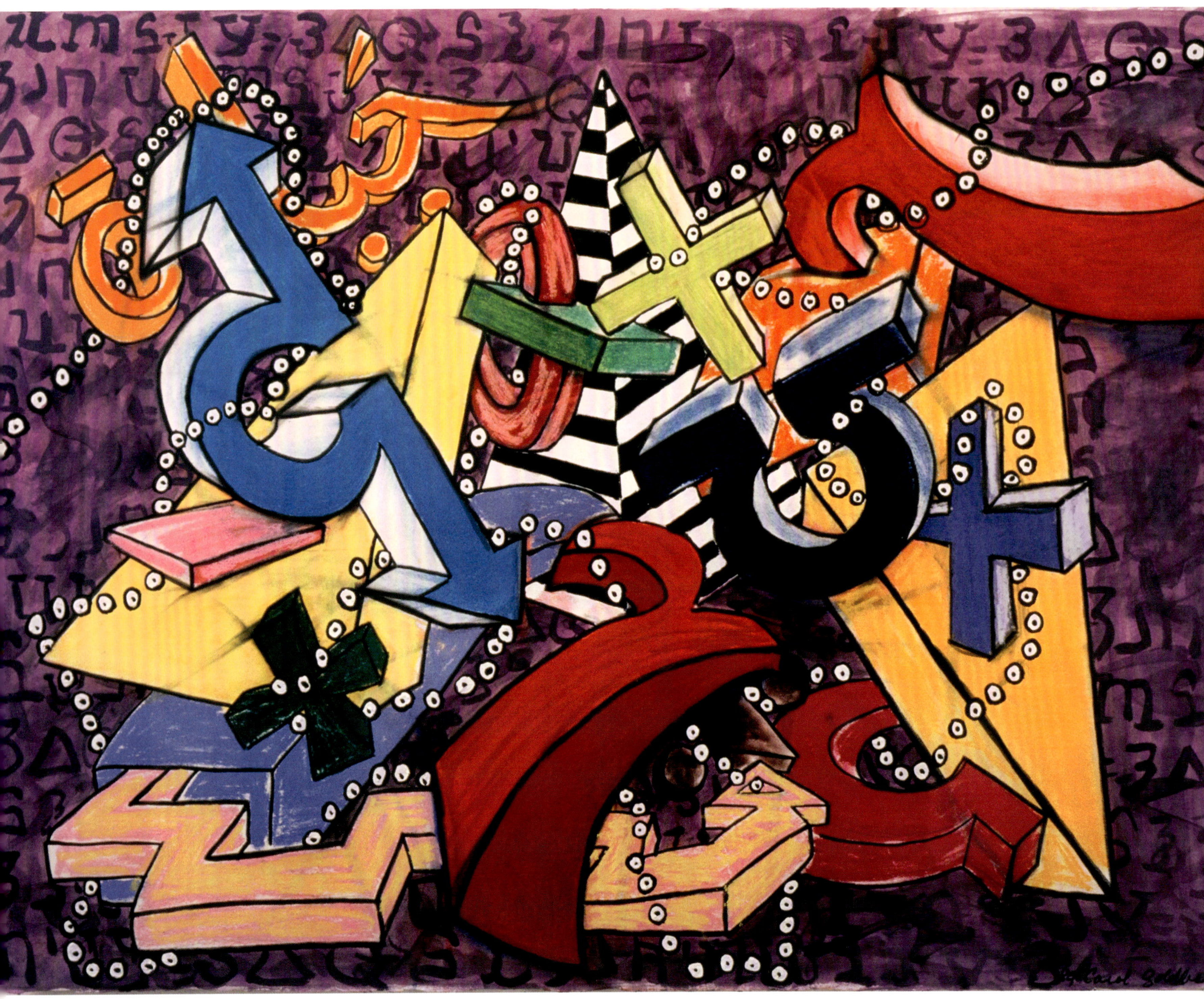

Purple Govts, 1989
Mixed media
22" x 30"
Private collection

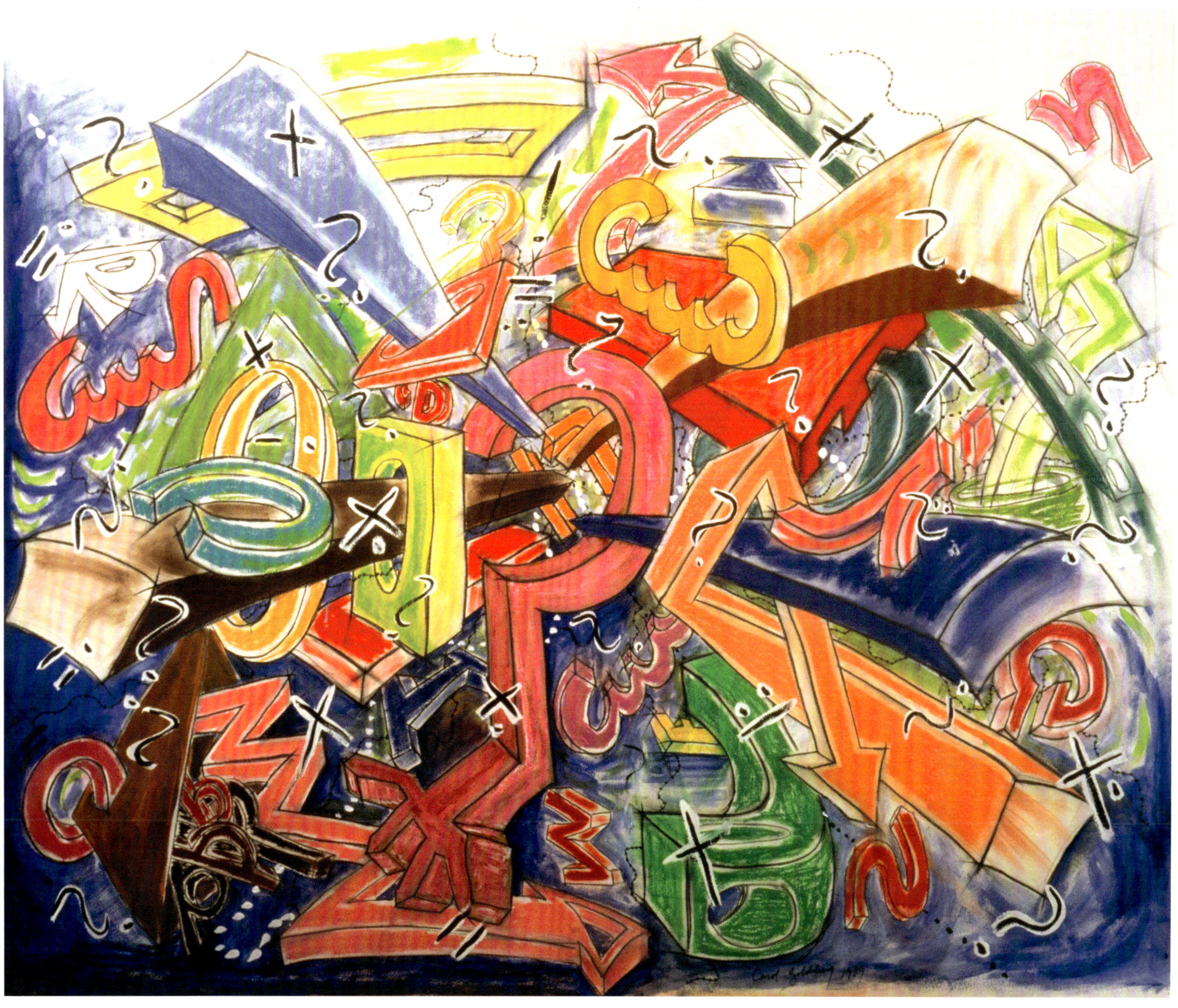

Einstein on the Beach, 1987
Mixed media
60" x 48"
Collection of Mr. and Mrs. Edwin Colodny

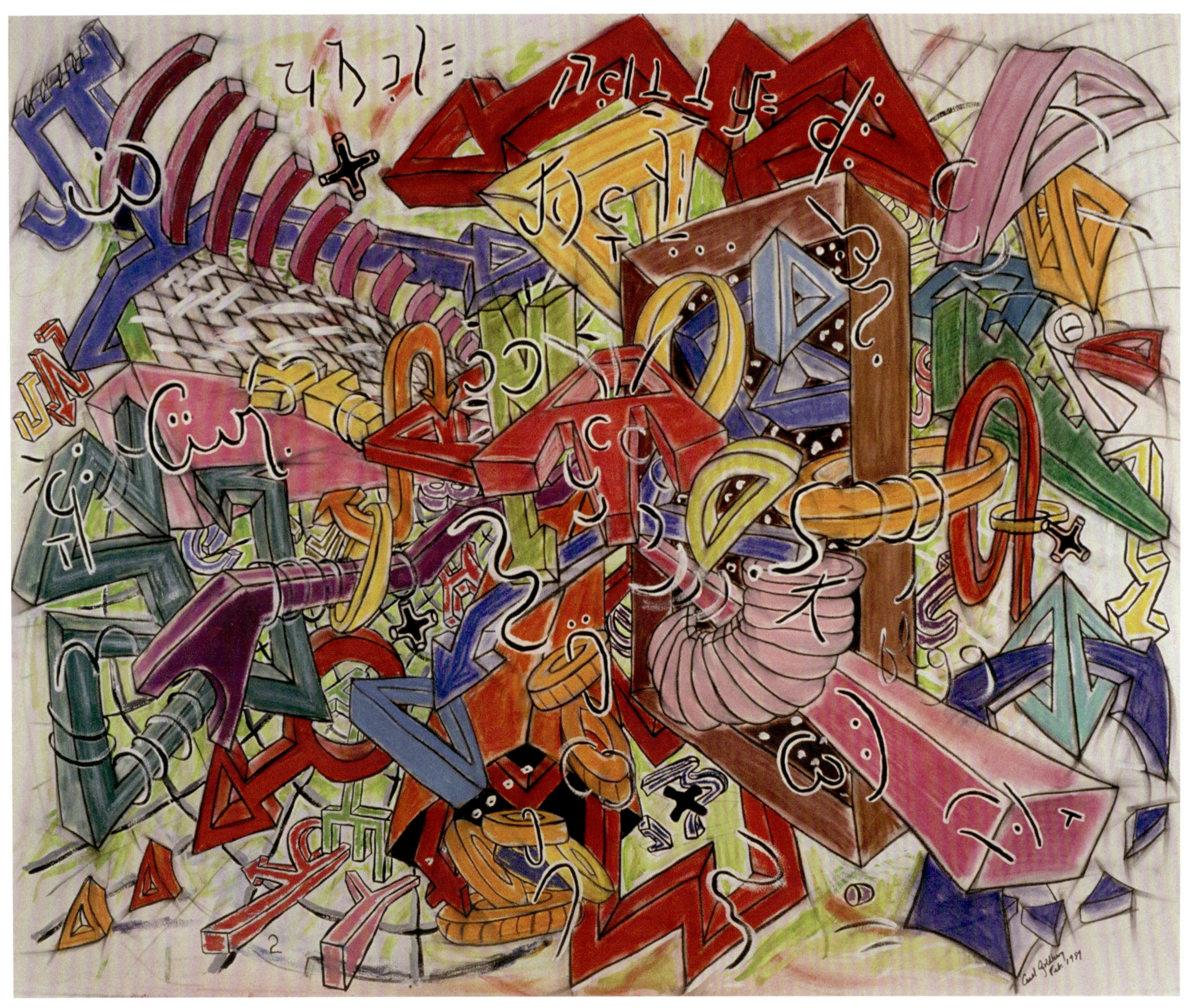

Sterling Universe, 1989
Mixed media
29" x 60"

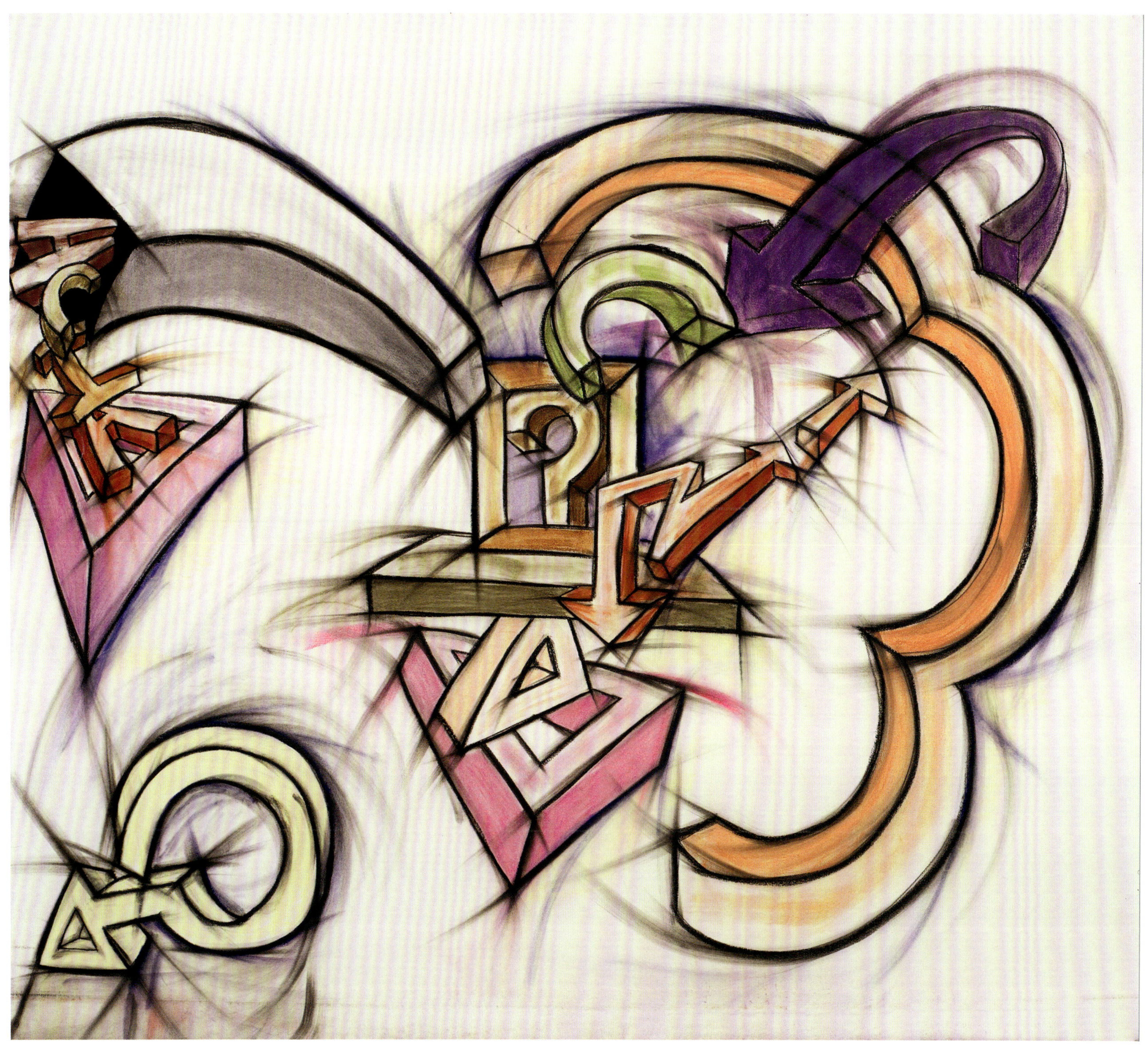

The Big No Know, 1989
Charcoal and pastel on paper
52" x 60"

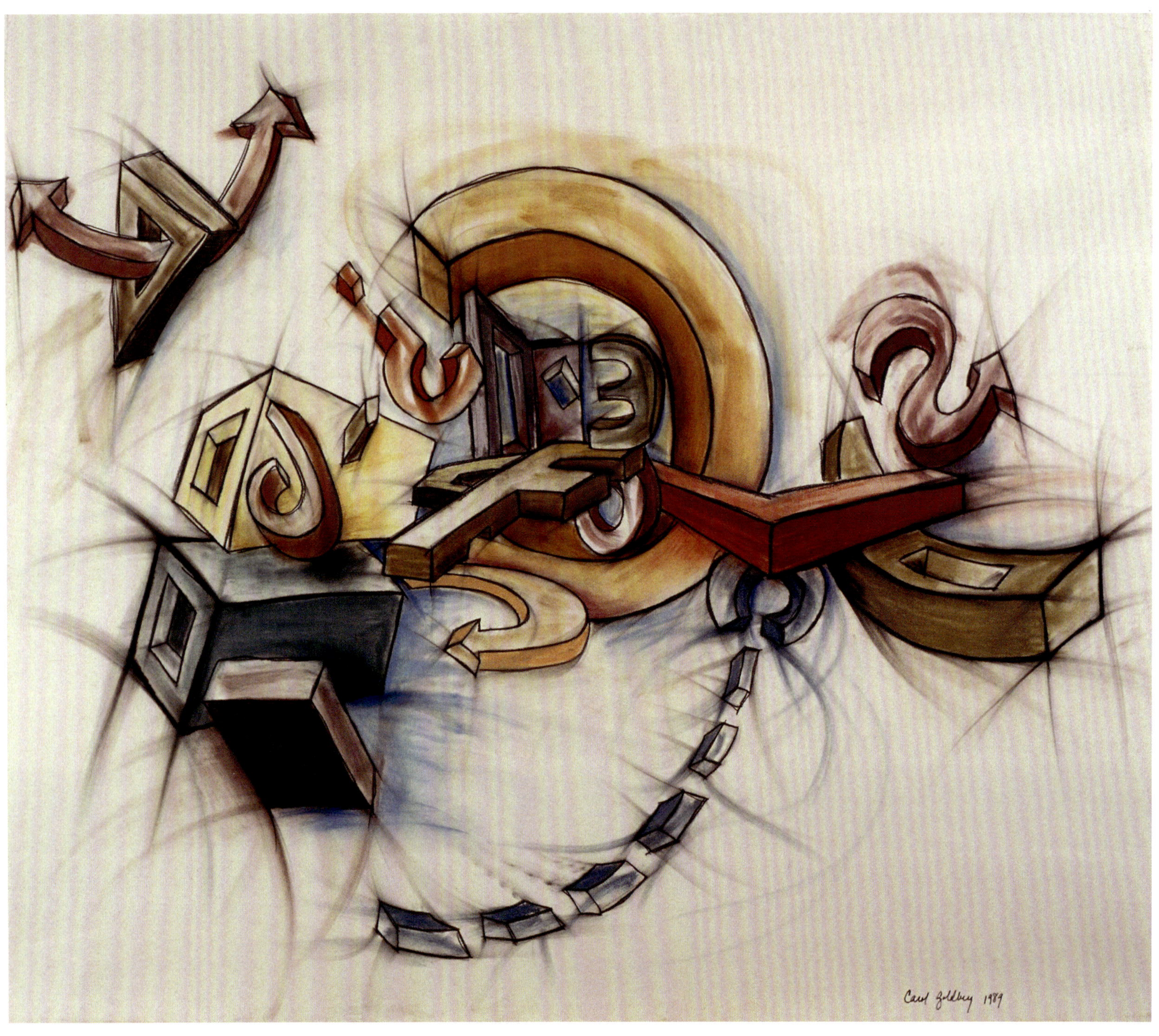

Andy's Light, 1989
Charcoal and pastel on paper
53" x 60"

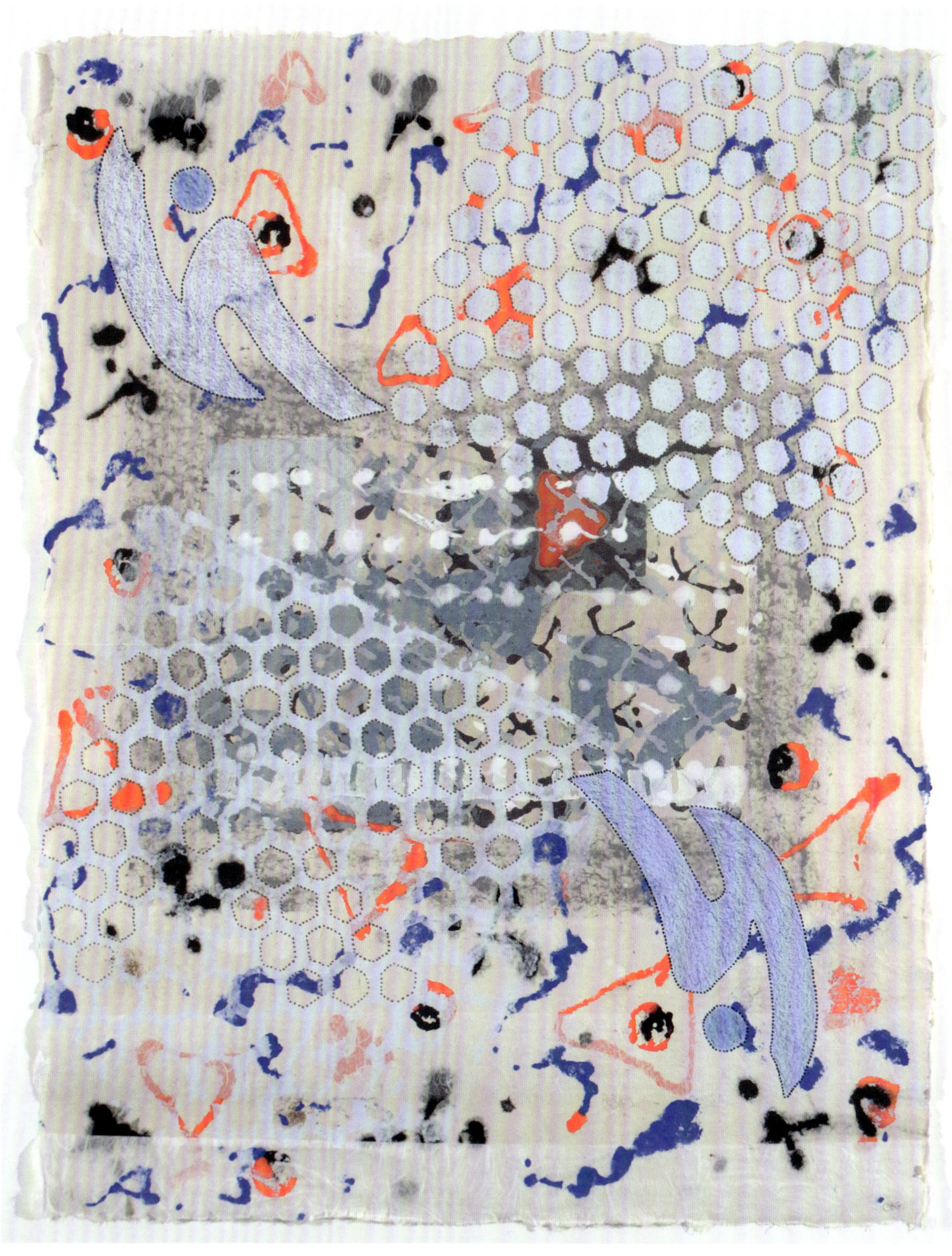

The Tranquility of Menemsha Bees, 1992-96
Pulp paint and mixed media on handmade paper
38" x 30"

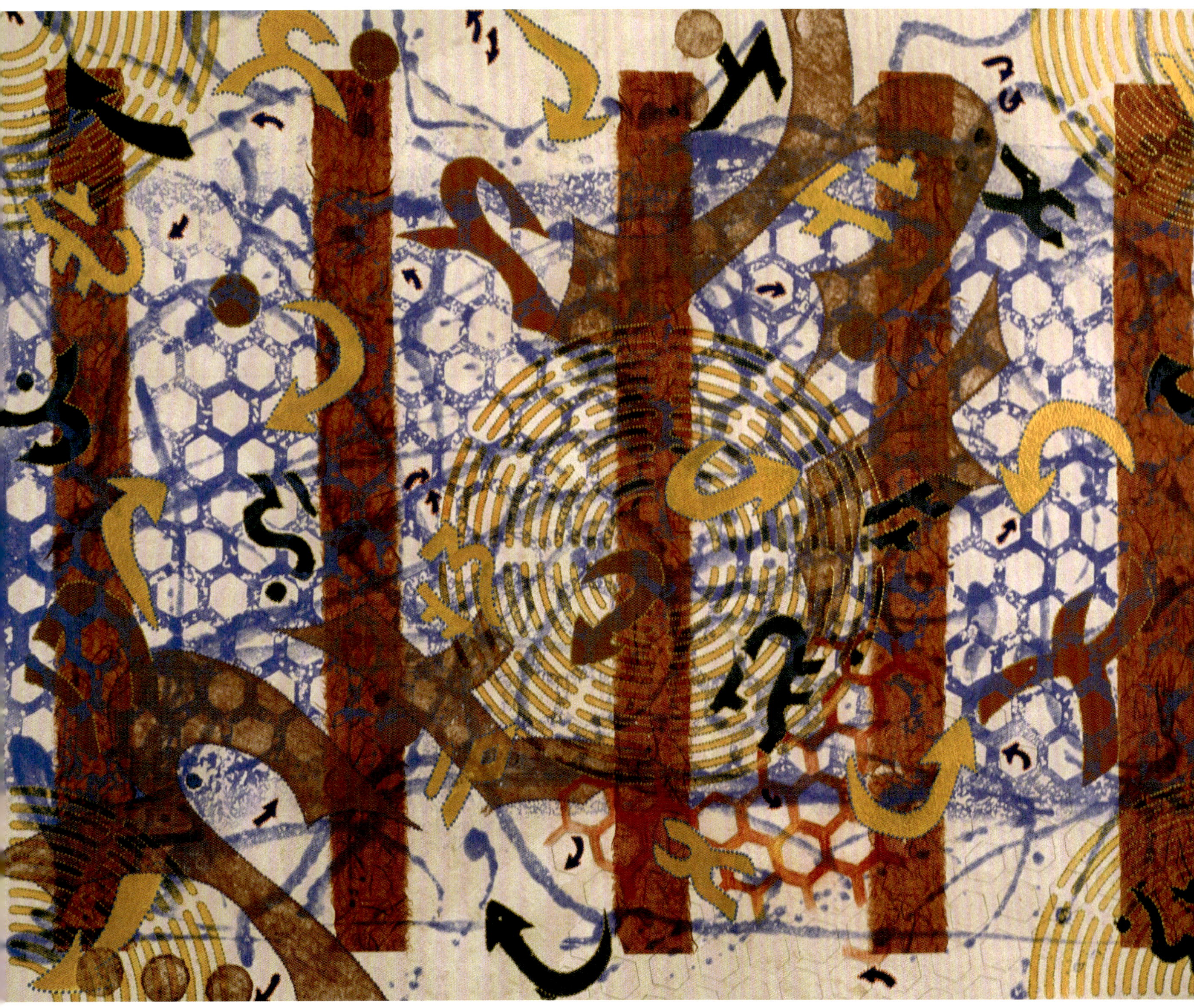

Emma, 1992-96
Pulp paint and mixed media on handmade paper
30" x 38"

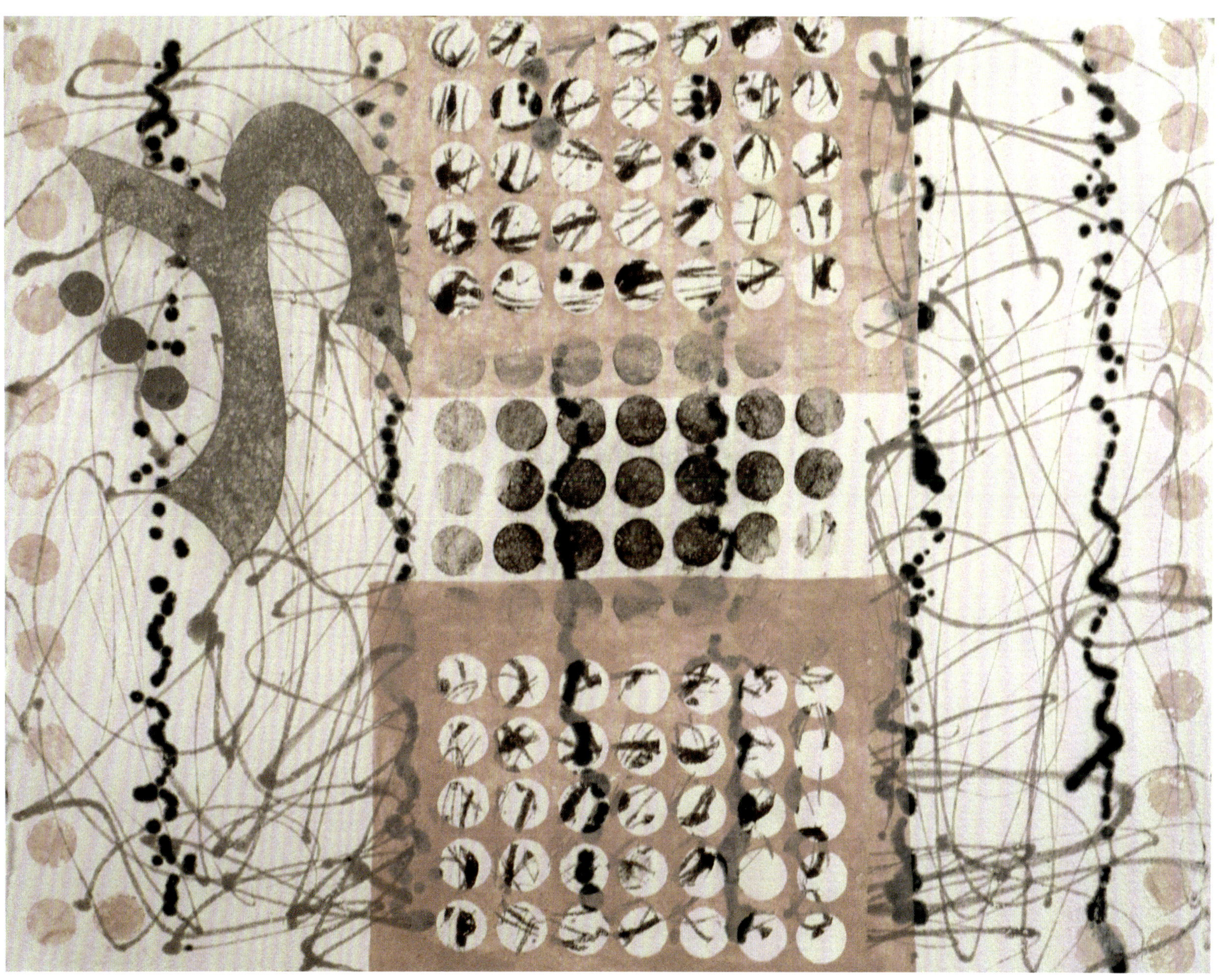

Chilmark on My Mind, 1992
Pulp paint and mixed media on handmade paper
30" x 38"

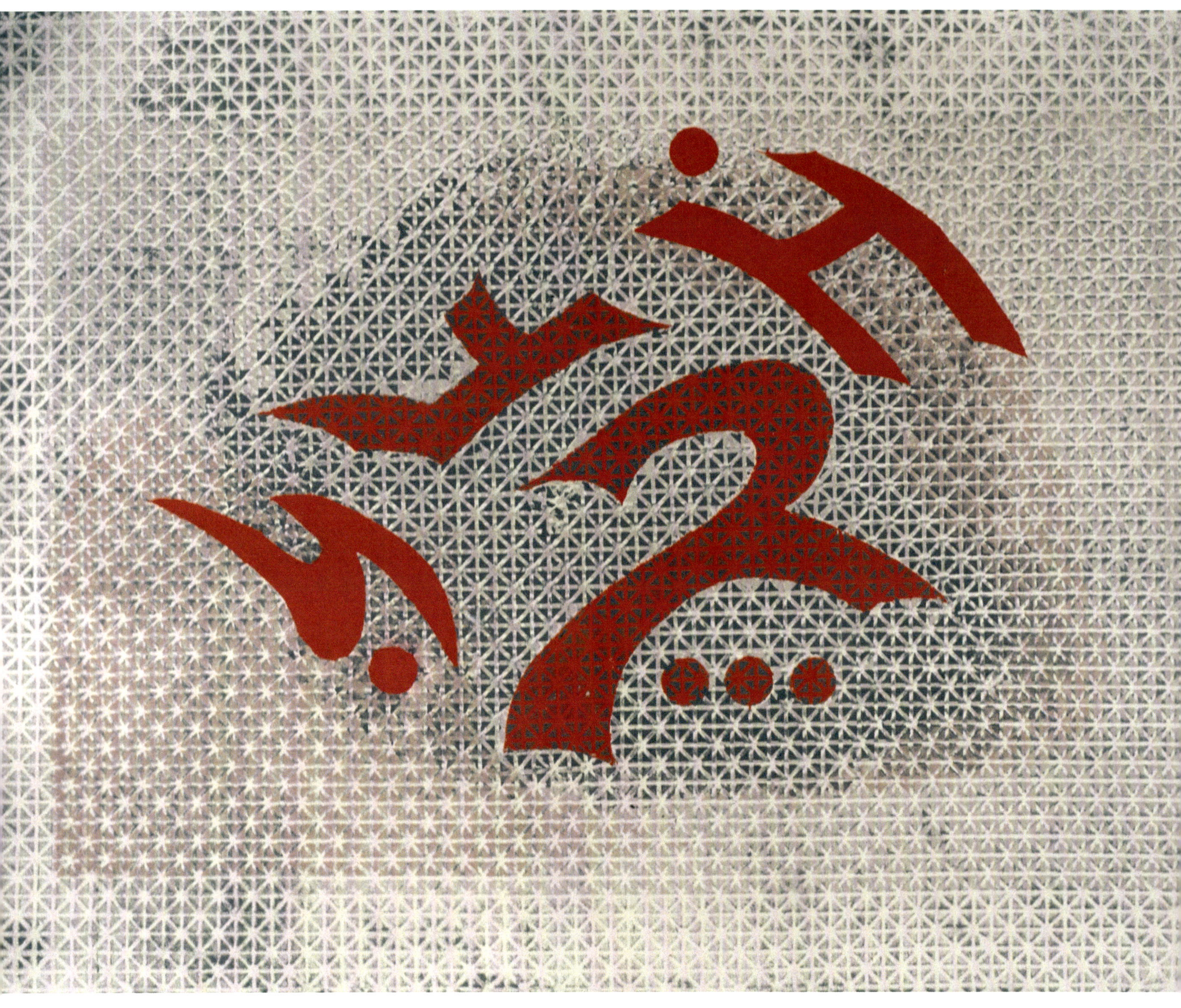

Paco, 1992
Pulp paint and mixed media on handmade paper
30" x 38"

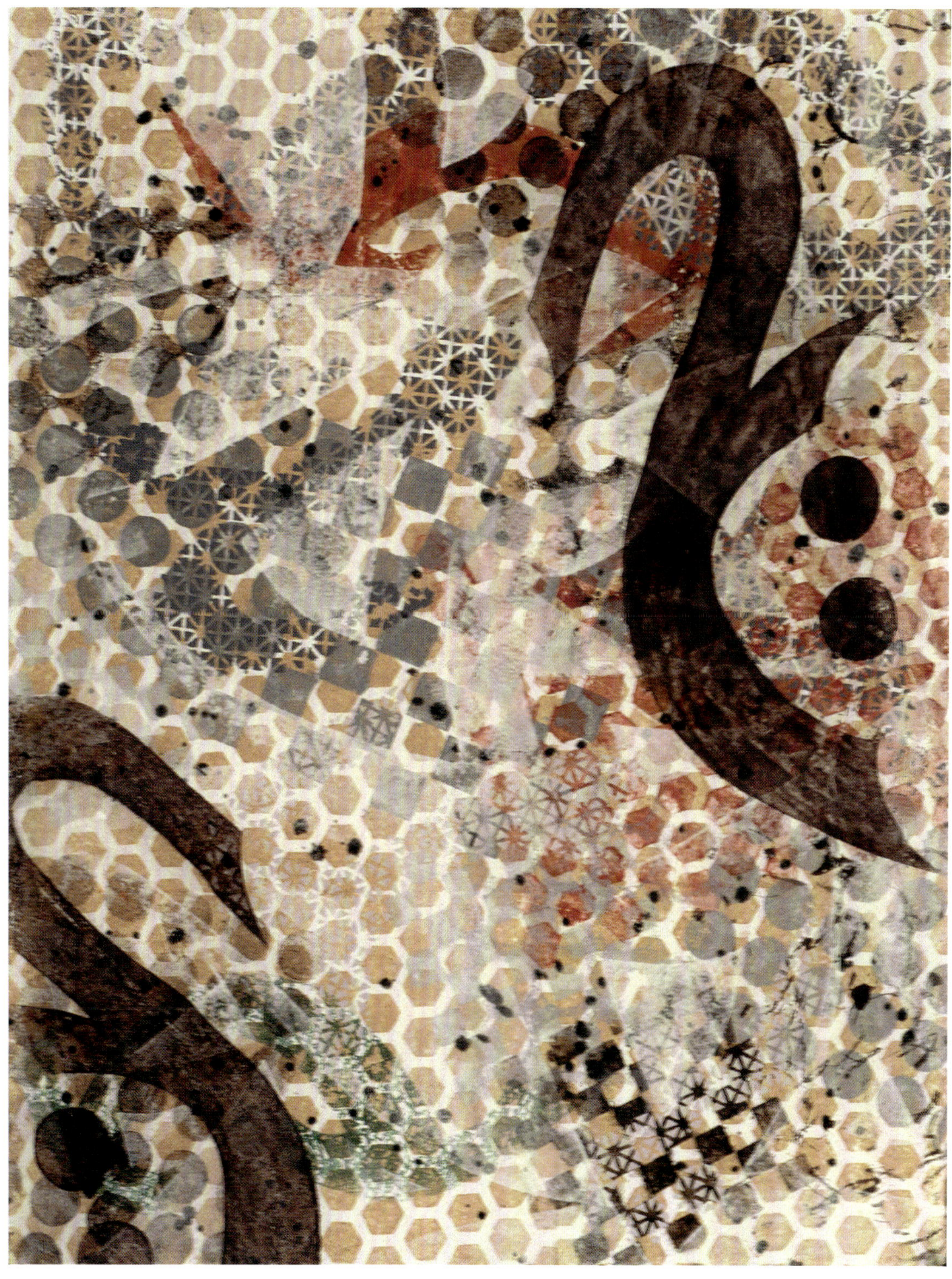

Untitled, 1992
Pulp paint and mixed media on handmade paper
30" x 38"
Collection of Cyrus and Myrtle Katzen

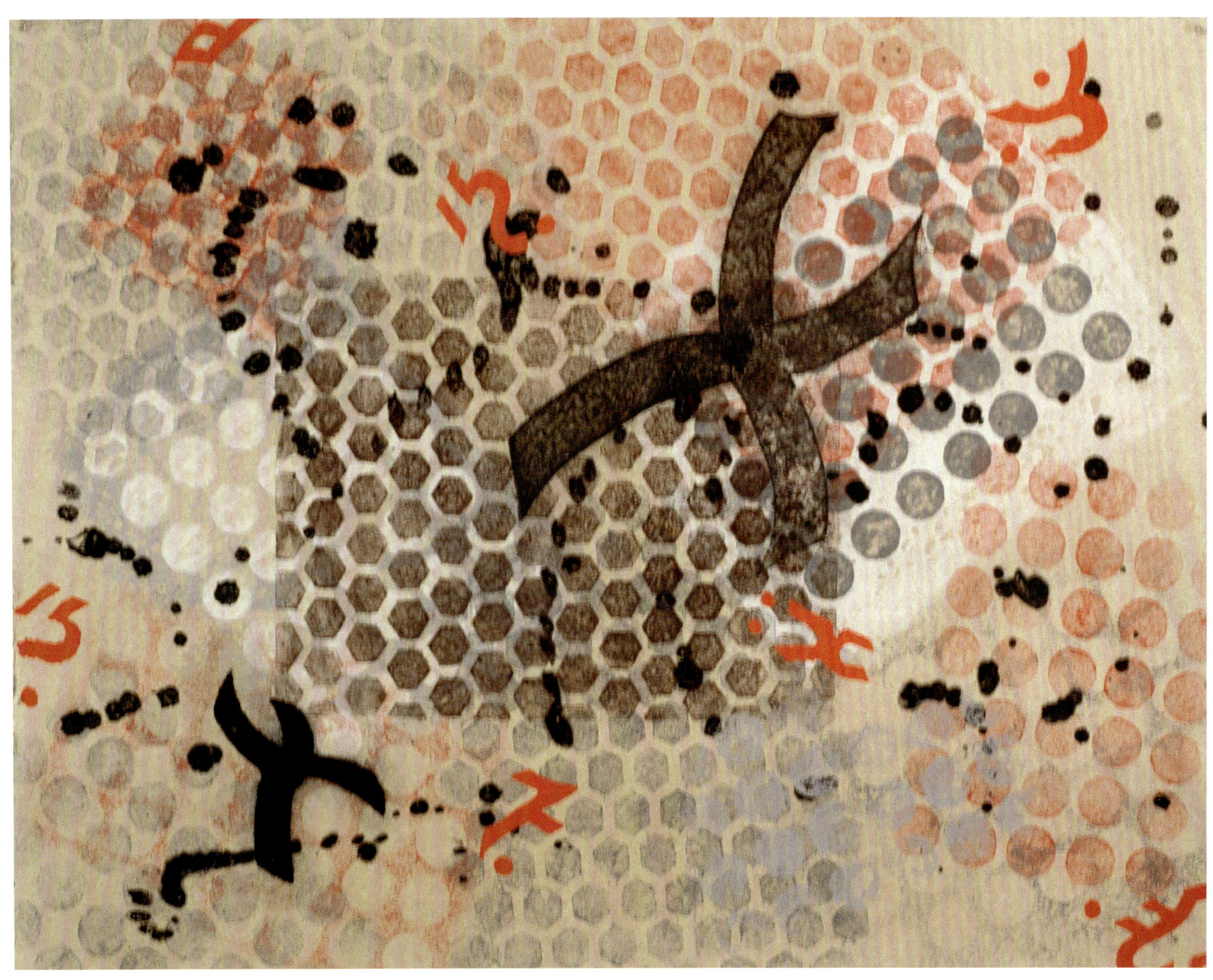

Dance of the Bees, 1992
Pulp paint and mixed media on handmade paper
30" x 38"

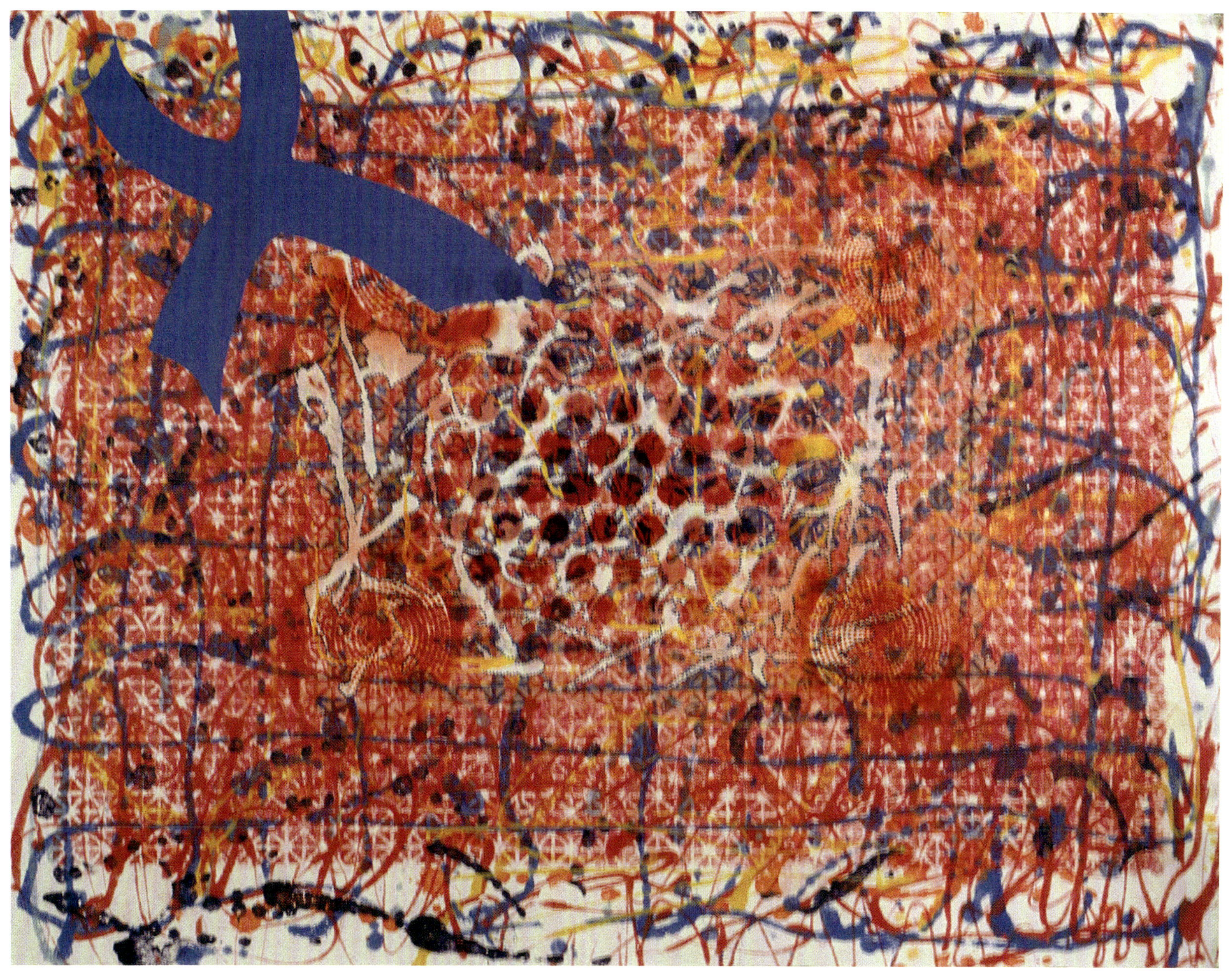

Clouds Over Saturn, 1992
Pulp paint and mixed media on handmade paper
30" x 38"

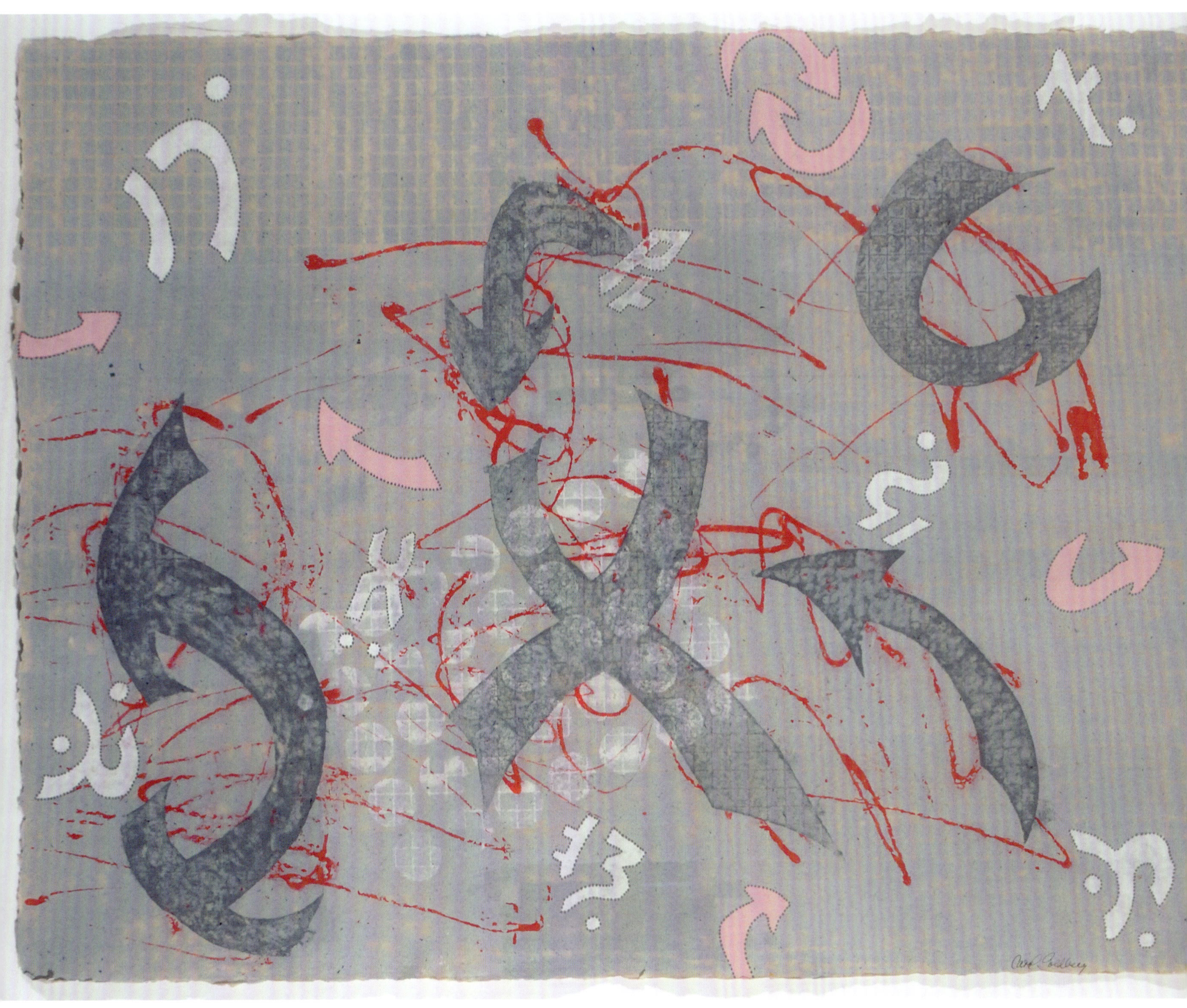

"With Liberty and Justice For All," 1992-96
Pulp paint and mixed media on handmade paper
38" x 30"

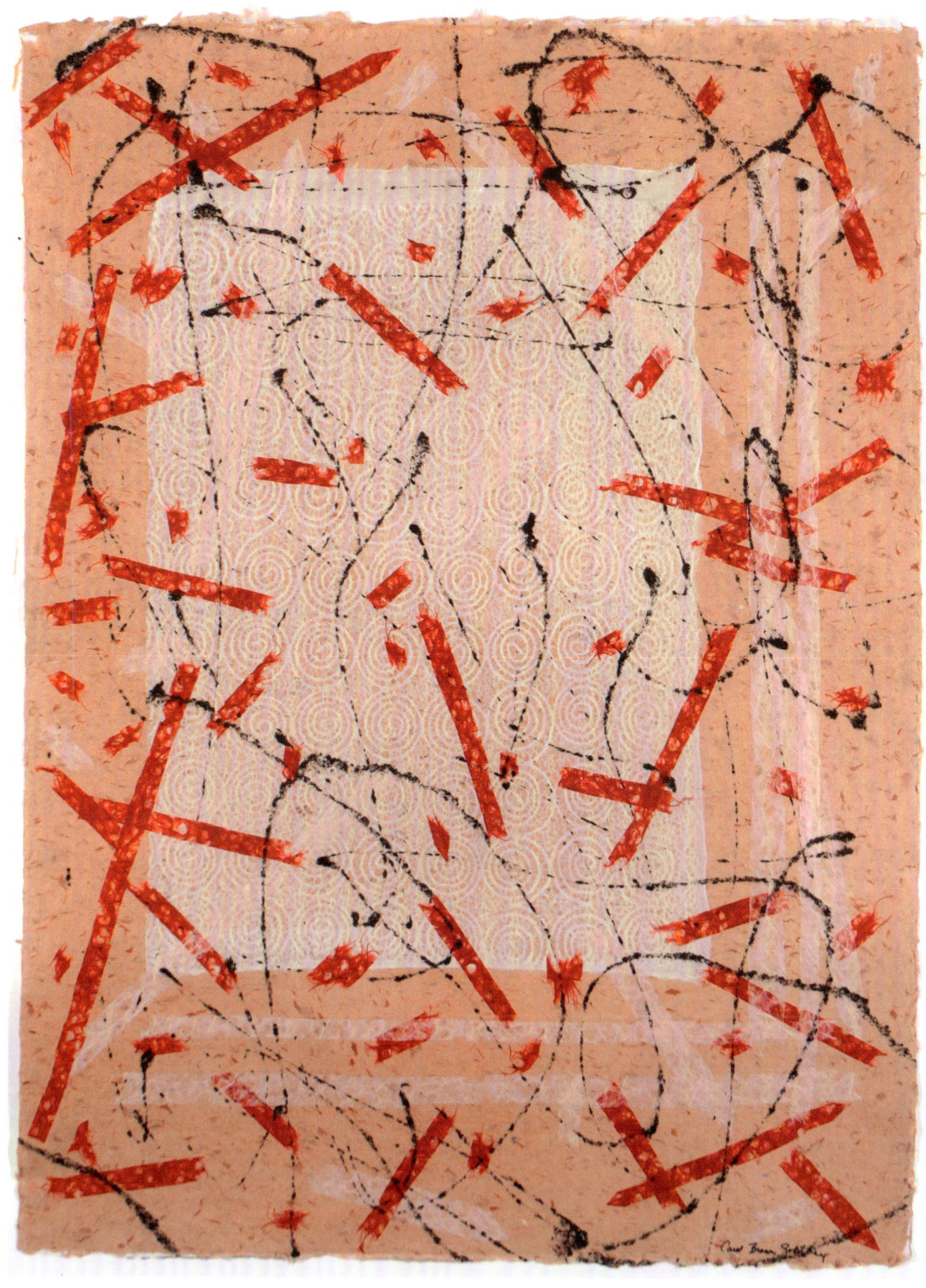

A Prayer for C&P, 2005
Pulp paint and mixed media on handmade paper
40½" x 30½"

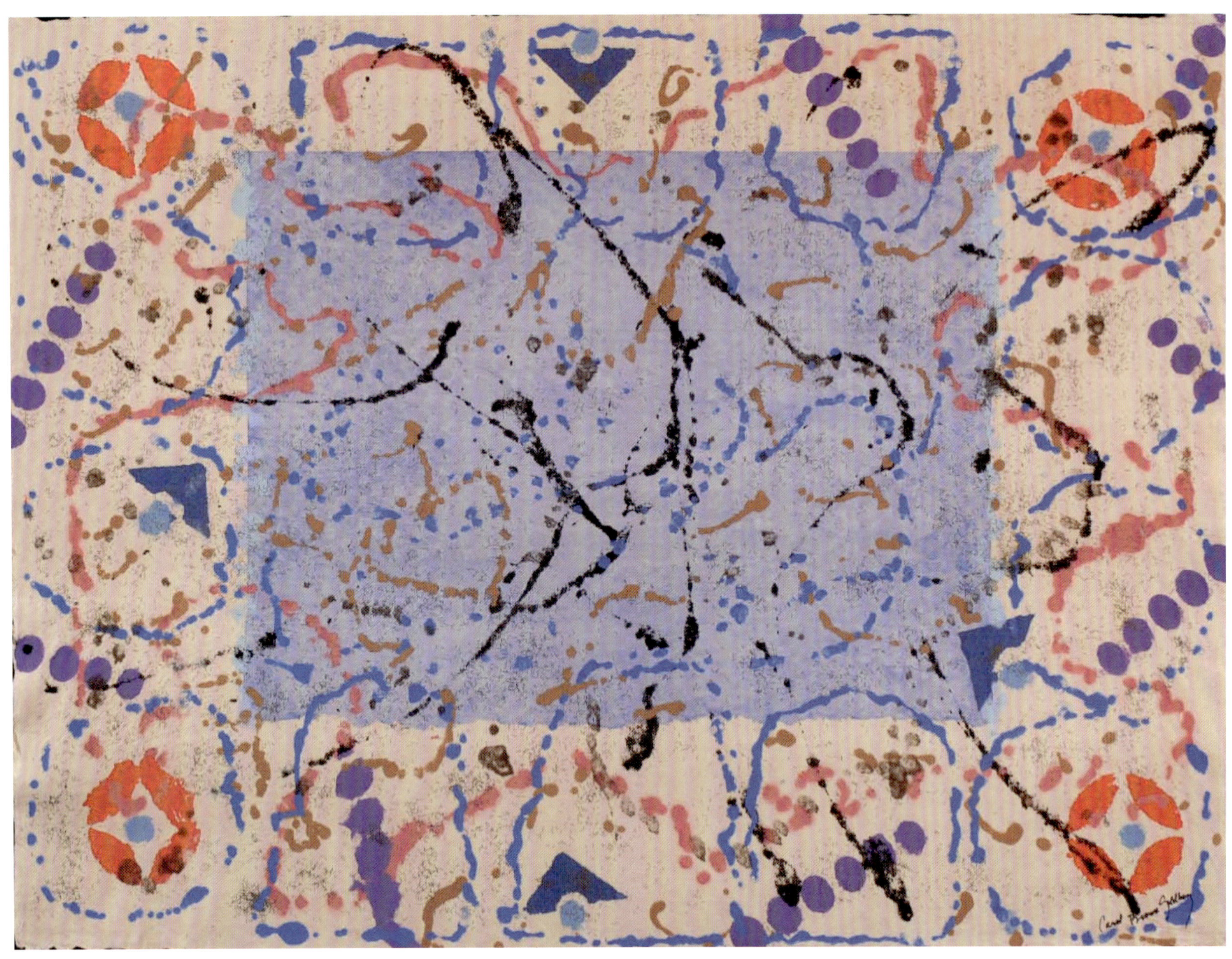

Sand Castles at Lucy Vincent, 2005
Pulp paint and mixed media on handmade paper
30½" x 40½"

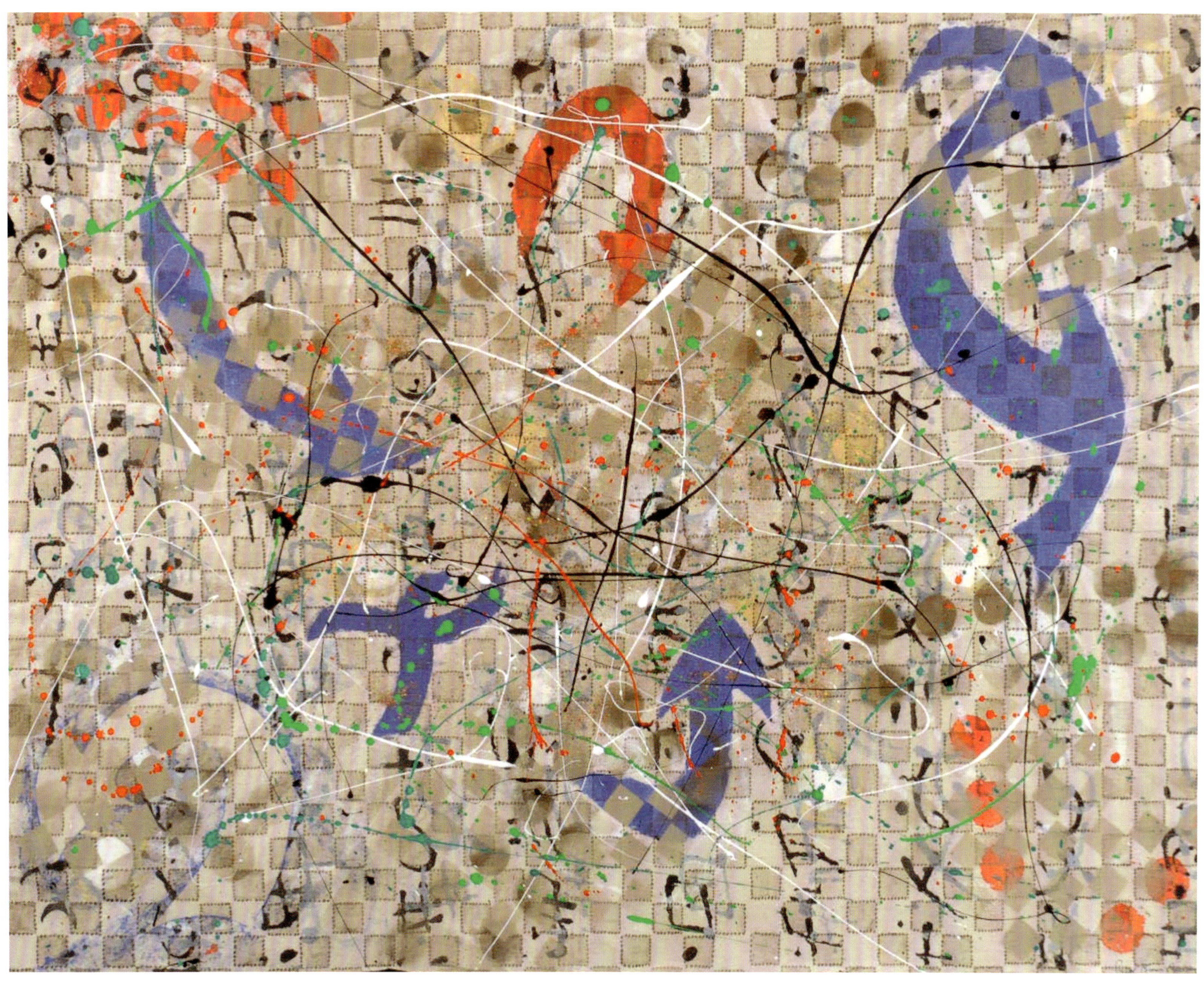

Conversations, 1992-2005
Pulp paint and mixed media on handmade paper
30½" x 40½"

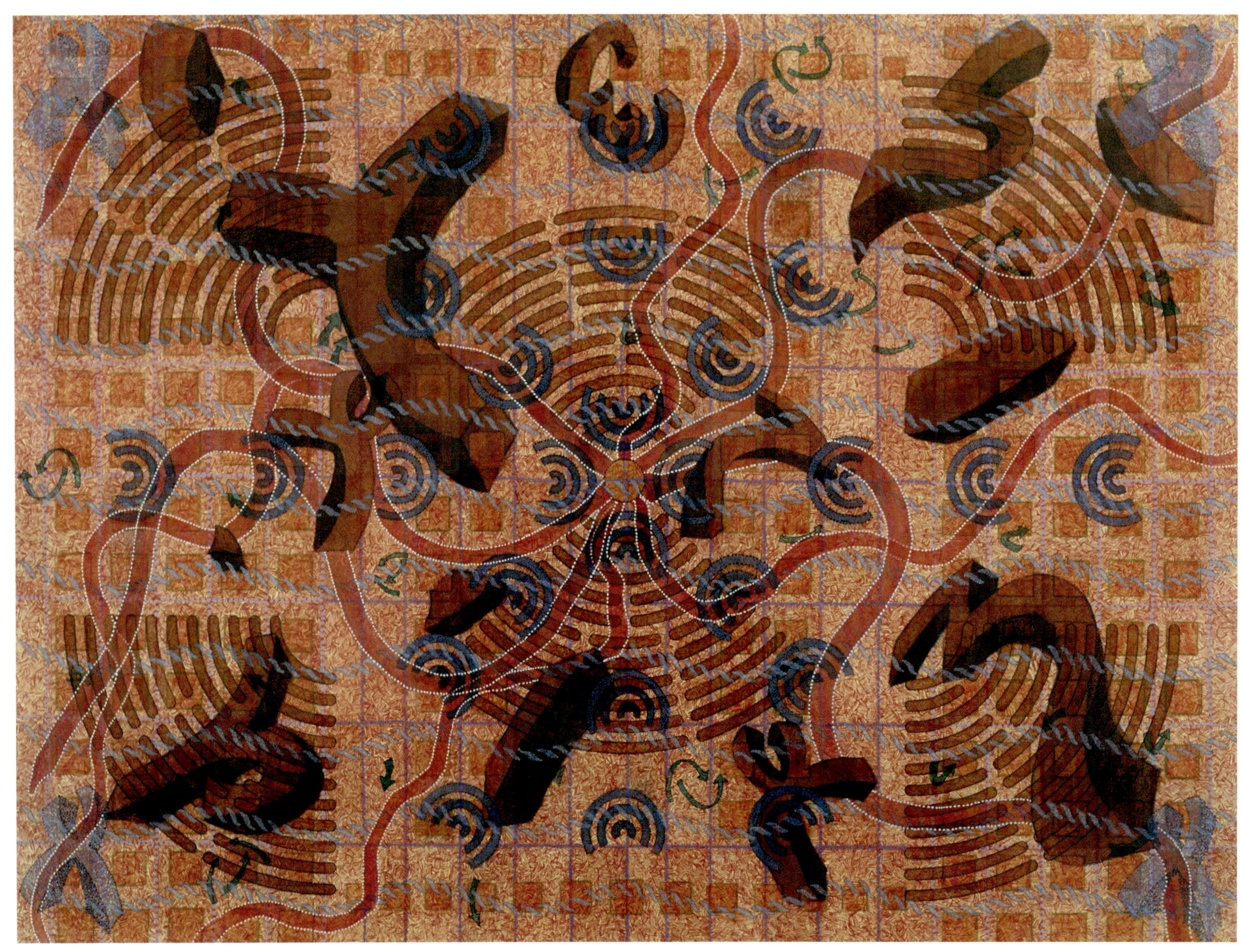

Untitled, 1989
Ink on paper
22" x 30"
Private collection

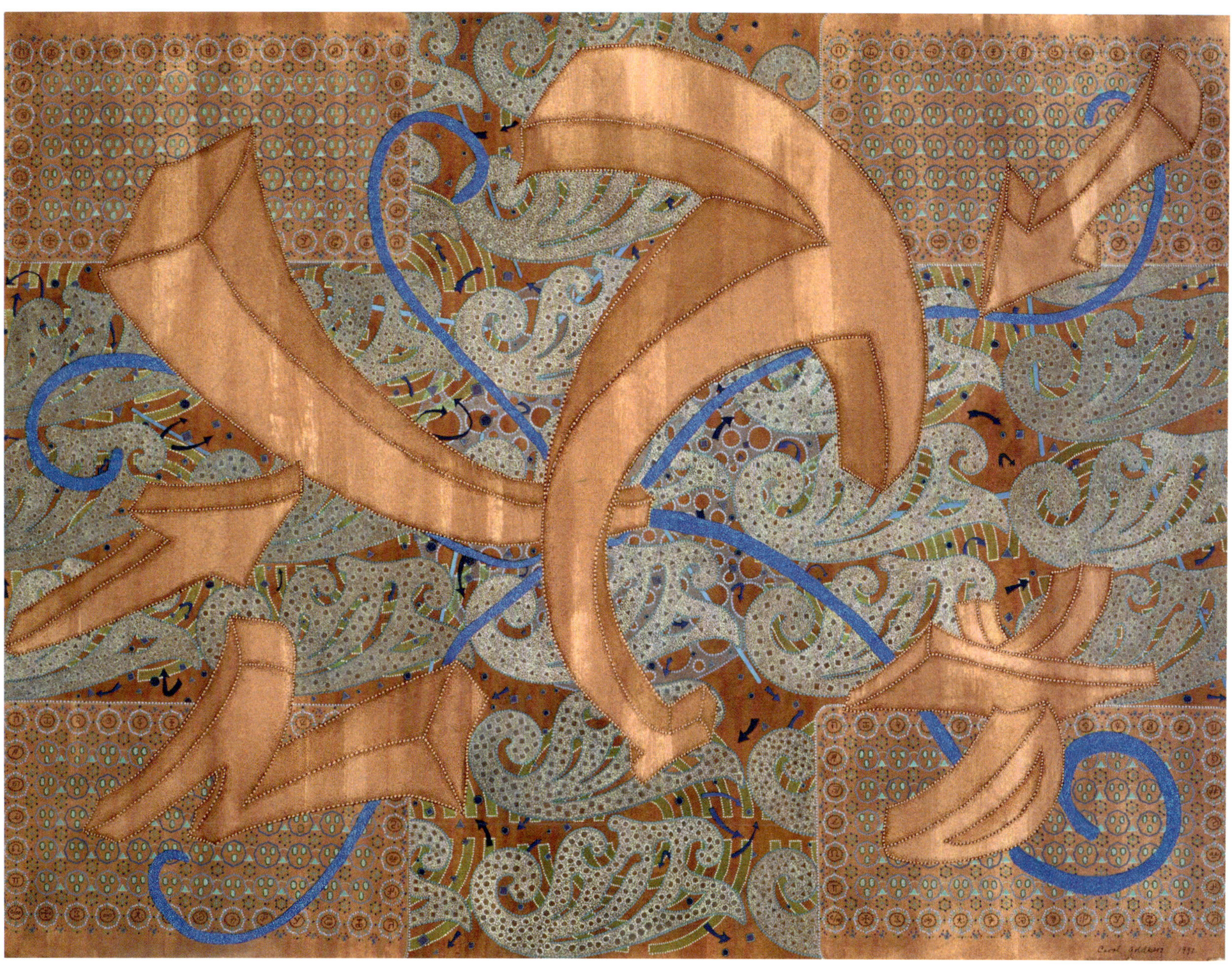

Mesons On Mari, 1992
Mixed media on Arches paper
20" x 30"
Private collection

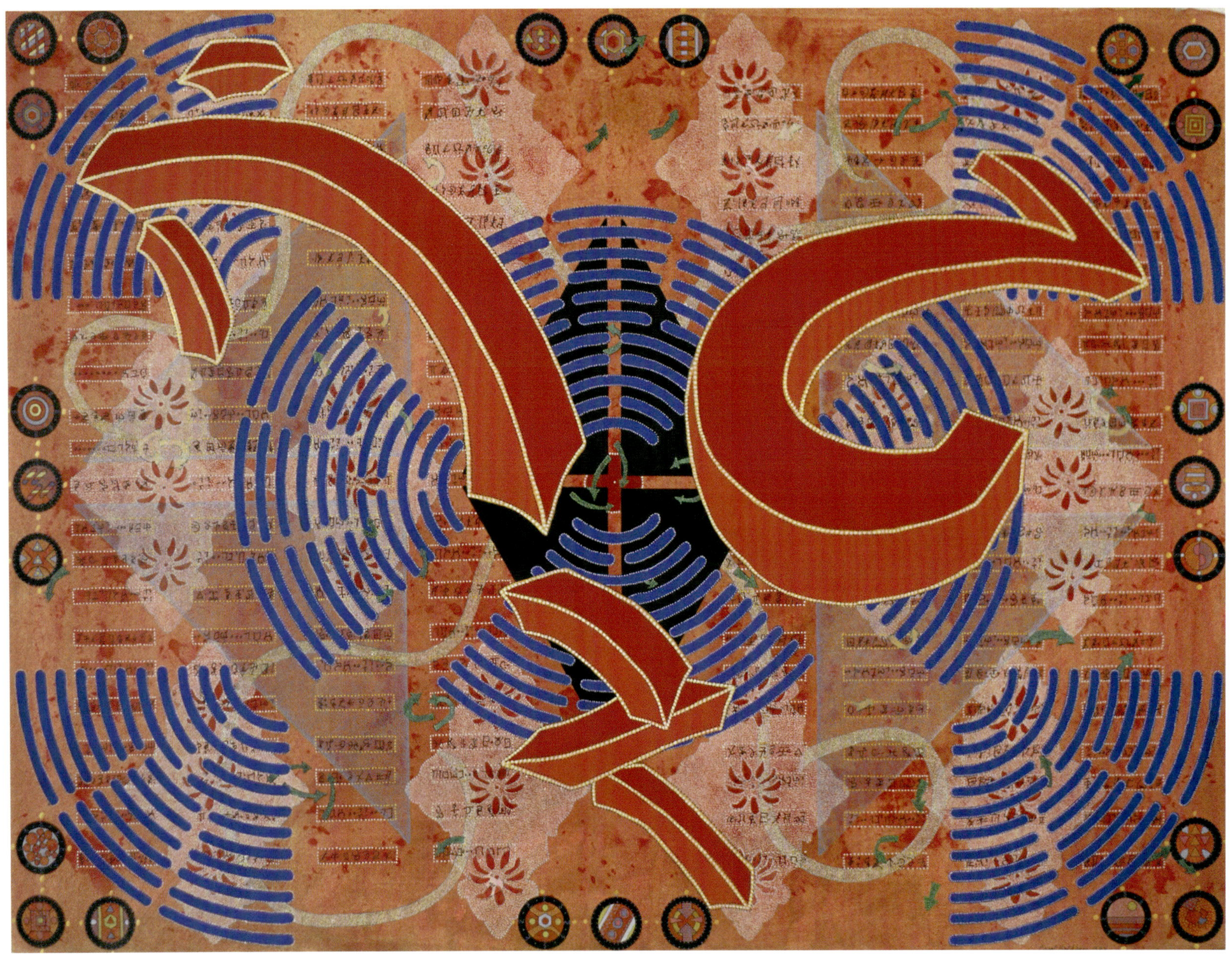

As Above, So Below, 1992
Acrylic and mixed media on Arches paper
33" x 38½"
Private collection

Detail ▶

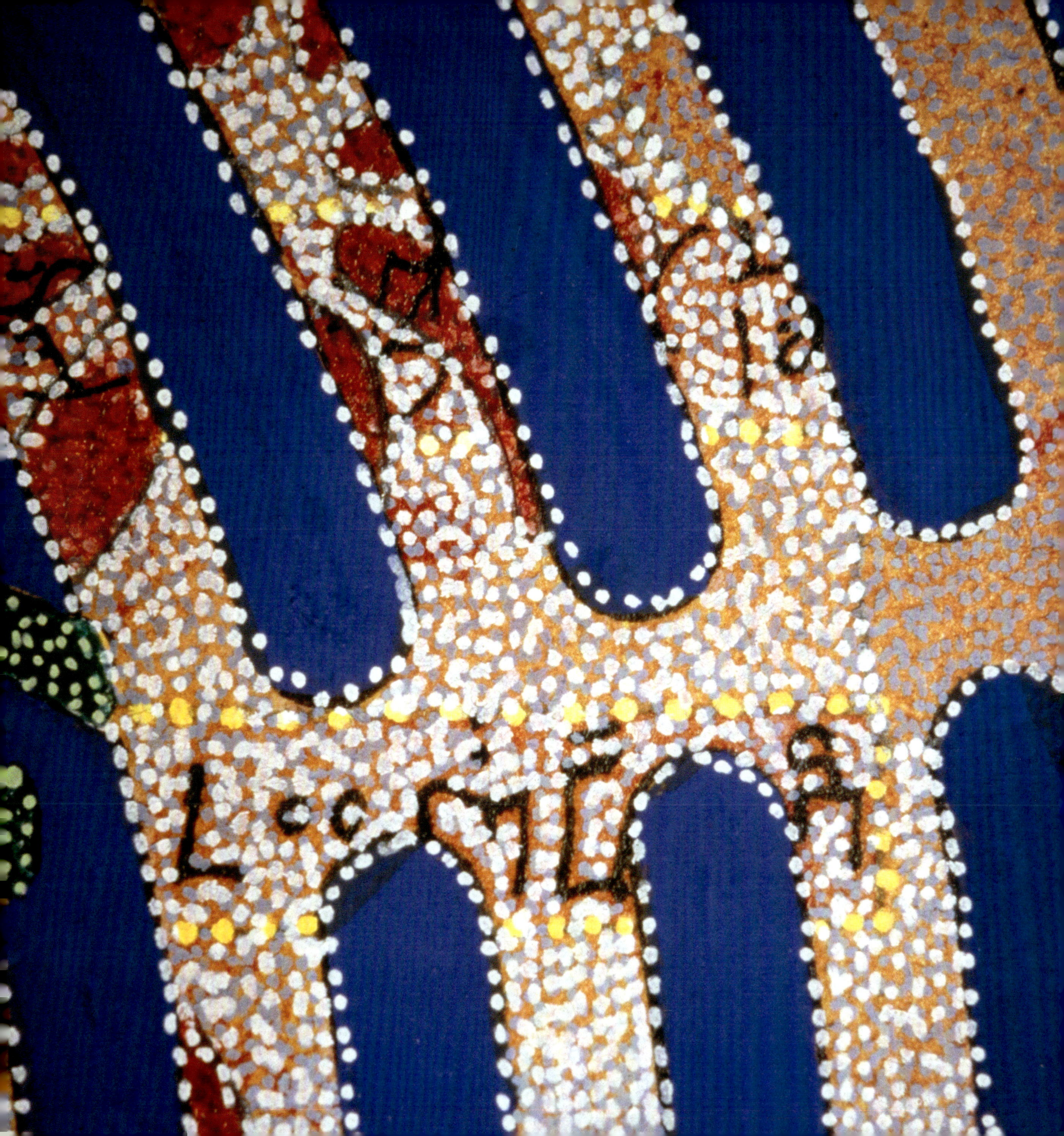

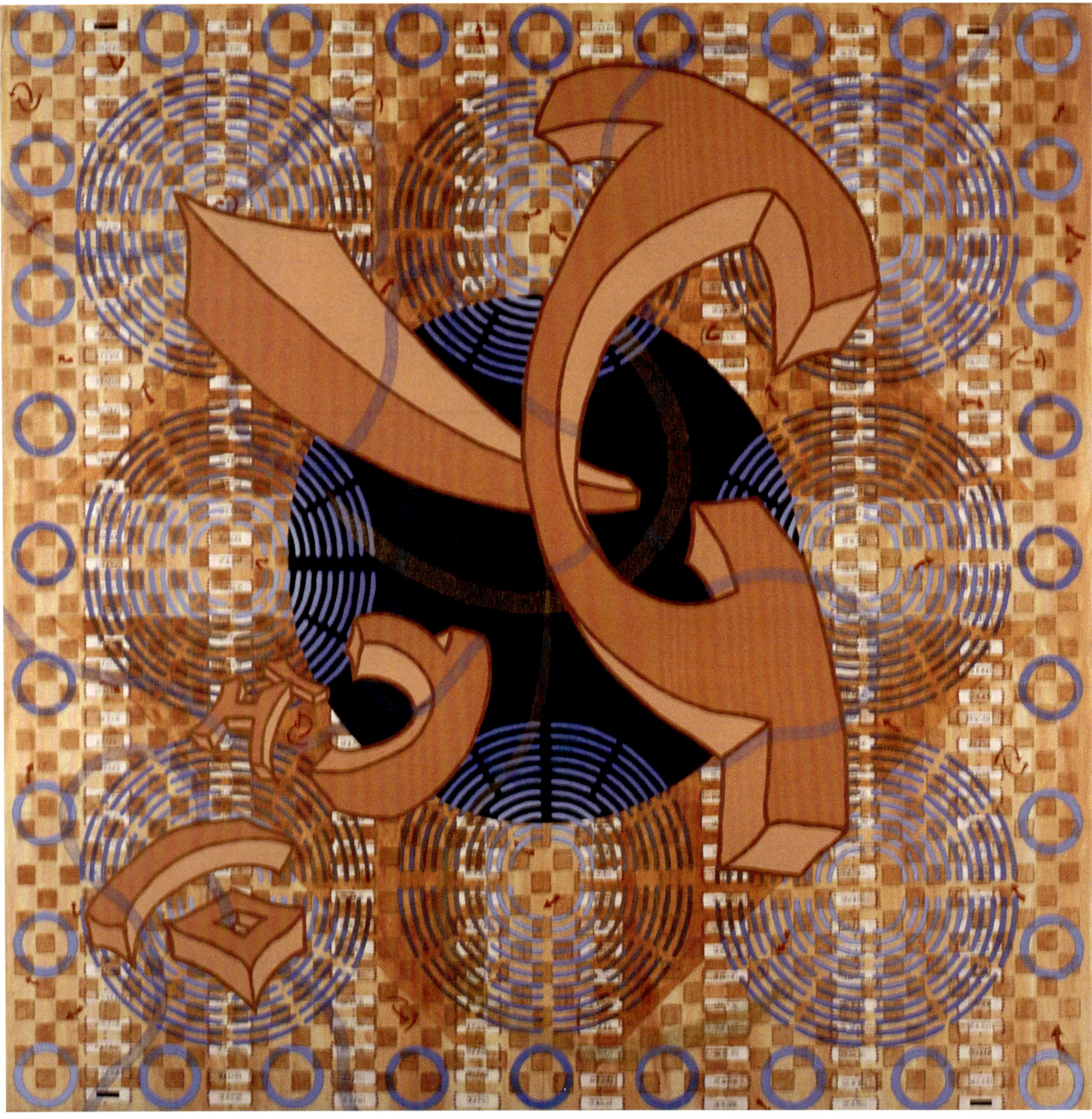

Adobe Visitors, 1996
Acrylic on canvas
50" x 50"

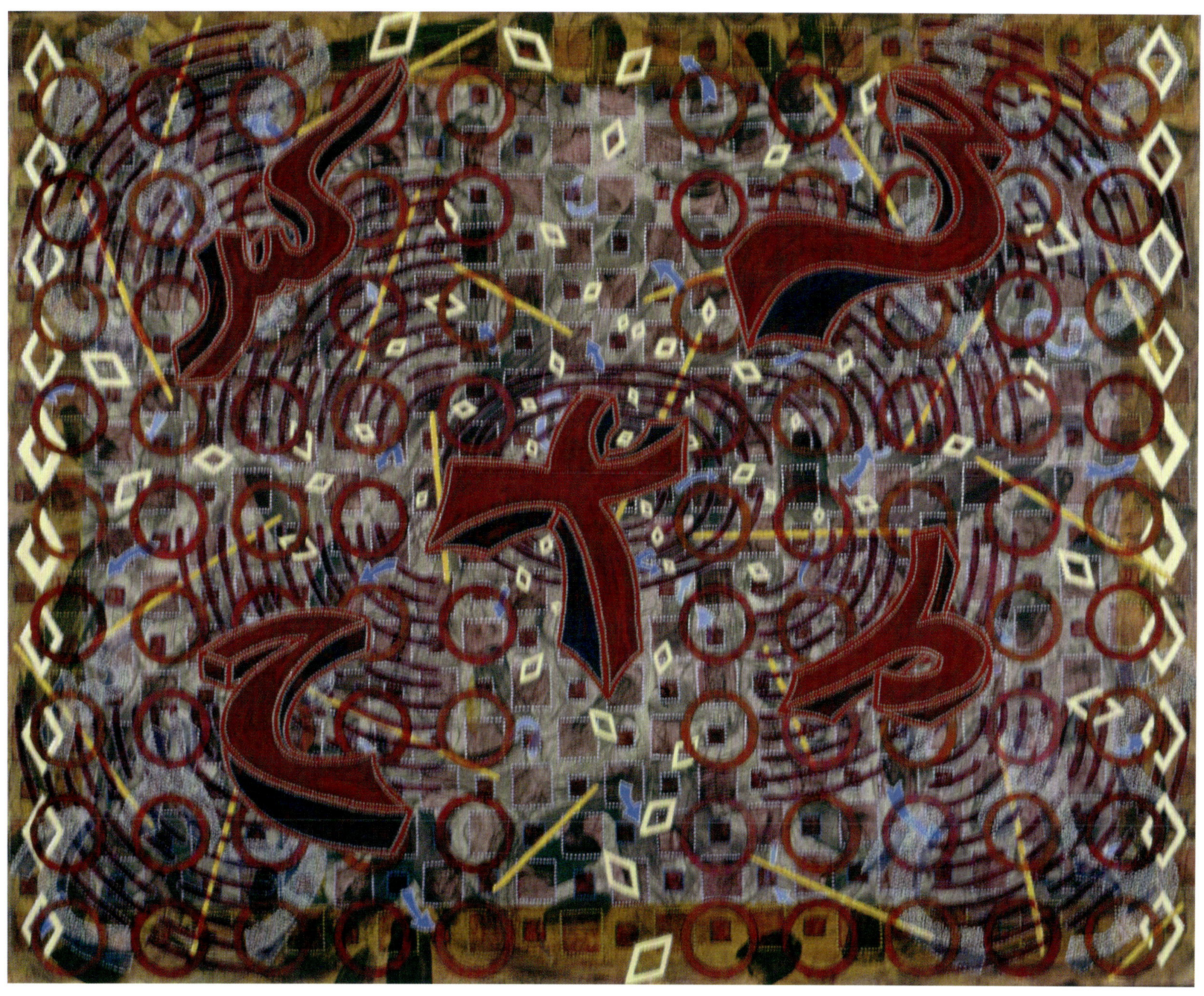

In My Father's Chair, 1994
Acrylic and mixed media on canvas
26½" x 32
Private collection

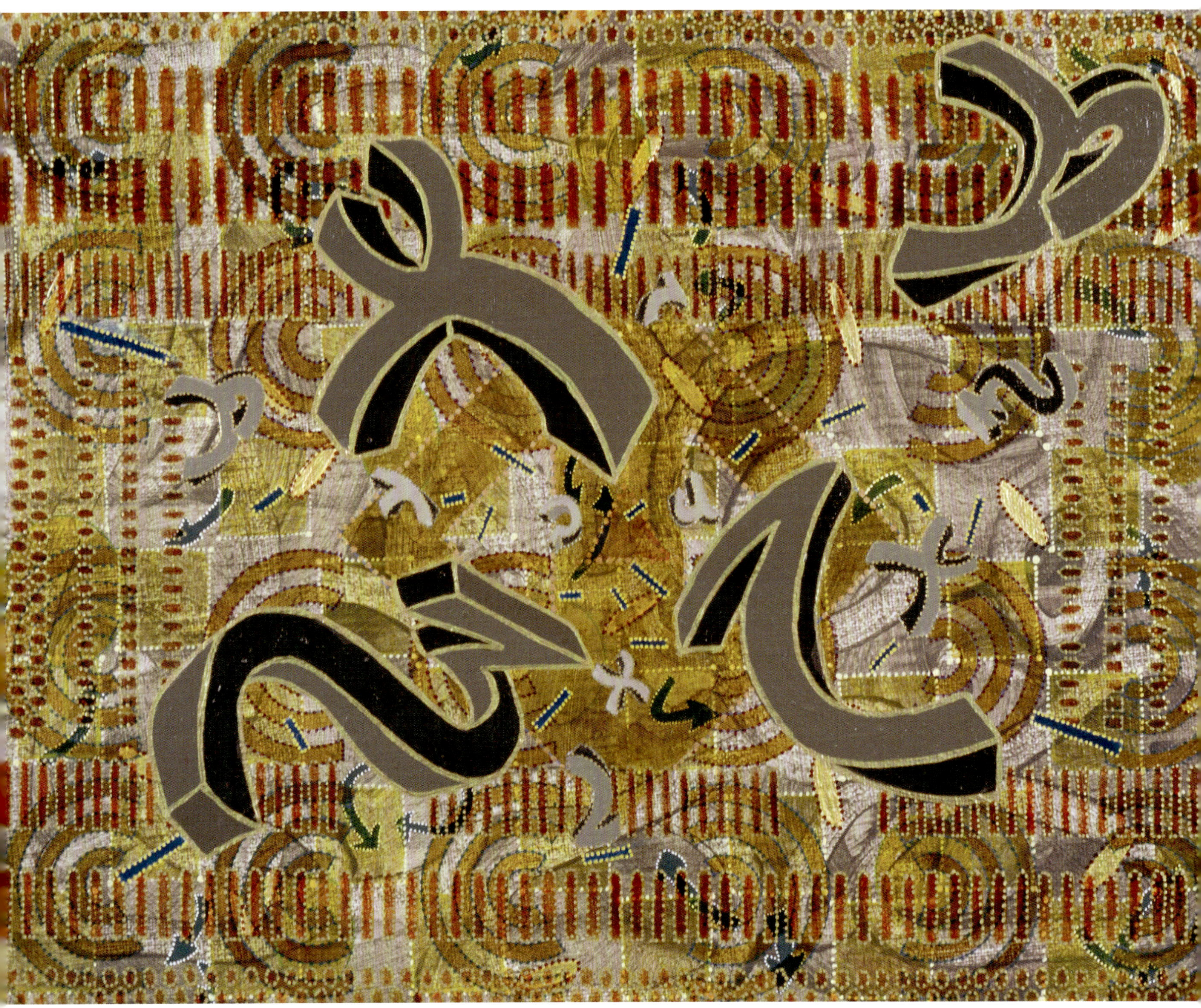

Atomic Library, 1995
Acrylic and mixed media on canvas
12 ½" x 15"
Private collection

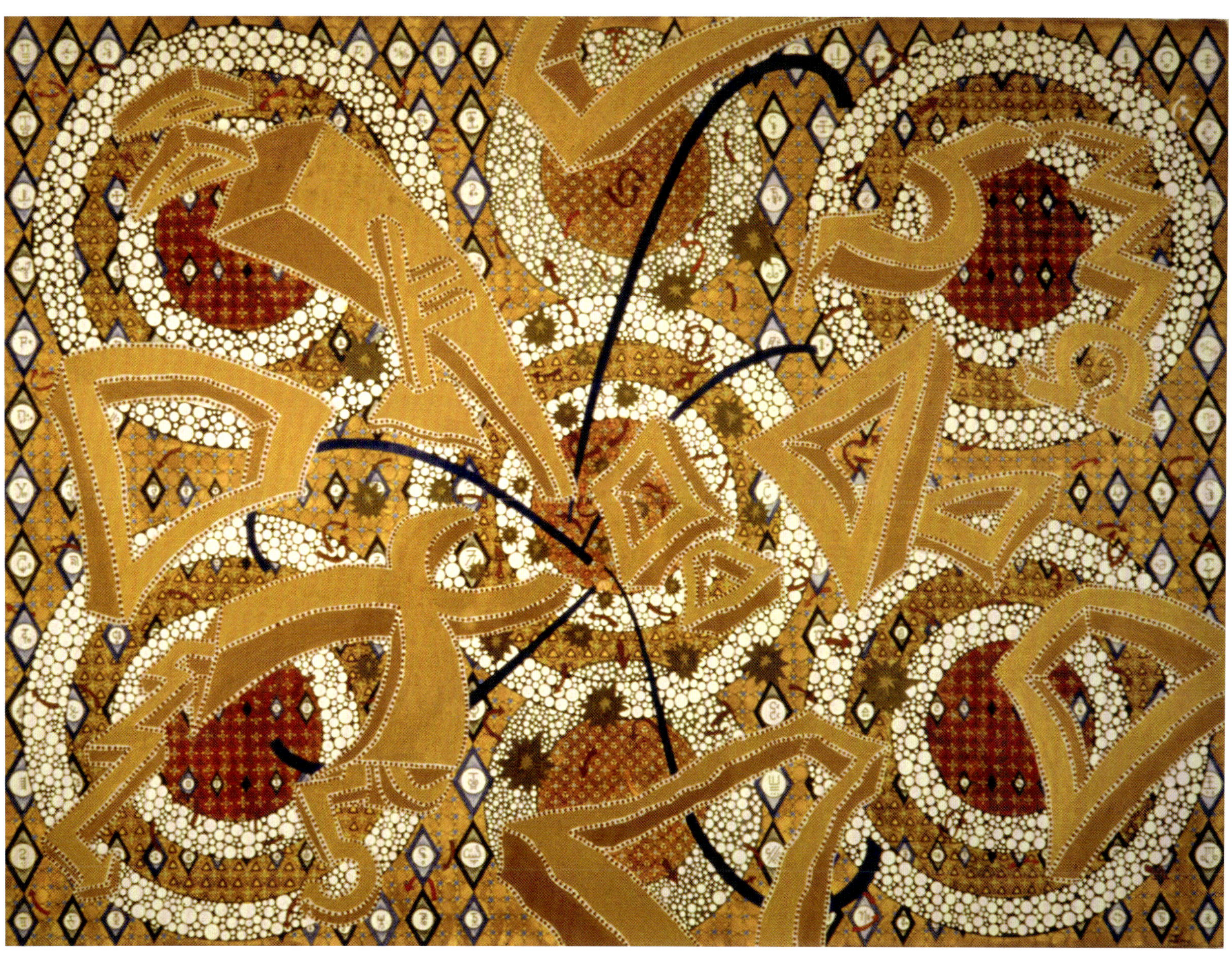

Mesons Over Nuzi, 1991
Acrylic and mixed media on canvas
33" x 38 ½"
Collection of Carolyn and Warren Kaplan

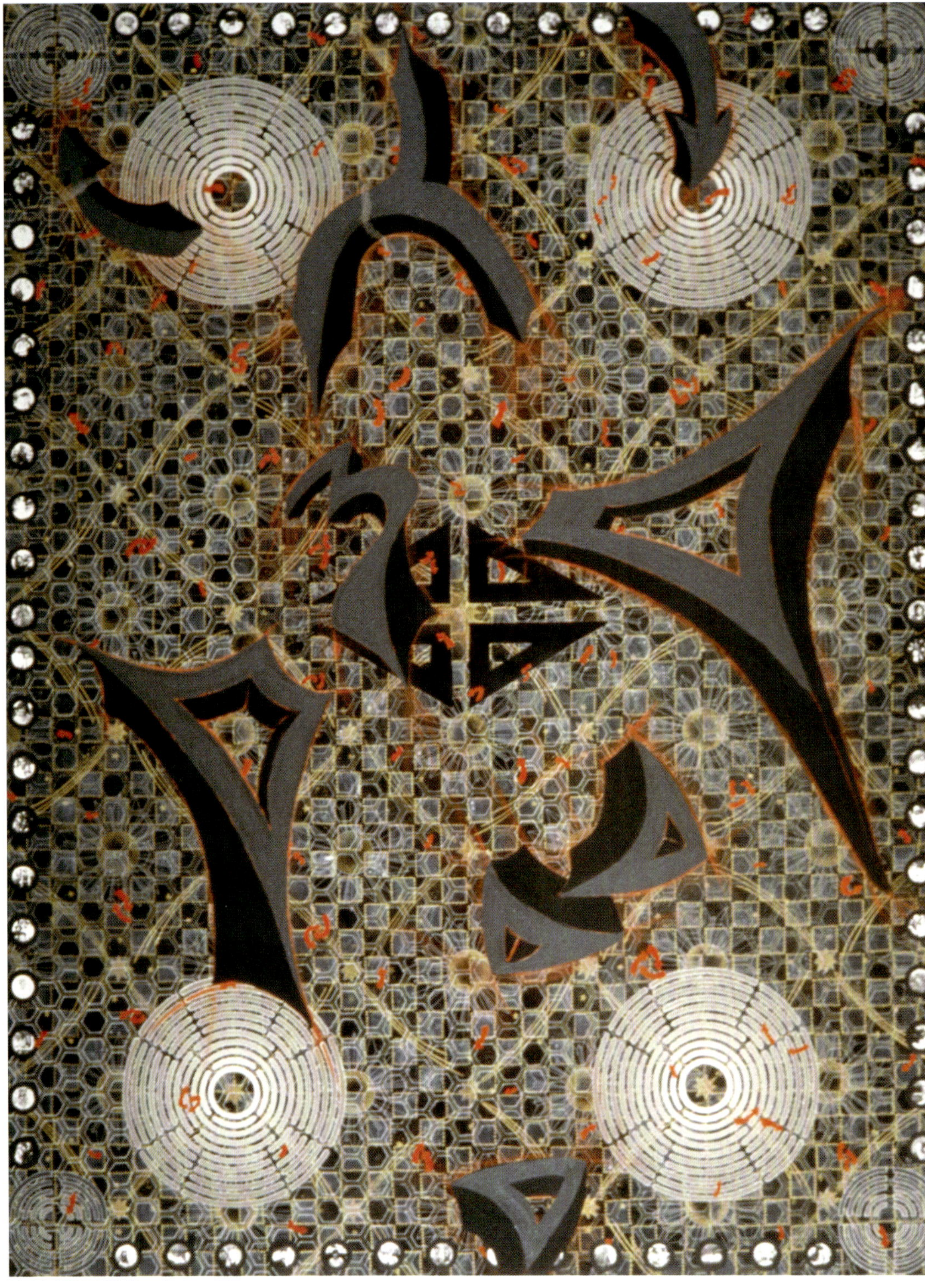

The Future of Memory, 1995
Mixed media on fabric
73" x 55½"
Collection of the National Museum of Women in the Arts

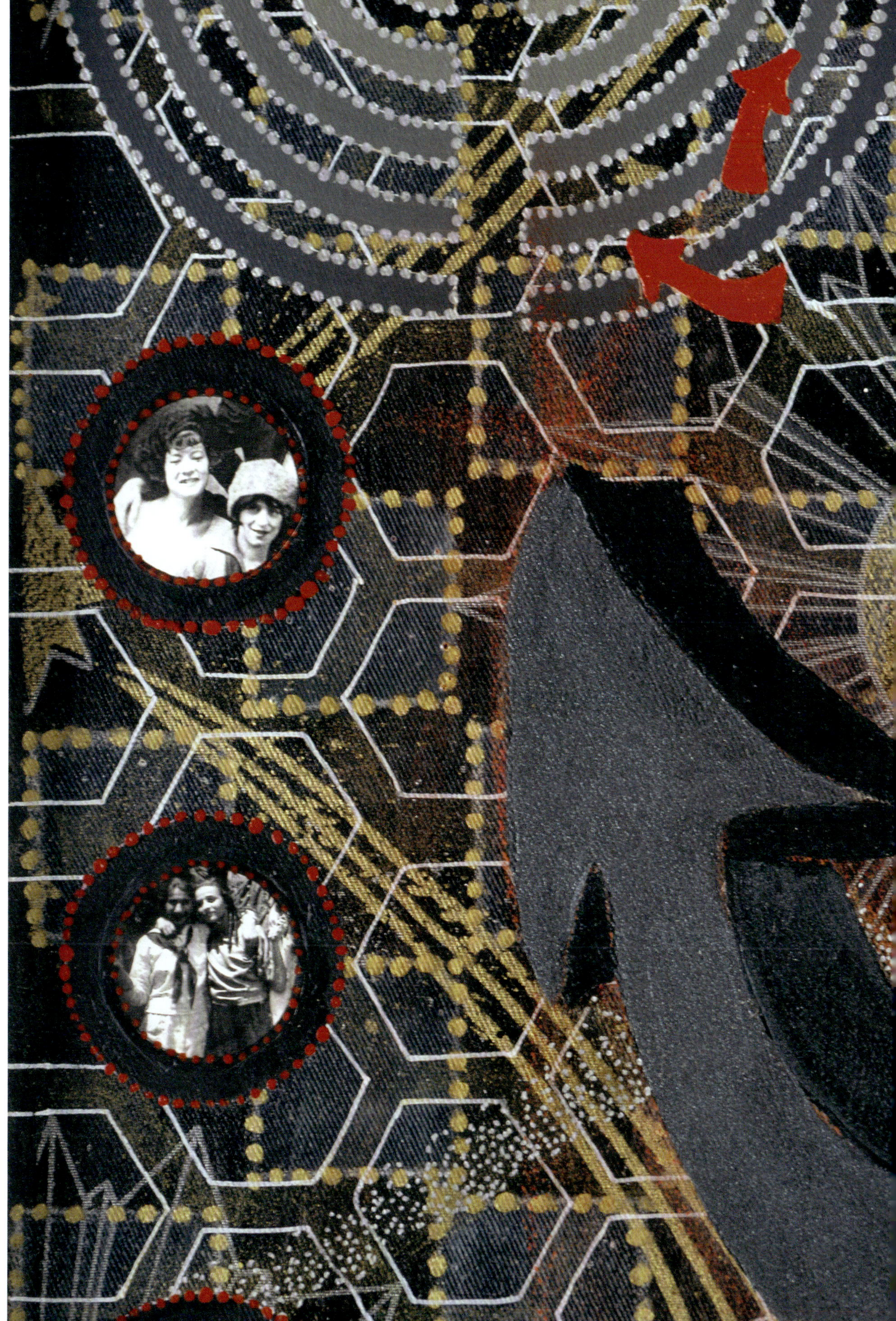

The Future of Memory
(detail: upper left corner)

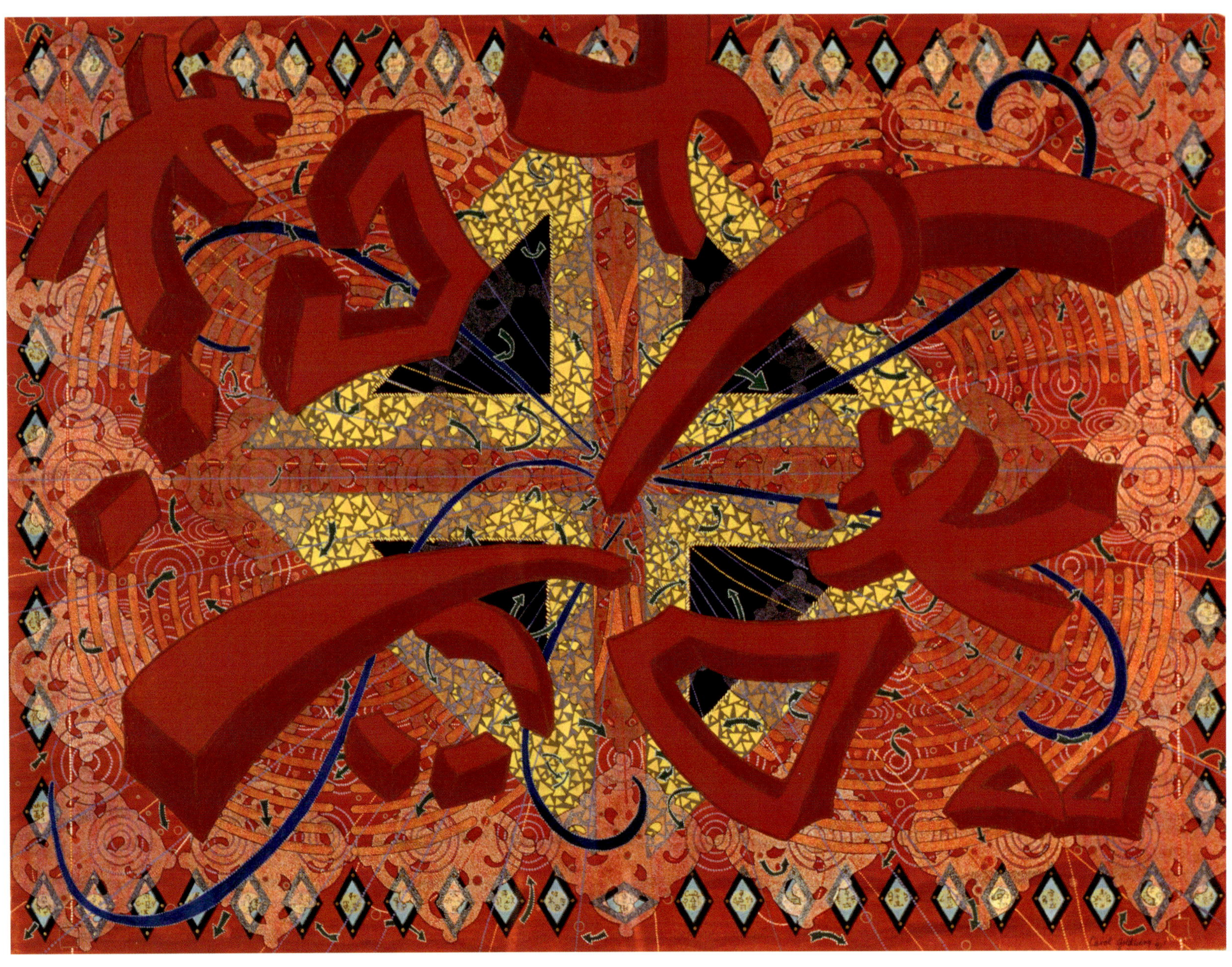

The Cycle of Ur, 1992
Acrylic, mixed media on canvas
32" x 26½"
Private collection

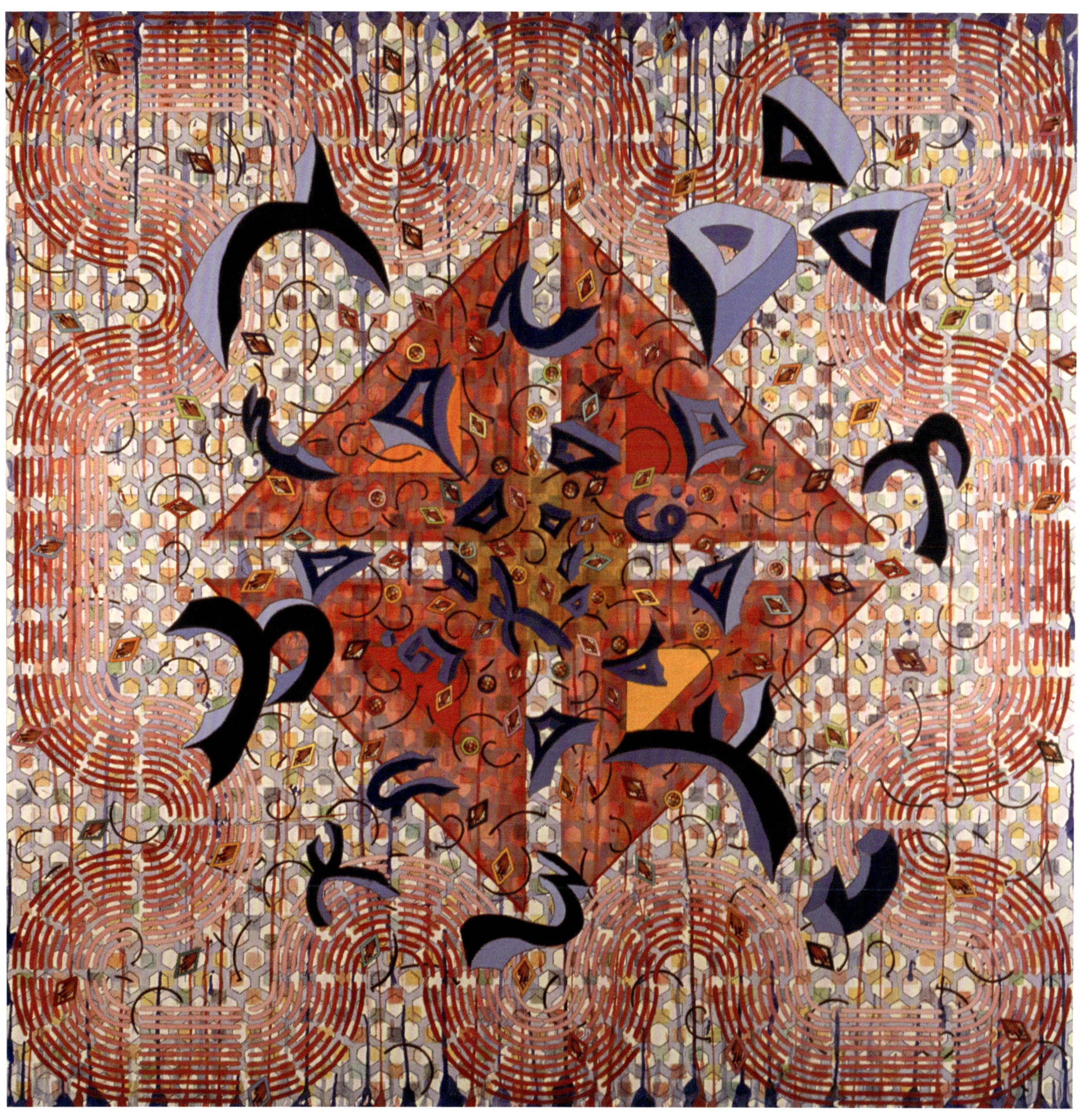

Touching Hands, 1996-97
Acrylic, ink and enamel on canvas
62" x 62"

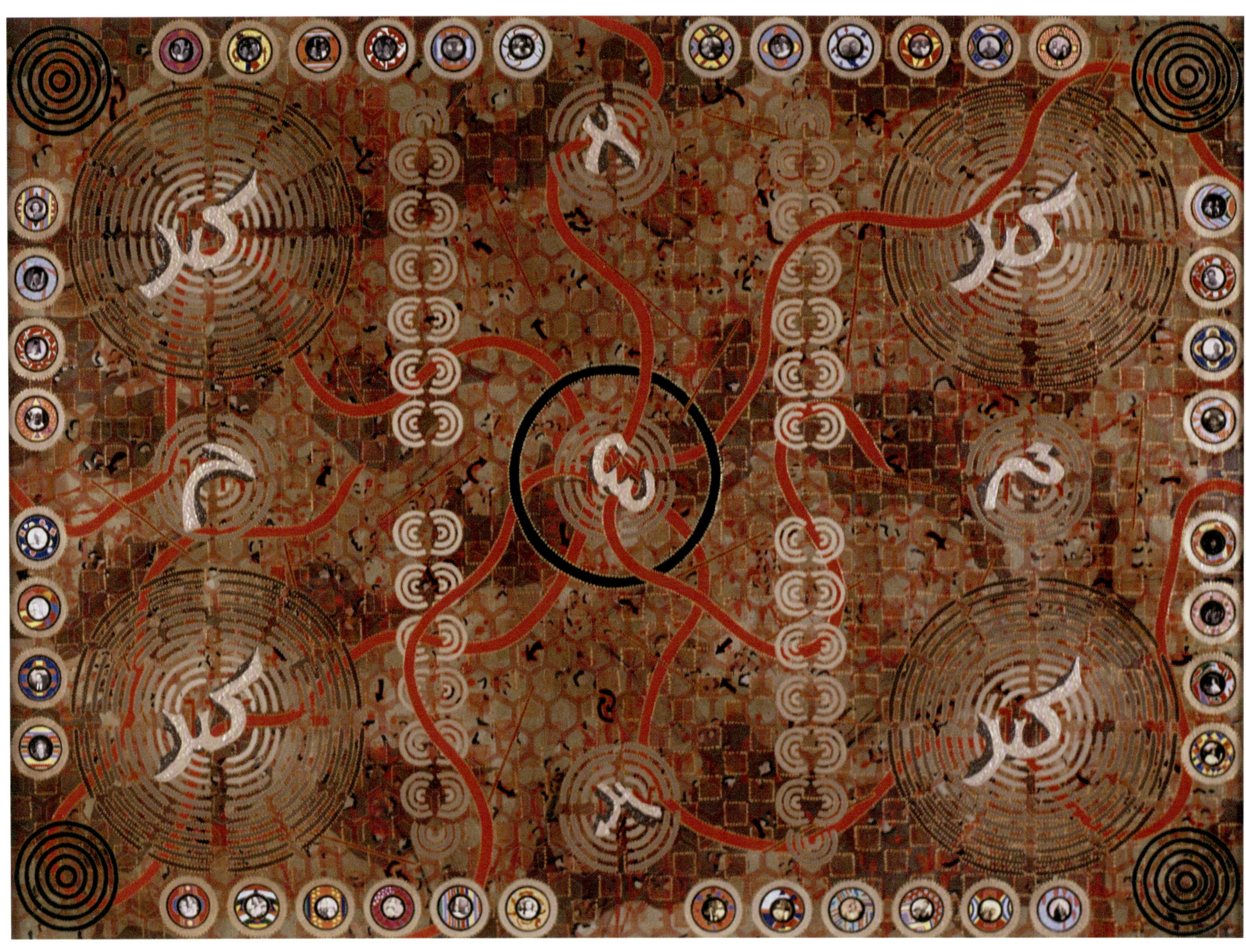

Long Ago in the 20th Century, 1995
Acrylic and mixed media on fabric
44" x 60"
Collection of Mr. and Mrs. Ben Huberman

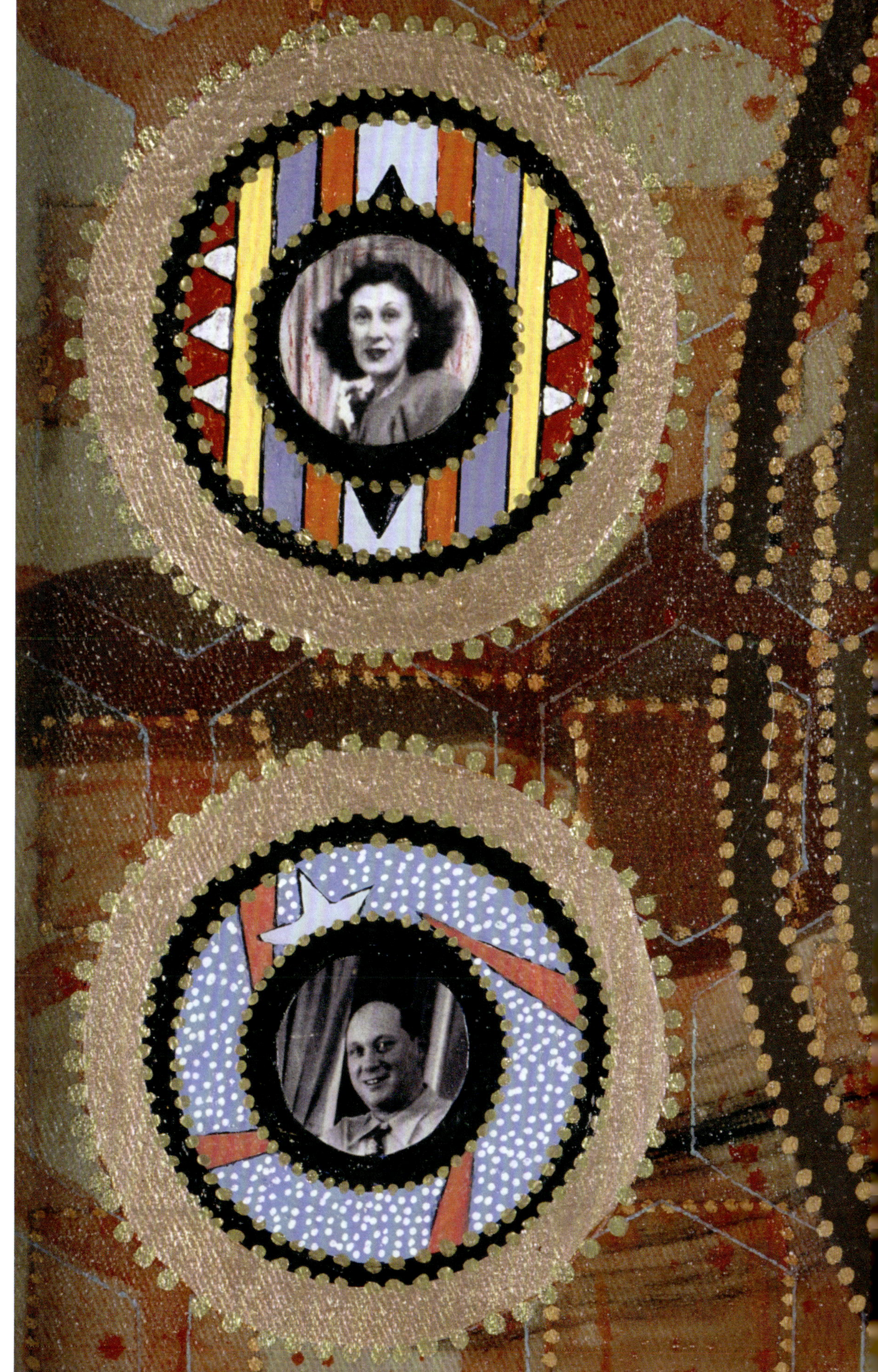

Long Ago in the 20th Century
(detail: upper left corner)

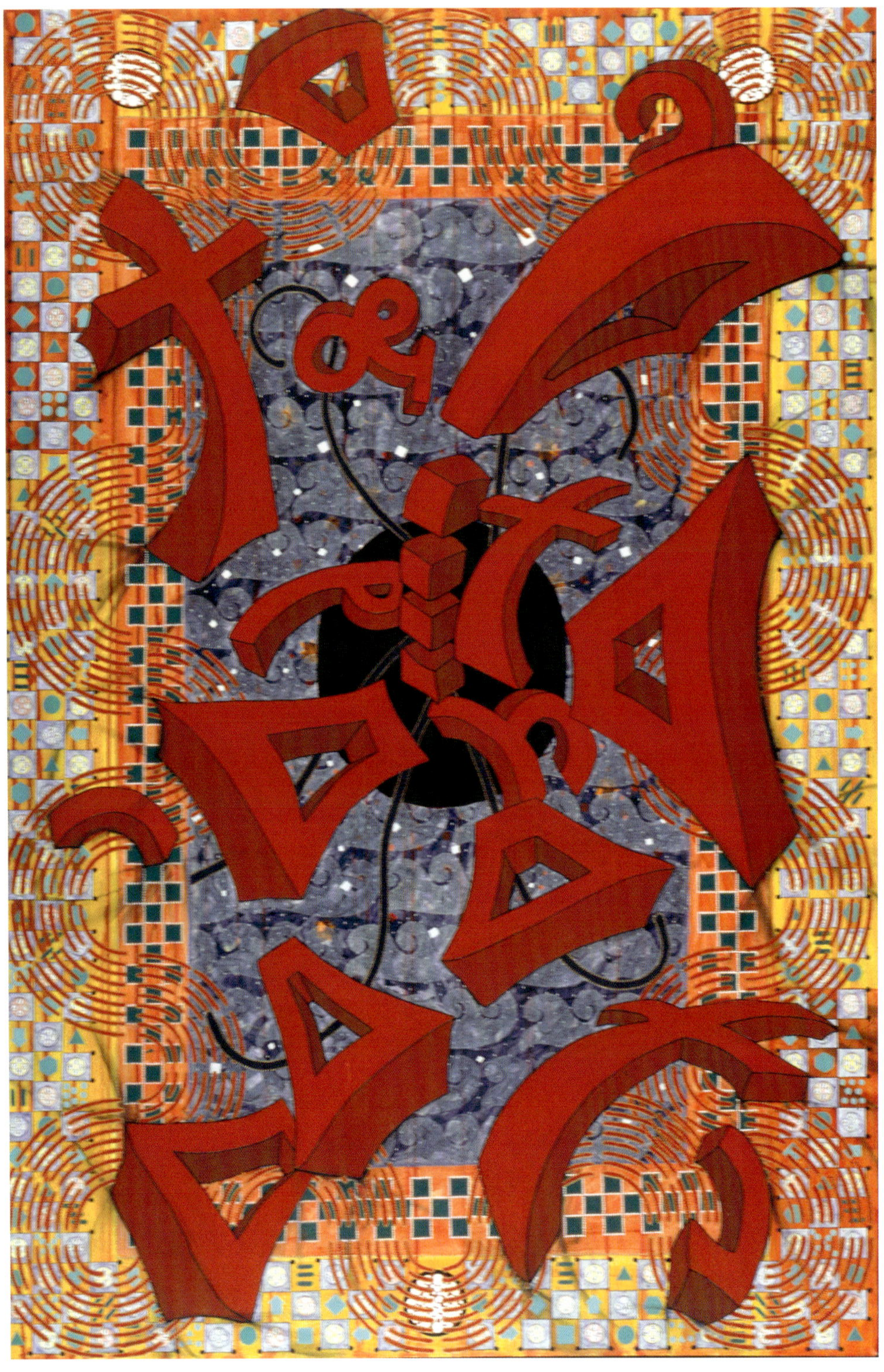

Dorothy's Laughter, 1995
Mixed media on canvas
68" x 46"
Collection of Mr. and Mrs. Elliot Hurwitz

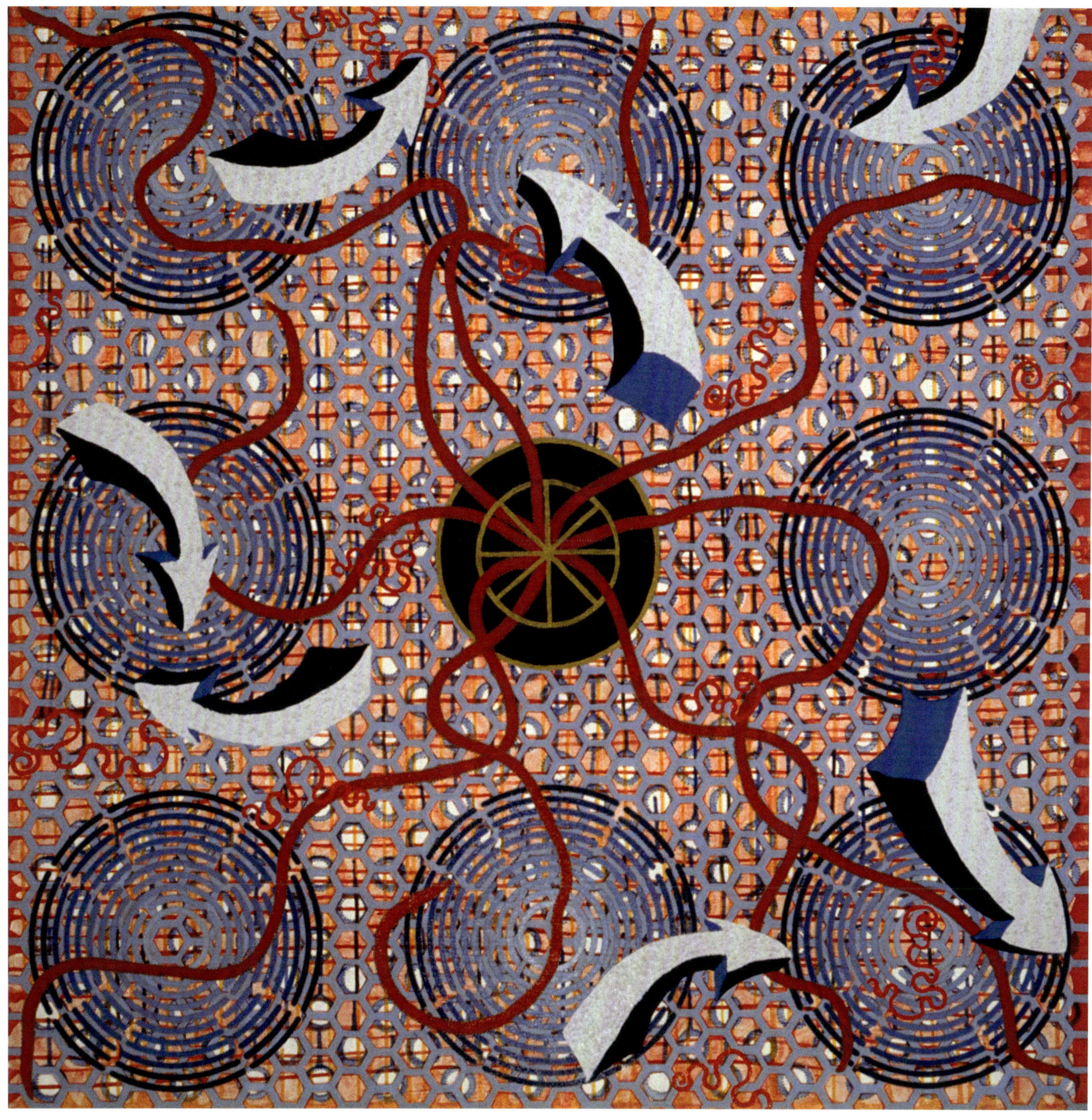

Blue Milk, 1995
Acrylic on canvas
50" x 50"
Collection of American University, Washington, DC

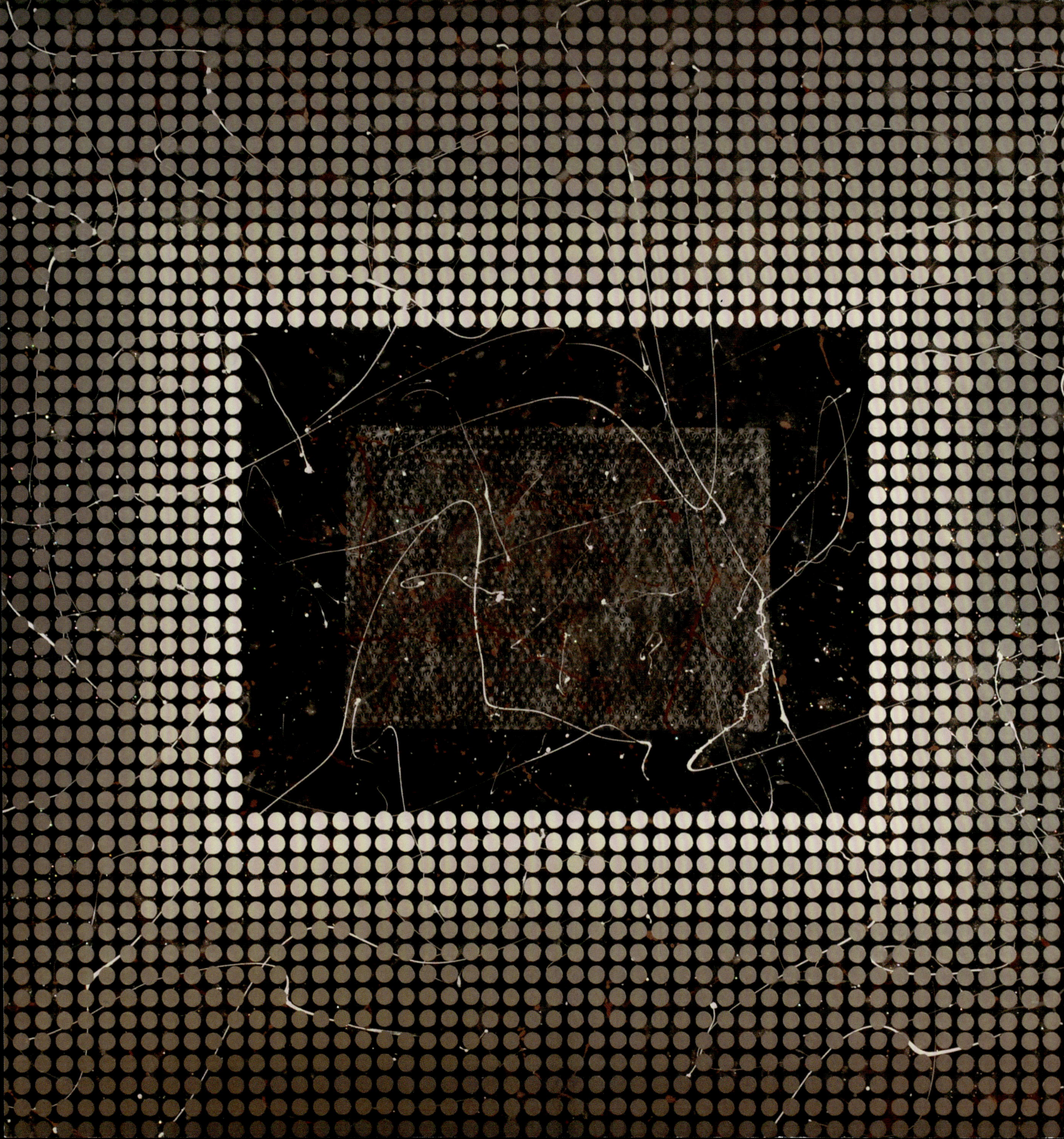

Afterword

By Jack Rasmussen

When artists make paintings, they are also constructing metaphors. Artists use their formal and iconographic means to create metaphors that exploit the expectations of viewers. Viewers expect to find sense or order (i.e. meaning) in a work of art, and artists expect them to look for it. Painting is, at its heart, a communicative act, and metaphor is its language.

The basic form of metaphor is analogy: A:B::C:D, or A is to B as C is to D. When viewers expect to understand a work of art and possess the relevant cultural knowledge artists assume they have, artists will be free to try out different values for the missing variables and arrive at their own interpretations.

We can test this hypothesis on a painting by Carol Brown Goldberg, *Bertrand Russell Visits Bancroft Road*, 2007 (opposite page). Carol began by taking a large (84" x 96") stretched and primed canvas and covering it completely with a pure Mars Black acrylic. Next, she divided the painting surface into quadrants and covered one quadrant at a time with glue. Before the glue could dry, Carol took iridescent, highly reflective, laser-cut particles of silver, white, and copper and scattered them across the deep, black space.

Bertrand Russell Visits Bancroft Road (detail), 2007 (Full image p. 48)
Acrylic on canvas with reflective chips and Japanese rice paper
84" x 96"

What looks so free and chaotic, when understood as part of the artist's process, becomes purposeful and meaningful. Already, even while Carol is preparing the first layers of her background and before she has introduced iconography of any sort, we find a metaphor waiting for us. Iridescence : Stars :: Black : Space. Iridescent particles are to stars as black paint is to space. Light comes from the void. Each subsequent act in her process enriches the metaphor, expanding its potential for meaning.

Carol next glues a rectangle of very thin, textured rice paper in the middle of her black and iridescent field. The rectangular shape brings structure to the void and also creates a plane in space, perhaps like the firmament dividing heaven and earth. Then, Carol takes a loaded brush and flings thin lines of white, red, copper, and bronze acrylic enamel at the painting, her gestures creating a controlled, rhythmic chaos over the other layers... a seemingly random, isotropic field.

Finally, Carol paints a grid of circles with a mixture of metallic silver and iridescent pearl, starting at the outside edges of the canvas, the circles getting progressively lighter as they move toward the center. She leaves the center open, an area slightly larger than the rectangle formed by the rice paper.

As we physically and mentally move from layer to layer, we feel the tension between order and chaos: the formal perfection of the circle against the formless space, the rectangle locking in the center of the larger rectangle, dividing the space into layers, front to infinity.

When I asked Carol where the fascination with physics and the cosmos originated, she mentioned reading her brother's copy of *The ABC of Relativity* by Bertrand Russell. The book sought to steer readers with no knowledge of mathematics or physics through Einstein's theories of special and general relativity, gravitation, and the hydrogen bomb. This book was the beginning of Carol's life-long affair with science, mathematics, and philosophy, making their concepts and theories the subject of, and inspiration for, her art. When questioned about her extended forays into the right side of her brain, Carol could have quoted Bertrand Russell: "Emotion that can be destroyed by a little mathematics is neither genuine nor valuable."

I used to think it was the job of the artist to impose order on the chaos around us, but watching Carol's work evolve over the years, I now think the artist may be discovering order in what to us only appears to be chaotic. The job of the artist would seem to require equal parts faith and science. Carol Brown Goldberg possesses both these gifts, and the sensitivity and skill to construct visual metaphors suggesting our place in a beautiful and mysterious universe. •

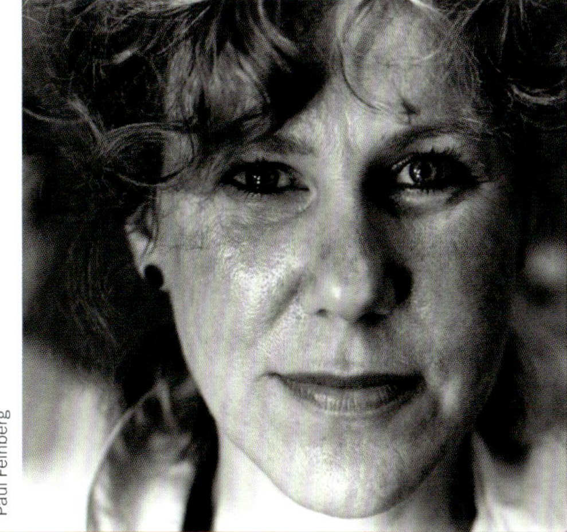
Paul Feinberg

Carol Brown Goldberg

Curriculum Vitae

Selected Solo Exhibitions

2008 National Arts Club, New York, NY
2007 Katzen Arts Center, American University, Washington, DC
2006 Pyramid Atlantic, Silver Spring, MD
2005 Osuna Art, Bethesda, MD
2004 Cosmos Club, Washington, DC
2003 John and Esther Clay Fine Arts Gallery, Cheyenne, WY
2002 Daryl Reich Rubenstein Gallery, Sidwell Friends School, Washington, DC
2002 Chautauqua Institute, Chautauqua, NY
2002 Anton Gallery, Washington, DC
1995 Troyer Fitzpatrick Lassman Gallery, Washington, DC
1993 Maryland Art Place, "Concertina" (Multi-Media), Baltimore, MD
1992 Osuna Gallery, Washington, DC
1990 Amnesty International, Washington, DC
1987 Virginia Polytechnic Institute, Squires Gallery, Blacksburg, VA
1985 G. Sander Gallery, Daytona Beach, FL
1983 FIAC Grand Palais, Osuna Gallery, Paris, France
1982 Osuna Gallery, Washington, DC, (1986, '87, '88, '89, '90, '92)

Selected Group Exhibitions

2007 Adamar Gallery, Coral Gables, FL
2006 "On the Verge," American Center for Physics, College Park, MD
2006 "Pulse 2006," Hillyer Art Space, Washington, DC
2005 "Faces of the Fallen," Women's Military Museum, Arlington, VA
2004 Chautauqua Institute, Chautauqua, NY
2002 "Math=Art," Frostburg University, Frostburg, MD
1999 "Artists for Amnesty International," International Visions, Washington, DC
1995 "Prints 1995," Baltimore Museum of Art, Baltimore, MD
1992 St. John's College, Collegeville, MN
1991 " The Critic's Choice," Watkin's Gallery, American University, Washington, DC
1990 "Moscow/Washington, DC Exchange," Moscow, USSR
1986 Driscoll Gallery, Denver, CO
1986 "Selected Group," G. Sander Fine Art Gallery, Daytona Beach, FL
1985 "Artists' Self Portrait," Jane Haslem Gallery, Washington, DC
1984 WPA Auction, Washington, DC
1981 "OPTIONS '81," Washington Project for the Arts, Washington, DC
1976 Corcoran Gallery of Art, Washington, DC

Selected Projects and Honorariums

Lecture: Kreeger Museum, Washington, DC
Adjunct Professor of Art: American University, Washington, DC, 1998 - present
"Art-Santa-Fe," Osuna Gallery, Santa-Fe, NM
VOICE OF AMERICA, Video Interview, "The Next Chapter"
Artist Residency/Instructor: Chautauqua Institute, Chautauqua, NY, 2001, 2002, 2003
Visual Artist Workshop, "Leadership Montgomery," Olney, MD, May 2000
Cosmos Club, "Art in the 21st Century," Washington, DC, March 2000
Curator: Internat'l Visions Gallery, "Amnesty Internat'l Artists," Washington, DC, 1999
Panelist: "Artists With Staying Power," Art Dealers Assoc., Washington, DC, 1998
Lecture: Sidwell Friends School, "Mothers/Daughters Graduation Banquet," Washington, DC, 1998
Essay, 'WRITING FROM THE HEART*,"* Nancy Slonum Aronie, Hyperion Press, NY, February 1998
Lecturer: "Painting in the 21st Century," Cosmos Club, January 1998
Bosnia Human Rights, "Solar Night," Print, 1996
Johns Hopkins University Hospital, "Child Life Project," Baltimore, MD, 1996
The band IVY, cover for "I Hate December" remix, Scratchie Records, 1995
Chair/Moderator: Southeastern College Art Conference, "Science and Poetry for Art," Georgetown University, 1995
Pyramid Atlantic Workshop Resident, "Exploration," 1995
AMANA Award, "Concertina," video
Maryland Art Place: Painting and Video, "Concertina," Baltimore, MD, 1993
Curator: MAP, "Mapping the Galaxies," Dr. Margaret Geller, Baltimore, MD, 1993
Curator: "Cystic Fibrosis Art Auction," Washington, DC, 1992
Producer: Lecture Series "Voices of our Time," Strathmore Hall Arts Center, Bethesda, MD, September - November 1991
Producer: lecture series "Voices of our Time," Strathmore Hall Arts Center, Bethesda, MD, September - November 1990
Book Cover, *The Empowered Woman,* by Riki Robbins, Ph.D., 1990
Poster, *The Empowered Woman*, 1990
Black Student College Fund, Silver Anniversary, silkscreen print, 1990
Amnesty International, painting, 1990
Poster, Amnesty International Human Rights Day for the 1990's – *The Poetry of Justice*, 1990
Visiting Artist: Mountain Lake Workshop, Blacksburg, VA, 1987
Federal Realty, honorarium, Willow Grove, PA, 1987
Outdoor Sculpture Honorarium, City of Rockville, Rockville, MD, 1987
Outdoor Sculpture Honorarium, Martin Luther King Park, Montgomery County, MD, 1987
Aspen Music Festival, theatrical masks for opera, *Houdini,* Aspen, CO, 1979
Eugene M. Weisz Memorial Award, Corcoran School of Art, 1976, Washington, DC
Corcoran School of Art, Washington, DC, BFA, 1976
University of Maryland, BA

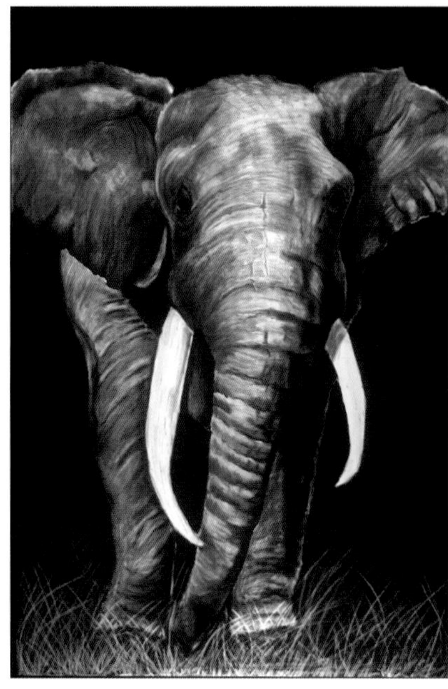
1

Selected Collections

2006 Art Bank, DC Commission on the Arts and Humanities, Washington, DC
Suzanne H. Arnold Gallery, Lebanon Valley College, PA
National Museum of Women in the Arts, Washington, DC
Museum of Arts and Sciences, Daytona Beach, FL
Deland Museum of Art, Deland, FL
Brevard Art Center and Museum, Melbourne, FL
The Artery Organization, Bethesda, MD
The Charles E. Smith Companies, Arlington, VA
Regional Center for Infants and Children, Rockville, MD
New England Contemporary Art Museum, Brooklyn, CT
The Francis Lehman Loeb Art Center, Vassar College, Poughkeepsie, NY
Peat Marwick Main & Company, Washington, DC
Federal Home Loan Mortgage Corporation, Vienna, VA
The Ruth and Marvin Sackner Archives, Miami Beach, FL
Amnesty International, Washington, DC
The George Washington University, Washington, DC
University of Maryland, College Park, MD
Howrey and Simon, Washington, DC
Fannie May Organization, Washington, DC
American University, Washington, DC
Republic of Fiji, Souva, Fiji, Art in Embassy
Republic of Malaysia, American Ambassador Residence, Kuala Lumpur, Malaysia, Art in Embassy
Arnold Gallery, Anville, PA

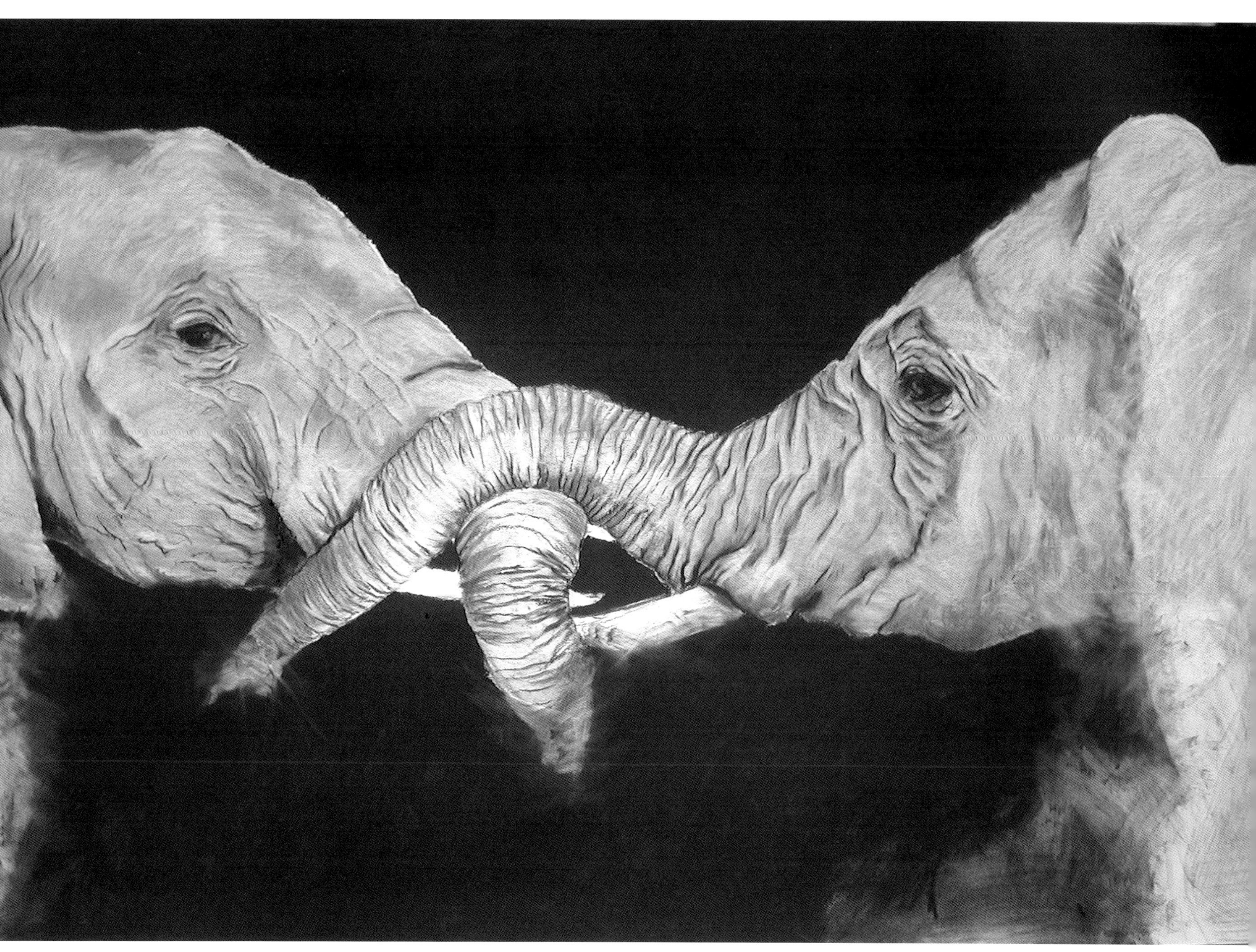

2

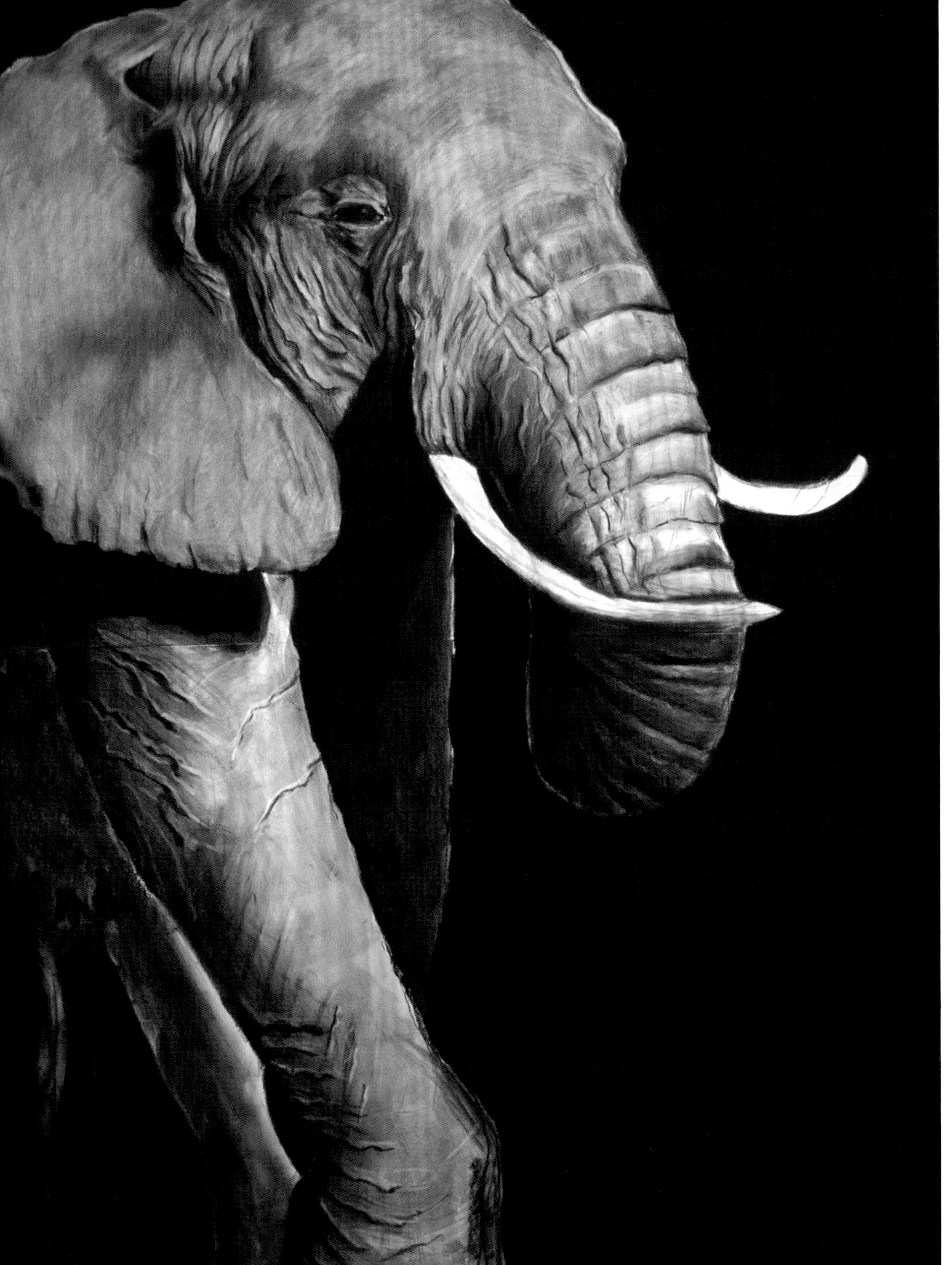

3

All elephant images:
Untitled, 2004
Charcoal on paper
Private collection

1 3' x 5'
2 3' x 5'
3 5' x 8'
4 3' x 5'

Selected Bibliography

The Washington Post, "Sunday Source Pick of the Week," September 3, 2006
Wingspan, "Abstract Artist to Show 9-11 Thoughts," Cheyenne, WY, September 22, 2003
Montgomery County Gazette, Bernice August, "Portrait of an Artist," March 10, 2000
Essay: in "Writing from the Heart," Nancy Slonum Aronie, Hyperion Press, NY, February 1998
George Washington Magazine, Paul Claussen, "George Washington and the Mystery of the Fifty Missing Share," Winter 1996
City Paper, Martha McWilliams, "George Washington...Past and Present," August 18, 1995
The Washington Post Weekend, Hank Burchard, "Washington Crossing the Spectrum," June 30, 1995
University of Maryland, undergraduate program, "Maryland Artists Collection," Summer 1994
Baltimore Alternative, Cecelia Meisner, "Patterns of Harmony and Anguish," October 1993
The Baltimore Sun, John Dorsey, October 9, 1993
The Baltimore Magazine, "At the Galleries," September/October 1993
The Baltimore Sun, John Dorsey, May 12, 1993
The Baltimore City Paper, Mike Giuliano, "Cracking the Codes," May 4, 1993
Art in America, J.W. Mahoney, "Carol Goldberg," July 1992
The Washington Review, Mokha Laget, "New Works on Paper," April/May 1992
The Washington Post, Michael Welzenbach, February 8, 1992
The Washington Post, Michael Welzenbach, October 6, 1990

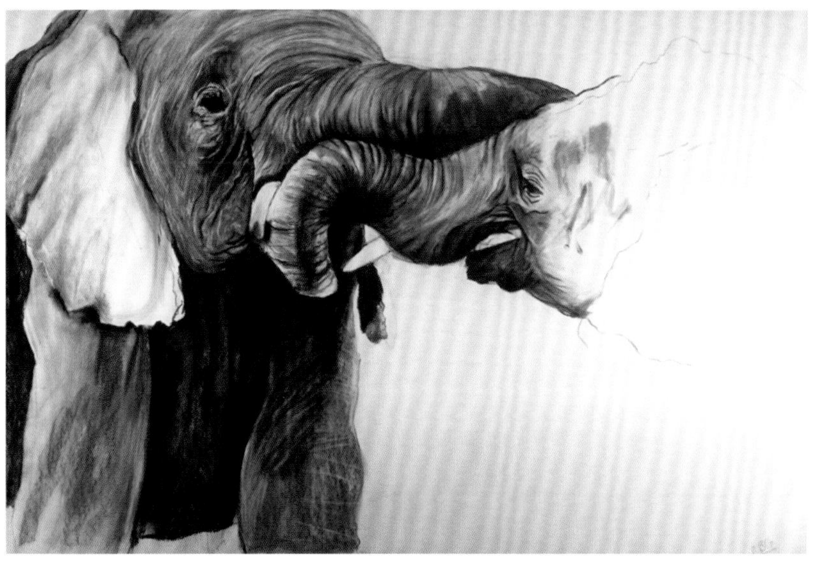

The New Art Examiner, Jane Addams Allen, March 1990
The Washington Times, Alice Thorson, "Exhibits Redefine Washington's Art Identity," January 4, 1990
The Chevy Chase Gazette, Ruth Palombo, "Artist Blends Physics with Chaos – Pastel Paintings," December 14, 1989
Eyewash, Ellen Gordon Gordon, "Carol Goldberg," December 1989
The Washington Post, Michael Welzenbach, "Goldberg at Osuna," December 2, 1989
The Baltimore Jewish Times, Alyssa Gabbay, "The Joyous Art of Carol Goldberg," November 24, 1989
The Washington Post Magazine, Jura Koncius, "Taking a Bough; Artists Deck Their Halls," December 15, 1988
Museum and Arts Magazine, A.J. Loftin, September/October 1988
New Art Examiner, M. Laget, June 1988
New Art Examiner, art review, Paul Bowman, 1987
Roanoke Times & World News, Ann Weinstein, April 19, 1987
Virginia Tech Collegiate Times, Andy Cohell and Terrie Gabriel, April 14, 1987
La Seine Magazine, Tokyo, Japan, "Three Women of Washington, DC," August 1987
Cover of *Hill Rag* magazine, March 4-18, 1987
Washington Review, Roz Kuehn, "Art & Function," December/January 1986 - 1987
Cover of *Hill Rag*, July 2-15, 1987
New Art Examiner, J. W. Mahoney, Washington, DC, "Carol Goldberg," Summer 1986
The Montgomery Journal, Linda Waters, June 6, 1986
The Washington Post, Jo Ann Lewis, "Goldberg's Winter Wonderland," May 17, 1986
The Washington Times, Michael Welzenbach, "Goldberg's Cutout Celebrate Joy of Color," May 8, 1986
The Washington Post Magazine, Paul Feinberg, "Artist's Fantasies," December 8, 1985
The Washington Times, Michael Welzenbach, June 20, 1985
Cover of *Volusia Magazine*, June 2, 1985
Daytona Beach Journal, Sharon O'Neill, May 28, 1985
The Washington Post Magazine, Joan Nathan, February 8, 1985
New Art Examiner, October, 1984
The Washington Post, Chuck Lonconi, September 1983
The Washington Post, Jo Ann Lewis, April 29, 1982
The Washington Star, Ben Forgey, "Dynamite Show of 'OPTIONS' at the WPA," April 20, 1982
The Washington Post, Jo Ann Lewis, July 16, 1976

Acknowledgments

The artist would like to thank those many people who have been so supportive of her work over the years: her family; her mentors, friends, and helpers; and her collectors. •